T0348431

The Independence of Credit Rating Agencies

The Independence of Credit Rating Agencies

How Business Models and Regulators Interact

Gianluca Mattarocci

AMSTERDAM • BOSTON • HEIDELBERG • LONDON
NEW YORK • OXFORD • PARIS • SAN DIEGO
SAN FRANCISCO • SINGAPORE • SYDNEY • TOKYO

Academic Press is an imprint of Elsevier

Academic Press is an imprint of Elsevier
The Boulevard, Langford Lane, Kidlington, Oxford OX5 1GB, UK
225 Wyman Street, Waltham, MA 02451, USA

First edition 2014

Copyright © 2014 Elsevier Inc. All rights reserved

No part of this publication may be reproduced, stored in a retrieval system or
transmitted in any form or by any means electronic, mechanical, photocopying,
recording or otherwise without the prior written permission of the publisher

Permissions may be sought directly from Elsevier's Science & Technology Rights
Department in Oxford, UK: phone (+44) (0) 1865 843830; fax (+44) (0) 1865 853333;
email: permissions@elsevier.com. Alternatively you can submit your request online by
visiting the Elsevier web site at http://elsevier.com/locate/permissions, and selecting
Obtaining permission to use Elsevier material

Notice
No responsibility is assumed by the publisher for any injury and/or damage to
persons or property as a matter of products liability, negligence or otherwise, or
from any use or operation of any methods, products, instructions or ideas contained
in the material herein. Because of rapid advances in the medical sciences, in particular,
independent verification of diagnoses and drug dosages should be made

British Library Cataloguing in Publication Data
A catalogue record for this book is available from the British Library

Library of Congress Cataloging in Publication Data
A catalog record for this book is available from the Library of Congress

ISBN: 978-0-12-404569-9

For information on all Academic Press publications
visit our web site at store.elsevier.com

14 15 16 17 18   10 9 8 7 6 5 4 3 2 1

  Working together
to grow libraries in
developing countries

www.elsevier.com • www.bookaid.org

Dedication

Remember loved ones never leave
They are forever near
For their love lives on in memories
Our hearts hold dear

Contents

Foreword

When I was approached to review a credit rating book manuscript by Professor Gianluca Mattarocci last year, I had in mind that any book in this area needed to be globally relevant and based on strong economic principles. Now the book *The Independence of Credit Rating Agencies: How Business Models and Regulators Interact* is in print and I am pleased that Professor Mattarocci's book exceeds my expectation by a large margin.

His book is perhaps the only book that discusses the rating agency industry and elucidates the "secrets" of operational details of credit rating agencies. It is based on strong academic research and yet offers many "insider" institutional details. It contains a detailed exposition of the credit rating agency industry with a global emphasis. The coverage of non-US credit agencies and their respective markets is excellent. The book is also very timely, given the recent European credit crisis and the US subprime crisis. The book will definitely help central bankers, regulators, academics, and any interested individuals to better understand credit rating agencies. Most importantly, during the crises, popular media and government officials unselectively blamed rating agencies for what they did or did not do. Professor Mattarocci's book provides a behind the scenes look into how credit agencies operate and helps us to understand why rating agencies chose what to do or what not to do.

Today, credit rating is important in serving many economic functions, such as providing information to the public and helping government and business to raise capital. However, potential conflicts of interest and their business practices cloud their independence and the reputation of the industry. Professor Mattarocci's book offers us a strong background about the industry. It is a special scholarly book on credit rating. Everyone who is interested in the topic should read this book.

Kam C. Chan Ph.D., CFA
Leon Page Chair of Finance and University Distinguished Professor,
Western Kentucky University, USA

Acknowledgements

The book has benefited greatly from comments given by all the anonymous reviewers who evaluated the first draft of the work. The quality of the current version of the book will be significantly lower without the independent and high-quality review service provided by all these academics.

Special thanks to Alessandro Carretta, University of Rome Tor Vergata, for his support since the development of the research idea, and to John Doukas, Old Dominion University, for his outstanding advice in refining and finalising the research project. I am also grateful to Scott Bentley, Melissa Murray and all Elsevier's staff for how they professionally managed the review and the publication process of the volume.

Last but not the least, special thanks to Kam C. Chan, Western Kentucky University, for the foreword to the book.

List of Tables

List of Figures

Introduction

Rating agencies are information providers that reduce information asymmetry by judging the quality of an issue or issuer (Ebenroth and Dillon, 1993). In doing so, they can increase transparency in financial markets (Cowan, 1991). However, it is only an opinion based on information available at the time of the analysis and does not imply any obligation for the evaluator if the judgment is not consistent with the issuer or issue's real risk exposure (Krahnen and Weber, 2001). This service is useful if the rating agencies are more skilled than the market in collecting, interpreting, and summarizing available information (Goh and Ederington, 1993). However, if this is the case, the market cannot directly assess the quality of the ratings, with such assessments typically based on the accuracy of ratings issued in previous years (Kuhner, 2001).

At present, supervisory authorities frequently use rating judgments to overcome certain problems in monitoring financial intermediaries and markets: For the first type of supervised entities the rating represents a measure of the risk of the lending portfolio, while for the latter the rating is used to define constraints on portfolio management choices in the asset management industry or delimit the investment opportunities of less financial skilled individuals. The current regulatory framework uses the rating judgments to control banks, insurance companies, other financial intermediaries, listed firms and, more generally, other investment vehicles (Cantor and Parker, 1996).

During the last century rating agencies assumed a primary role in the financial markets, and only for extraordinary events (such as Enron) were they not able to correctly evaluate the risk exposure related to an issuer or issue due to the complexity of the entity evaluated (Sinclair, 2003). The current financial crisis reveals the limits of the evaluation procedure adopted by rating agencies, such as the scenario where judgments based on new information cannot be revised on time (Langhor and Langhor, 2008). Rating industry misjudgments are more frequent in certain business sectors, and structured finance products tend to be more frequently misevaluated during crises (Benmelech and Dlugosz, 2009). Many issues have been downgraded directly from investment-grade to junk bonds, demonstrating the limits of rating agencies in predicting and understanding the default risk related to complex financial products (Coval, Jurek, and Stafford, 2009). Errors repeated by the main rating agencies lead to loss in investor confidence in their service, with a greater impact on agencies that adopt an issuer fee model, and have higher risk of collusion with the evaluated entities (Coffee, 2004).

Nowadays investors are worried about the business models adopted by the rating agencies and interested in understanding the rating procedure adopted and the main drivers of their annual income. The main concern about the rating agency business is that it allows a risky sector, structured finance, to have a greater role in determining overall annual income of the rating agency (Partnoy, 2006): Because the evaluation procedure is less accurate for such complex types of financial instruments, a rating agency focused too much on this sector is less useful in reducing information asymmetry in the financial market.

Moreover, critics of rating agencies question their independence with respect to the main market players (Utzig, 2010), which are generally those customers that request the most services from a rating agency. The issuer fee model is frequently criticized in favor of the user fee model, currently adopted only by small to medium-sized rating agencies that can ensure a degree of independence in the evaluation procedure (White, 2010).

The current financial crisis demonstrates some limits of the current supervisory process that are regarded as among the causes of the systemic crisis (McVea, 2010). Since their inception, supervisory authorities have had opportunities to make direct or indirect intervention in the rating markets: The first method allows direct control of the maximum number of agencies authorized and their evaluation procedures, while the latter assumes that the market is able to efficiently self-regulate itself. Even if the rating market is not too competitive with the main entry barrier being a reputational requirement (Guttler, 2005), the supervisory authorities of almost all countries have adopted a market-oriented approach in which the only direct control applied to the market is represented by accreditation principles that all rating agencies must respect to be recognized for monitoring purposes (Lucas, Goodman, and Fabozzi, 2008). To create other incentives for offering high-quality service to the market, the supervisory authorities periodically publish information about the quality and affordability of the rating judgments defined by different agencies (Committee of European Securities Regulators, 2004).

The USA was the first country to adopt this supervisory approach, with the US Securities and Exchange Commission (SEC) in 1975 defining the criteria for a nationally recognized statistical rating organization (NRSRO). In recent years, the same approach has been adopted in Europe, where the Basel Committee has defined comparable requirements for rating agencies to be recognized as external credit assessment institutions. The main aspects considered in identifying higher-quality standards of service are quality and accuracy of judgment and the evaluator's independence from different types of stakeholders (Champsaur, 2005).

In the literature, the quality of service offered for different counterparties and financial instruments is normally measured by considering the rating prediction's accuracy, the timing of judgment revisions when new information becomes available, and the most frequent types of errors committed by each rating agency (e.g. Cheng and Neamtiu, 2009). Regulators note that, for supervisory purposes, transparency must also be taken into account: If only investors are able to understand the meaning and main reasoning behind a judgment, the service may be considered an instrument to reduce information asymmetry in financial markets (Goodhart, 2008).

The degree of independence considers both organizational and economic features. Only a deep analysis of the business strategy adopted by each rating agency allows an evaluation of the impact of business choices on judgmental independence. Analysis of economic features requires information about the types of services offered, the annual reports' main features, pricing policies, and the length and other characteristics of customer relationships. Organizational independence considers all the different stakeholders engaged in the rating evaluation process (i.e. shareholders, customers, and employees) and the firewalls eventually used to reduce the risk of their interaction with the evaluation committee.

This book proposes a detailed analysis of the main aspects of economic and organizational independence with respect to different stakeholders, pointing out the methods adopted by the rating agencies and the monitoring procedures selected by the supervisory authorities. The available literature points out relevant differences in the business practices adopted by the major rating agencies and others (Purda, 2005). The analysis therefore focuses not only on the main players but also on the minor rating agencies to determine any differences in the practices adopted by the main market players and the others.

The organizational structure analysis points out methods that may significantly reduce the risk of conflicts of interest and collusion in the rating sector, even for rating agencies that adopt an issuer fee model, and highlights key features to be monitored in stakeholder relationships. The analysis of economic independence notes some limits of the current supervisory approach that could be overcome using a well-established approach in the marketing literature to obtain more complete measures of customer dependence.

The main characteristics of the rating business and the main customers in the rating market are prerequisites to understanding rating evaluations based on the degree of the market's information asymmetry. In Chapter 1, Section 1.2 defines the rating service and discusses the standard classification based on the object of the analysis (issue versus issuer ratings) and the relationship between the rater and the rated entity (solicited versus unsolicited ratings), while Section 1.3 focuses on the usefulness of the service for different types of users (investors and financial intermediaries).

Rating services have a direct role in the capital markets and any judgment that is unexpected by the market can significantly affect financial market dynamics. The current financial crisis demonstrates some limits of the business model adopted because big failures in the evaluation process caused a decrease of their reputation and pointed out the usefulness of sector reform. Chapter 2 discusses the role of the new ratings (Section 2.2) and existing ratings (Section 2.3) on the financial market and evaluates the current regulatory framework (Section 2.4). Section 2.5 looks at the financial crisis, points out the main differences in the raters' attitude and performance (Section 2.5.1), and summarizes the main future perspectives for the regulation after the crisis (Section 2.6).

Since its development at the beginning of the nineteenth century, the rating market has changed radically, even if entry barriers can still negatively affect the degree of competition in the market. Chapter 3 presents some information about the history of the market (Section 3.2) and discusses the role of entry barriers in a rating market that can justify a low degree of competition. The last two sections present a detailed description of the current degree of market competition (Section 3.4) and some statistics on the evolution of the degree of competition in the last decade (Section 3.5).

Rating agencies are often criticized for taking advantage of lesser competition in the market to maximize profits, but there is no clear evidence, either medium or long term, of any extra performance thus achieved. Chapter 4 analyzes the annual reports of a set of rating agencies compared with a benchmark constructed considering different types of information providers. Once the main characteristics of the business approach of all information providers and differences related to the type of service provided are identified (see Section 4.3), a standard annual report analysis on a 10+-year time horizon is performed on a heterogeneous set of information providers: Section 4.3 examines the balance sheet, Section 4.4 the income statement, and Section 4.5 the financial statement, highlighting the main differences of the principal items for rating agencies with respect to information providers.

Due to the prominent role assumed by the core business in determining the yearly performance of a rating agency, a more detailed analysis of the pricing model adopted by raters is presented to identify their best practices and implications. Chapter 5 starts with an analysis of the characteristics of the information providers that may have an impact on firm business models and must be taken into account for a complete business analysis (see Section 5.2). Focusing only on the rating market, Section 5.3 describes in detail the types of fees for the different types of services offered. Section 5.4 compares the issuer and user fee models, pointing out their main advantages and risks and describing their relevance in the worldwide market.

Chapter 6 examines the worldwide rating agency market and points out the main characteristics of the organizational structure adopted by these firms, focusing on their implications for the quality of service offered. The first aspect involves the ethical code of the employees and the control procedures adopted to prevent any conflicts of interest for rating committee members (see Section 6.2). The study of the organizational structure also considers the organization rating and evaluation committee, examining the roles and relationships between analysts and supervisors in the rating committee and the relationship of the rating committee to the rest of the firm (see Section 6.3). After examination of their internal structure, Section 6.4 focuses on the legal status of rating agencies and shareholder concentration and their implications for independence. Section 6.5 analyzes the relationship between the rating agency and other members of the affiliation group, and Section 6.6 examines the advantages and risks related to the role of public authorities and the government in the promotion and development of rating agencies.

Chapter 7 discusses the approaches available to measure the relevance of each customer and the concentration of the overall customers' portfolios in the rating industry. Section 7.2 studies customer relationships in the industry to determine the frequency and value of the service requested by each entity evaluated and the mean retention rate. Section 7.3 analyzes the methods available for measuring the value of customers and portfolio concentration, considering the main approaches adopted by the main supervisory authorities worldwide. Section 7.4 presents a simulation approach to identify the best method on the basis of rating industry features and discount policies normally adopted for the best customers.

A rating is the rater's opinion of the risk of an issue or issuer and the value and significance of the service varies on the basis of the issuer's or issue's complexity. Rating agency service users can be differentiated by their financial investors and intermediaries, which are subject to different regulatory constraints and whose evaluations of counterparty risk therefore have different levels of usefulness.

Even if the rating market cannot be considered a competitive environment due to entry barriers, current market developments demonstrate an increase in competitiveness. At present the role of the three main worldwide players (Fitch Ratings, Moody's Investor Service, and Standard & Poor's) is significantly bigger that other raters, but in the last decade the degree of concentration has gone down.

Rating agencies do not differ significantly from other information providers available in the market, and the only differences that balance sheet analysis proposed pointed out involve short-term asset liability management and cash flow dynamics. Agencies normally show higher asset liquidity, their core business is normally the most important item in their cash flow statements, and their risk exposure is lower than that of other information providers.

An issuer fee model is the pricing policy most frequently adopted, and the market is thus significantly exposed to the risk of collusion between evaluators and evaluated entities. Moreover, for retention purposes, rating agencies normally adopt a discounted fee policy as well, and thus the relationship established is a long-lasting one that can increase the risk of collusion.

The organizational independence analysis determines the best practices adopted worldwide to ensure the independence of the evaluation committee with respect to firm stakeholders. The results show that the rating sector has defined an efficient mechanism to avoid any risk of collusion between customers and evaluation committees and to eliminate any flow of information from the marketing area that could affect judgment objectivity. The main limit of the organizational structure concerns shareholder concentration, especially in small firms, and the role of the government in firm ownership. Moreover, the analysis of affiliated rating agencies demonstrates that the rating business is normally among the more profitable and, due to the characteristics of other affiliated members, the risk of cross-selling exists for almost all groups.

Raters and rated entities normally establish long-term relationships. Frequently older customers are the ones who increase the number of services requested the most and represent the main source of income for the rating agency. The current supervisory approach does not consider long-term relationships and focuses only on a one-year time horizon. The results obtained demonstrate that the higher the number of top customers considered, the more sensitive is the concentration measure to changes in the pricing policy, and the effect is significantly greater for smaller raters with respect to larger ones. Independent of the measure selected, the greatest relevance of the majority of the customers is persistent over time and so a multi-year measure could best fit the evaluation of the relevance of raters' customers.

Chapter one

Rating Agencies and the Rating Service

1.1 INTRODUCTION

Financial investors do not have access to the same information set among themselves, and the existence of horizontal asymmetric information (Ramakrishnan and Thakor, 1984) can be a disincentive for capital flows to the financial market and lead to the inefficient allocation of available financial resources (Stiglitz and Weiss, 1981). Information asymmetry increases the impact of a firm's reputation on the cost and amount of capital that can be raised through the financial market: In this scenario, smaller and younger firms are penalized and may be more financially constrained than bigger players (Diamond, 1989).

To overcome the problem of information asymmetry, firms can hire information providers to obtain an objective evaluation of their business. If the market trusts the evaluators, such firms can reduce the cost of capital or increase capital collected by publishing the judgment obtained due to the expected market reaction to any decrease in information asymmetry (Kerwer, 2002).

Rating agencies provide judgments of an issuer or issue that summarize all available public and reserved information (Cowan, 1991). The main advantage of the rating service is the opportunity to signal to the market the expected impact of reserved information without making it public, due to the confidentiality constraint that characterizes the relationship between the entity evaluated and the agency (Goh and Ederington, 1993).

The rating service is not comparable with the (implicit) judgment of lenders due to the different purposes of the evaluations: In the first case the judgment is only an opinion on an issue or an issuer, whereas the latter case involves direct financial exposure for the lender (Krahnen and Weber, 2001). Moreover, the information given to the market by the rating agencies is more clearly readable for those who are not skilled financial investors.

This chapter analyzes the service offered by rating agencies and presents an updated analysis of the market. Sections 1.2 and 1.3 identify the main characteristics of the service and the users respectively. Section 1.4 presents

1

The Independence of Credit Rating Agencies.
© 2014 Elsevier Inc. All rights reserved.

a detailed outlook of the worldwide market, pointing out the current level of competition and expected trend for the next years. Section 1.5 analyzes the expected characteristics of the service, examining the main requirements established by the supervisory authorities. Finally, Section 1.6 summarizes the chapter and concludes with some policy implications.

1.2 THE RATING SERVICE

Rating agencies are information providers that reduce the level of information asymmetry in the market by defining a judgment (the rating) on an issue or an issuer (Ferri and Lacitignola, 2009). A unique definition of the rating service is not available but, on the basis of business declarations given by the rating agencies, some common characteristics can be identified (see Table 1.1).

A rating is a synthetic judgment that summarizes, using an alphanumeric scale, the main qualitative and quantitative characteristics of an issue or issuer (Nickell, Perraudin, and Varotto, 2000). The agency does not assume any

Table 1.1 Rating Service Definitions

SCRiesgo	The risk ratings granted by SCRiesgo are the results of an extensive analytical process that includes an exhaustive revision of quantitative and qualitative factors.
Demotech Inc.	Our rating process provides an objective baseline for assessing solvency, which in turn provides insight into changes in financial stability. Financial Stability Ratings® are based upon a series of quantitative ratios and quantitative considerations, which together comprise our Financial Stability Analysis Model®.
Ecuability S.A.	The credit risk assessment is an opinion based on both qualitative and quantitative data that can be more or less relevant according to the economic environment of each industry or sector. Each type of rating also varies according to the nature of the issue, the issuer, its history, and its corporate culture.
MARC	Rating assesses the likelihood of timely repayment of principal and payment of interest over the term to maturity of debts.
PACRA	Rating is an interactive process relying primarily on gathering information from the issuer and supplementing it with strategic information obtained from outside independent sources. The entire process is aimed at evaluating (a) financial risk and (b) business risk. Information with regard to (a) is generally provided by the company requesting for rating and, only when necessary, such information is corroborated or complemented by information from other sources.
RAM	Rating is an objective and impartial opinion on the ability and willingness of an issuer to make full and timely payments of their financial obligations. It represents a ranking within a consistent framework showing the degree of future default risk of a particular debt, relative to other rated securities in the market.
TURK Rating	The rating reflects the company's current financial strength as well as how the financial position may change in the future. In this respect, extensive research on the outlook of the sector in which the firm operated is also an integral part of the rating methodology.

Source: Rating agency websites (accessed 03.01.2013).

responsibility for inaccuracy in the rating because they explicitly declare that it represents only an opinion (Bussani, 2010). The judgment is stated using the rating classes (i.e. AAA, BB, A1, etc.) as main segmentation criteria and, when necessary, the agency may offer a more detailed classification using secondary segmentation criteria, defined as notches (i.e. $+$, $-$, $+ / -$, etc.). Each agency can define different levels of detail for their rankings, and frequently defines different rating scales for different types of issuers and issues and/or different time horizons (see Table 1.2).

The information given to the market may be supplied by further information about the perspectives of the issue or the issuer that are summarized in the outlook or credit watch. The purpose of these two instruments is the same, but while the first is normally used for medium- to long-term horizons, the latter relates more to the short term (Gropp and Richards, 2001) (see Table 1.3).

The role of qualitative information in defining a rating judgment with respect to quantitative information depends on the rating criteria adopted and is affected also by the characteristics of the entity evaluated (Resti and Omacini, 2001). The rating agencies normally assign a greater role to qualitative data when they think that any change in the qualitative features may impact significantly on the default risk of the issuer or the issue.

The service offered by the rating agency is immaterial, and thus the value recognized by the market changes significantly based on the agency's reputation acquired over the years: The more affordable the rating agency is considered, the greater the market reaction to any new information available (Mann, 1999). This reputation mechanism is the main incentive for offering a high-quality service to the market because, on the basis of reputation change, an agency can modify market share over time (Kuhner, 2001).

To ensure the usefulness of the service, the agency must constantly monitor the market to modify judgment if any relevant event occurs (Loffler, 2005). The procedure normally implies the use of a watch list that identifies the issuers or issues currently under revision (Hand, Holthausen, and Leftwich, 1992). At the end of the revision process, the rating agency publishes the new ratings and normally, if change is anticipated by an outlook, the market reaction is less significant (Fayez, Wei, and Meyer, 2003).

Independently of the rating agency considered, qualitative and quantitative features impact differently on rating changes. Normally, qualitative changes require more time to be incorporated in the judgment, while quantitative changes are almost immediately recognized in a rating. The different time lags in rating reactions may be explained by examining the characteristics of the information: The first type requires a long time to collect and evaluate, while the latter is standardized and can be immediately included in the rating model (Guttler and Wahrenburg, 2007).

The next subsections analyze separately the main characteristics of the different types of rating classified on the basis of the entity evaluated (issuer versus issue rating) and the relationship between the entity evaluated and the evaluation (solicited versus unsolicited ratings).

Table 1.2 Rating Scales for Bond Issues in the Short and Medium to Long Term

A.M. Best		DBRS		Egan-Jones Ratings Company		Fitch Ratings		JCR		LACE Financial Corp		M		Morningstar		Standard & Poor's	
ST	MLT	ST	MLT	ST	MLT	ST	MLT	ST	MLT	ST	MLT	ST	MLT	ST	MLT	ST	MLT
AMB-1	Aaa	R-1	AAA	A-1	AAA	F1	AAA	J-1	AAA	K1	AAA	P-1	Aaa	–	AAA	A-1	AAA
AMB-2	Aa	R-2	AA	A-2	AA	F2	AA	J-2	AA	K2	AA	P-2	Aa	–	AA	A-2	AA
AMB-3	A	R-3	A	A-3	A	F3	A	J-3	A	K3	A	P-3	A	–	A	A-3	A
AMB-4	Bbb	R-4	BBB	B	BBB	B	BBB	NJ	BBB	B	BBB	NP	Baa	–	BBB	B	BBB
D	Bb	R-5	BB	B-1	BB	C	BB		BB	C	BB		Ba	–	BB	B-1	BB
	B	D	B	B-2	B	RD	B		B	D	B		B	–	B	B-2	B
	Ccc		CCC	B-3	CCC	D	CCC		CCC		CCC		Caa	–	CCC	B-3	CCC
	Cc		CC	C	CC		CC		CC		CC		Ca	–	CC	C	CC
	C		C	D	C		C		C		C		C	–	C	D	SD/D
	D		D	D	D				D		D		D	–	D		
Rs																	R
Number of Notches																	
23		26		22		19		20		22		21		20		22	

Source: SEC (2012), Report to Congress Credit Rating Standardization Study, available at < www.sec.gov > (accessed 03.01.2013).
Notes: – = Information not available

Table 1.3 Credit Watch Definitions

SCI Seoul Credit Rating & Information Inc.		Emerging Credit Rating Ltd	
Positive Review (↑)	When a probable cause for upgrade of a rating occurs	Positive	Indicates that a rating may be raised
Negative Review (↓)	When a probable cause for downgrade of a rating occurs	Negative	Indicates that a rating may be lowered
		Stable	Indicates that a rating is likely to remain unchanged
Evolving (↕)	When possible direction of a rating adjustment is uncertain	Developing	Indicates that a rating may be raised, lowered or remain unchanged

Source: Rating agency website (accessed 03.01.2013).

1.2.1 Issuer Rating

An issuer rating considers all the characteristics of a firm or institution and its future growth perspective on the basis of existing and planned investments/expenditures. The preliminary analysis released considers the balance sheet and computes some relevant indexes useful in evaluating the economic and financial condition of the entity evaluated (Klinger and Sarig, 2000). Information collected is not compared with the hurdle rate defined by the rating agency and is used in a multivariate statistical model to measure the issuer's default probability and thus identify its risk level (Kaplan and Urwitz, 1979).

The service offered by the rating agencies is quite heterogeneous, and normally there are different evaluating procedures based on the characteristics of the evaluated counterparty (Lanzoni and Patarnello, 2010). The choice to identify different procedures for issuers that pertain to different sectors is normally adopted for inclusion in the evaluation procedure features and information is sector specific (see Table 1.4).

The number of criteria and segmentation principles depend on the features of the historical database available to the rating agency. Normally, the higher the number of segmentation criteria adopted, the higher the quality of the rating judgment, because it is defined by comparing the issuers against a set of more homogeneous, comparably rated entities. Rating agencies may also define various subcategories to define specific rating criteria to better evaluate the distinctive features of the issuer or issue. This method is normally adopted only for the more important business segments (such as corporate segments) and may imply some relevant differences in the rating criteria adopted to evaluate each sub-segment (see Table 1.5).

Independent of the type of rating considered, to define the final judgment, the agency may organize a meeting with the entity evaluated to collect information related to qualitative features—such as the organization's

Table 1.4 Issuer Rating Criteria Segmentation

JCR, Japan Credit Rating Agency Ltd.	Clasificadora de Riesgo Humphreys Ltda.
Corporate	EmpresasBancarias y Financieras
Financial institutions	Empresas de Leasing
Public sector	Compañías de SegurosGenerales
Sovereign and supranational	Compañías de Seguros de Vida
Medical institutions	Empresas no Financieras
Educational institutions	Gobiernos Locales y Regionales
	Empresasdomiciliadas en el exterior

Source: Rating agency websites (accessed 03.01.2013).

Table 1.5 Corporate Rating Criteria Detailed Segmentation

P.T. PEFINDO Credit Rating Indonesia	Companhia Portuguesa de Rating, SA (CPR)
Otomotif	Healthcare
Kimia	Infrastructure
Minyakkelapasawit	Property and A-REITS
Makanan & Minuman	Mining and resources
Media	Retailing
Pertambangan	Utilities
Properti	
Perdagangan Eceran	
Perkapalan	
Tembakau	
Jalantol	

Source: Rating agency websites (accessed 03.01.2013).

structure—that could not be obtained from the economic and financial documents available (Fight, 2001). On the basis of the public criteria available, the main aspects considered pertain to governance, ownership, stakeholder rights, transparency, and the composition and efficiency of internal committees (Ashbaugh-Skaife, Collins, and LaFond, 2006). The final judgment considers not only the characteristics of the issuer but also the main features of the environment that may impact on its risk (De Laurentis, 1999).

Table 1.6 Issue Rating Criteria Segmentation

Dominion Bond Rating Service (DBRS)	Korea Investors Service Inc. (KIS)
Abcp	Corporate bond rating
Auto Abs	CP rating
Cmbs	Structured finance rating
Covered bonds	PF rating
Credit card and consumer lending	Stock valuation
Equipment	Venture rating
Rmbs	
Split shares and funds	
Structured credit	
Student loans	
Other	

Source: Rating agency websites (accessed 03.01.2013).

A wealthy and safe country can impact positively on the reputation of all its firms and ensure a high quality of public services necessary to support firm growth. Especially for developing economies and small and medium enterprises, rating agencies apply the so-called country ceiling, a constraint such that the maximum rating assigned to each firm in that country can never be higher than the country rating itself (Altman, 2005).

Sectors can be differently affected by economic trends, and for issuer evaluations it is necessary to consider the possible impact of sector features on riskiness (Kerwer, 2002). Analysis of the sector dynamics must also consider if any current or expected change in the regulation can affect the performance of these types of firms and, moreover, evaluate if there is an expected change in the market share of the entity evaluated that could impact sector risk exposure (Crouhy, Galai, and Mark, 2001).

1.2.2 Issue Rating

An issue rating summarizes the risk exposure of an issuer on the basis of all information (public and reserved) available (Blume, Lim, and Mackinlay, 1998), corrected for the specific contract features of the financial instrument evaluated (Pinches and Mingo, 1973). Agencies normally define different criteria on the basis of the characteristics of the issue evaluated and the availability of a sufficiently detailed database to construct a specific evaluation model (see Table 1.6).

A misalignment between the issuer rating and the issue rating frequently appears when the issue features can increase or decrease the risk exposure of the investment (Ritter and Miranda, 2000). Independent of the type of financial instrument evaluated, features always considered are (Crouhy, Galai, and Mark, 2001) the following:

- Expiration date
- Main contractual clauses
- Degree of subordination
- Real or personal guarantees.

The length of the contract represents the time horizon of the rating evaluation, and the longer it is, the higher the probability that unexpected events may cause the issuer's default. All other conditions being equal, the rating of short-term issues will always be higher than those assigned to medium- and long-term or open-ended ones (Galil, 2002). The contract clauses that must be taken into account in the issue risk evaluation procedure are quite heterogeneous, and normally the greater the complexity of the financial instrument, the greater the number of features that must be considered. For example, in the case of structured finance, the evaluator must consider not only the characteristics of the financial instrument (i.e. size, number of issues, expected rate of return, etc.), but also the placement procedure adopted (i.e. arrangers, number of rating agencies involved, role of the issuer, etc.) (Vink and Thibeault, 2008).

Subordination between different tranches of the same issue can significantly modify the default risk exposure for investors, and rating agencies assign higher ratings to tranches that are less subordinated (John, Ravid, and Reisel, 2010). Normally, secured and unsecured debt is rated differently by at least one notch, and the same distinction is made between junior and senior subordinated debt (John, Lynch, and Puri, 2003).

In every financial contract, the existence of real or personal guarantees can impact positively on the results of the recovery process in case of default and must therefore be considered in the issue rating definition (Schwarz, 2002). Real guarantees can justify the stickiness of a rating, even in the case of some negative event, if the value of the guarantee is sufficient to satisfy all the rights of the stakeholders (Strier, 2008). Personal guarantees impact on the risk evaluation of the instrument because the default risk must consider not only the default risk of the issuer, but also that of the guarantor (Dermine and Neto de Carvalho, 2006). The issuer rating will be improved by the personal guarantee only if the rating agency evaluates it as affordable and does not consider the risk of joint default of the issuer and guarantor probable.

Given all the features related to an issue risk evaluation process, the main problems normally concern the recovery process in the event of default. Construction of the necessary detailed database is time-consuming and expensive, and the rating agency can thus decide to render an incomplete evaluation of the risk to avoid the cost of estimating the loss given default (Altman and Karlin, 2009). The probability of a split rating increases when the complexity of the issue increases, because the agencies can adopt different measures and proxies for the risk exposures related to the financial instrument (Skreta and Veldkamp, 2009).

1.2.3 Solicited Ratings

Solicited ratings are defined using all public and private information available on an issue or issuer (Cannata, 2001), and represent a complete evaluation of all the main features of the entity evaluated (Nickell, Perraudin, and Varotto, 2000). The overall process includes phases in which the rating agency works alone and stages in which there is interaction and discussion with the entity evaluated (see Figure 1.1).

A firm hires a rating agency to make a judgment on the quality of an issue or issuer on the basis of the information made available by the evaluated entity. The agency identifies the rating committee that, after a preliminary analysis of all the public information, collects qualitative information through meetings with the firm's management (Jewell and Livingston, 1999). At the end of the evaluation process, the agency presents a preliminary rating to the customer, who normally has the right to authorize or reject the judgment's publication (Sangiorgi, Sobokin, and Spatt, 2009). The authorization mechanism that characterizes the solicited rating can create an upward bias in the rating available because the firm has an incentive to publish the rating only if a positive market reaction is expected (Mahlmann, 2008).

The analysis of rating agency criteria does not allow an identification of all the variables used in the evaluation procedure and the weights assigned to quantitative and qualitative features (Ederington, 1986). However, the role of qualitative features is never residual, because empirical evidence notes that the relevance of new ratings or rating revisions has increased since the agencies started using this type of data (Jorion, Liu, and Shi, 2005).

During the evaluation process, a rating can also give advice on increasing the firm's efficiency and its capacity to maximize value for the stakeholders. Especially for complex financial instruments, a rating agency could define the best structure of the transaction to maximize the rating assigned (Fender and Mitchell, 2005).

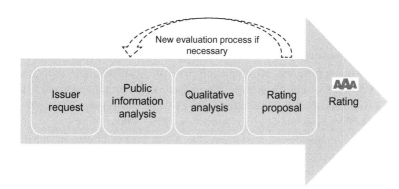

FIGURE 1.1 Solicited rating process.

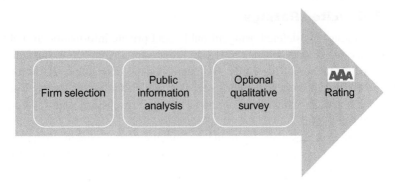

FIGURE 1.2 Unsolicited rating process.

1.2.4 Unsolicited Ratings

A rating agency can define the rating of an issuer or issue without the request of the evaluated entity (Behr and Guttler, 2008): The rating thus assigned is normally defined as unsolicited, or a shadow rating, to distinguish it from standard, solicited ratings. The evaluation process is normally simple because the interaction between the evaluator and the entity evaluated is only optional, and so the overall process may be significantly shorter than for solicited ratings (see Figure 1.2). The rater's purpose behind issuing an unsolicited evaluation is normally to increase its reputation and experience in a market (Bannier and Tyrell, 2005), and/or create an incentive for the rated entity to ask for a solicited rating (Mukhopadhyay, 2006).

The agency collects all the public information available and summarizes it in a judgment that is useful to the potential users of the service offered. These data may be integrated with other information directly provided by the managers but, due to the absence of any contractual relationship between the agency and the firm, the entity evaluated is not obliged to provide a complete or detailed set of information to the rater (Poon and Firth, 2005). To collect qualitative data, the rating agency can send surveys or organize meetings with the firm's top management, as well as discuss the preliminary ratings (Golin, 2001).

Investors seeking more affordable rating services consider the agency's market coverage and reputation, and normally the greater the number of the agency's ratings, the more important its evaluation in the market (Mattarocci, 2005). Unsolicited ratings are frequently used by small national rating agencies to reduce their reputation gap with respect to the main players and to construct a database of ratings that allows them to offer a service requested by the market (Bank for International Settlements, or BIS, 2000).

The use of unsolicited ratings by the main market players is normally restricted to issuers or issues not evaluated by other rating agencies (Butler and Rodgers, 2003). Empirical evidence shows that these ratings are normally less favorable for the entity rated (Poon, 2003), and so frequently it has an incentive to request a solicited rating, even if this implies a fee (Van Roy, 2006).

In some cases, unsolicited ratings also attain issuers or issues evaluated by other agencies to avoid rating shopping and to signal to the market rating agencies that are currently offering overly favorable ratings (BIS, 2000).

Even if the set of information used in the unsolicited rating is normally more incomplete than for a solicited rating, the market takes care of any changes (downgrades or upgrades) defined by the rating agencies. Empirical evidence shows that price sensitivity to changes in rating is higher for unsolicited ratings (Byoun and Yoon, 2002). The market's attention to this type of service demonstrates the relevance of independence in the rating industry, and normally the absence of the evaluated entity's formal authorization to publish the judgment is considered a key feature in ensuring the rating's objectivity (Shimoda and Kawai, 2007).

1.3 RATING SERVICE USERS

Users of the service offered by a rating agency can be classified by the type of investments evaluated, with two main categories: financial investors and financial intermediaries. The classification is useful due not only to the different purposes but also the different regulatory constraints applied to the two types of users. The next subsections present a detailed analysis of the characteristics and needs of the two types of users.

1.3.1 Financial Investors

In the context of capital rationing, ratings can be used to select investments available in the market on the basis not only of expected revenues but also (default) risk (Pagano and Volpin, 2003). The role of ratings in the selection of investment opportunities differs according to the financial skills of the user, and thus normally the approach is quite different for institutional and individual investors.

Individual investors consider a rating as a proxy of the default risk of the issuer, and they use this information, combined with other features—such as the rate of return and financial risk—to select the best investment opportunities (Fabozzi, 2007). To compare different investments, the user considers the mean default rate related to the rating class and computes the expected return corrected for the default risk for each available investment (Kerwer, 2005). If the investor is evaluating an indirect investment released though investment vehicles, the rating acts as an instrument to control the manager and avoid any excessive risk exposure due to this behavior. Empirical evidence demonstrates that this simple type of control is effective and the benefits for the investor are comparable with those in more complex procedures (Loffler, 2004).

Institutional investors normally create specialized offices for investment analysis that, using public information, evaluates the economic/financial convenience of an investment (Sinclair, 2001); frequently the quality of the evaluation is comparable or even superior to the judgment produced by an agency (Eamount, 2003). Institutional investors use rating agencies mostly only to define general guidelines of portfolio strategy (Ang and Patel, 1975) and/or define some prerequisites to investment that will be considered in the investment selection process (Ellis, 1998). More generally, the higher (lower) the amount and quality of the reserved information available for the institutional investor, the lower (higher) the relevance of the rating in the investment selection process (Bannier, Behr, and Guttler, 2010).

Whether individual or institutional, if an investor works as a dealer or a broker in the market, the regulator can define some minimum capital requirement based on the rating of the instrument traded. The supervisor assumes that the rating represents a proxy of the risk assumed in the trading activity, and so every investor must consider the rating to evaluate the opportunity cost of the capital requirement necessary for the type of investment selected (Feinberg, Shelor, and Jiang, 2004).

Due to the high heterogeneity of the rating market, the supervisory authorities defined a recognition process for those rating agencies interested in providing ratings recognized for the definition of capital requirements (Schwarz, 2001). The procedure establishes the documents (public and reserved) the agency must provide, and all the agencies that respect certain quality requirements of the service and constraints related to organizational structure are thus recognized for supervisory purposes.

The SEC was the first authority to define a procedure to recognize a rating agency as an NRSRO (Pinto, 2006), and the number of recognized raters changed over time due to the failures of some agencies and the merger and acquisition (hereinafter M&A) activities (White, 2010). Nowadays nine rating agencies satisfy these recognition requirements (see Table 1.7).

Not all are recognized for all the services they offer. Normally those agencies recognized only for some services are the smallest agencies, which ensure high-quality standards only for their core business (Morningstar, for example, is recognized only for securitization).

Other countries, such as France and Japan, define comparable accreditation criteria for their rating agencies, but there are no global standards that can be used to define a unique accreditation for the global market. The absence of a unique procedure is normally justified on the basis of the cost of the project, but the absence of international standards may have a negative impact on market competition and the rise and development of new rating agencies (Schwarz, 2002).

1.3.2 Financial Intermediaries

Financial intermediaries are supervised to ensure the stability and efficiency of the financial system. One of the main aspects considered is capital adequacy with respect to overall expected and unexpected losses related to lending activities. Evaluation of credit risk exposure considers the probability of default, the loss given default, and exposure at default (Sironi and Resti, 2007).

New capital standards consider the problems related to collecting all the information necessary for evaluating customers and provide some options for

Table 1.7 Complete NRSRO List

	Registration Date	Financial Inter-mediation	Insurance	Corporate	ABSs	Sovereign
A.M. Best Company Inc.	September 24, 2007	☑	☑	☑	☑	☑
Dominion Bond Rating Service	September 24, 2007	☑	☑	☑	☑	☑
Egan-Jones Rating Company	December 21, 2007	☑	☑	☑	☑	☑
Fitch Ratings Ltd.	September 24, 2007	☑	☑	☑	☑	☑
Japan Credit Rating Agency Ltd.	September 24, 2007	☑	☑	☑	☑	☑
Kroll Bond Rating Agency Inc.	February 11, 2008	☑	☑	☑	☑	☑
Moody's Investors Service	September 24, 2007	☑	☑	☑	☑	☑
Morningstar	June 23, 2008	☐	☐	☐	☑	☐
Standard & Poor's	September 24, 2007	☑	☑	☑	☑	☑

Source: <http://www.sec.gov/divisions/marketreg/ratingagency.htm> (accessed 01.03.2013).
Notes: The market categories are defined coherently with the Section 3(a)(62)(B) of the Exchange Act (1934).

reducing the information needs related to exposure measurement. If the information available is insufficient, the probability of default can be measured using a rating assigned by a rating agency (Basel Committee on Banking Supervision, 2006).

The choice to use a rating is subject to constraints ensuring the quality of the risk evaluation procedure and preventing any opportunistic choice by the financial intermediary. Due to misalignment between the ratings assigned by different agencies for the same issue or issuer (so-called split ratings) (Cantor, Parker, and Cole, 1997), the supervisory authority obliges financial intermediaries to select only one reference rating agency for each business segment and does not allow "cherry picking" to minimize capital requirements (Basel Committee on Banking Supervision, 2006).

The choice of rating is also constrained by a recognition procedure of the evaluator that defines agencies that guarantee high-quality standards in the rating process and affordability of judgment. The Basel Committee gives each national supervisory authority the right to define a list of authorized rating agencies and also allows them also to only partially recognize such agencies, recognizing only some of the services offered (Basel Committee on Banking Supervision, 2006) (see Table 1.8).

Table 1.8 Number of European Countries in Which the Rating Agencies are Recognized, 2010

Rating Agency	No. of Countries
Banque de France (BdF)*	2
COFACE	4
Creditreform Rating AG (CRAG)*	1
DBRS	8
Fitch	27
ICAP S.A. Research and Investment Company Management Consultants*	2
Japan Credit Rating Agency Ltd (JCR)	6
Lince*	1
Moody's Investors Service	28
Rating and Investment Information Inc. (R&I)	2
Standard & Poor's	27

Source: Committee of European Banking Supervision data processed by the author.
*The rating agency definition used by the Basel committee is wider with respect to the one proposed in the literature and so there are some recognized agencies that are not strictly definable as rating agencies.

Only the main international players (Fitch Ratings, Moody's Investors Service, and Standard & Poor's) are recognized in almost all the countries adopting the Basel II capital requirements, because they are able to satisfy all the requirements established by the supervisory authorities, whereas the smallest agencies (such as Creditreform Rating AG and Lince) are recognized only in one country.

Intermediaries that, due to the lack of internal data, use the information produced by the rating agencies to measure the probability of default for computing capital requirements are identified as the "standard model", and this method is frequently adopted in all European markets (see Table 1.9).

In over 75% of the countries listed here, more than 90% of the financial intermediaries use the standard methodology, and in some of the smallest countries (nine countries) that percentage may rise to 100%. Considering the value of a portfolio managed by a financial institution, the percentage of the portfolio evaluated using rating agency information decreases (72%). The difference between percentages computed on the number of intermediaries and the value of the portfolio demonstrates that, normally, small and medium lenders use rating agencies' judgment more frequently to define their credit risk exposure.

Larger financial intermediaries use rating agency evaluations as supplementary information to identity a benchmark for comparing the results

Table 1.9 Credit Risk Measurement Model in Europe in 2009

	% of Intermediaries			% of the Value of the Credit Portfolio		
	Standard	FIRB	AIRB	Standard	FIRB	AIRB
Austria	91.81	0.27	0.12	71.61	18.43	9.95
Belgium	84.78	4.35	10.86	30.11	18.64	51.25
Bulgaria	100.00	0.00	0.00	100.00	0.00	0.00
Cyprus	100.00	0.00	0.00	100.00	0.00	0.00
Germany	100.00	0.83	1.50	57.14	17.49	30.01
Estonia	100.00	28.60	0.00	81.60	18.40	0.00
France	31.83	0.00	68.17	55.11	0.00	44.89
Greece	100.00	5.70	0.00	83.40	16.60	0.00
Hungary	99.46	2.17	1.63	85.95	11.49	2.56
Ireland	91.84	20.41	18.37	64.58	26.13	9.29
Italy	96.35	2.30	1.35	79.61	11.27	9.12
Latvia	90.50	9.50	0.00	62.30	37.70	0.00
Liechtenstein	100.00	0.00	0.00	100.00	0.00	0.00
Lithuania	71.40	14.30	14.30	56.50	32.70	10.80
Luxembourg	82.00	7.20	10.80	64.10	15.10	20.80
Malta	76.92	15.38	7.69	76.93	22.14	0.94
Norway	91.60	3.70	4.70	73.90	16.00	10.10
Poland	100.00	0.00	0.00	100.00	0.00	0.00
Portugal	100.00	3.50	5.30	84.50	0.99	5.60
Romania	96.88	3.12	0.00	96.07	3.93	0.00
Slovakia	86.67	13.33	0.00	65.18	23.67	10.26
Slovenia	95.00	0.00	5.00	99.78	0.00	0.22
Spain	100.00	3.45	5.91	64.07	7.44	28.50
UK	99.53	4.72	22.17	33.25	17.61	24.27

Source: CEBS data processed by the author.
Data for Finland, the Netherlands, the Czech Republic, and Sweden are not available. Overall percentage could be higher than 100% because financial intermediaries can use different evaluation methodology for the different segments.

obtained by their internal rating systems or to evaluate market segments that are residual to their core business and do not justify the investment necessary to develop a specific internal evaluation procedure (Jameson and McNee, 2002).

1.4 CONCLUSIONS

A rating is only an opinion given by a specialized agency of the creditworthiness of an issuer or an issue based on quantitative and qualitative information. An issuer rating measures the default risk of a firm, while an issue rating considers the specific characteristics of an issue that can affect the risk of default and the result of the recovery process.

The evaluated entity can be actively engaged in the evaluation process (solicited rating) or the judgment can be defined autonomously by an agency (unsolicited rating). The two procedures can affect the amount of information used in the evaluation process and, generally, the more the evaluated entity is involved in the evaluation process, the greater the amount of information available for the analysis.

The rating market competition is restricted by the entry barriers related to reputation requirements, and nowadays few agencies are active in the market. The three top players own a market share that far surpasses that of the other players, and the overall competition is reduced even further by strategic affiliation between the biggest players and small agencies.

The quality of the service offered depends on the characteristics of both the service offered (objectivity, accessibility, and transparency) and the agency (human resources, reputation, and independence).

Now that the characteristics of the service offered are identified, the next chapter focuses on the role of ratings for the financial markets and the effects of the financial crisis on the reputation of the raters.

Chapter | two

Rating and Financial Markets

2.1 INTRODUCTION

The purpose of rating judgments is to provide investors with a simple gradu-ated system by which an issue's or issuer's relative investment qualities may be noted (Pinches and Mingo, 1973). Especially since the second half of the twentieth century, a vast literature has tried to evaluate if there is any relation between the rating assigned and firm characteristics and whether, on the basis of results, ratings could be considered a useful instrument in selecting invest-ment opportunities (Pogue and Soldofsky, 1969).

Many studies have evaluated the impact of newly issued and/or changed ratings. They point out that the effect is significant for almost all finan-cial instruments traded in the market and that the impact is higher when the event is unexpected (Hand, Holthausen, and Leftwich, 1992). After the 1929 crisis, investors were no longer very interested in purchasing ratings, partic-ularly given the agencies' poor track record in anticipating the sharp drop in bond values beginning in late 1929. The rating business remained stagnant for decades (Cheick, 2011). During the current crisis rating agencies have not been able to correctly define the ratings assigned, especially for complex issues. This has led to a heated debate on the solution to reforming the sec-tor to increase the objectivity and quality of the information provided by raters and overcome the risk of more decades of stagnation for the rating business.

The chapter presents a detailed literature review on the effects of new rating issues (Section 2.2) and the revision of existing ratings (Section 2.3), and points out the main guidelines followed by the supervisory authorities to ensure rating service quality (Section 2.4). An analysis of the crisis scenario is presented separately and considers the main failures since the bursting of the real estate bubble (Section 2.5.1), the main rating changes that had a relevant impact on the financial markets (Section 2.5.2), and, finally, proposals to learn from the crisis mistakes (Section 2.5.3). The final section presents a conclusion and implications of the analysis.

The Independence of Credit Rating Agencies.
© 2014 Elsevier Inc. All rights reserved.

2.2 THE IMPACT OF NEW RATINGS ON ISSUERS AND ISSUES

Initial ratings attest to the accuracy of a firm's financials and accounting statements, and their judgment reduces investor uncertainty and enables new issues to command higher prices (Wakeman, 1984). The reduction in uncertainty affects not only the cost of the capital issued but also existing financing sources with non-fixed returns (e.g. shares), which reduce the return required immediately after the disclosure of a new rating (Barron, Clare, and Thomas, 1997).

The reduction of the cost of capital caused by an initial rating issue is normally justified for the following reasons: Information supplied to the public market requires costly verification or costly signaling, firms are reluctant to expose information publicly that they provide confidentially to evaluators, and a firm's excessive use of capital market funding opportunities can be viewed by the market as an attempt to bypass the banks' monitoring role.

Ratings summarize financial and economic information publicly disclosed by a firm and there is always a direct relation between the information disclosed and the rating assigned even if, on the basis of the methodology adopted by the rater, sensitivity levels with respect to the information disclosed can differ (Ziebart and Reiter, 1992). Rating agencies are specialized information providers that, due to their experience and opportunity to use scale economies, can offer a service at a reasonable price to the customer. The effect of a new rating issue is related to the rater's reputation, with higher market reactions, normally, for ratings issued by the main rating agencies.

Raters are normally able to collect a more complete set of information for each issue or issuer with respect to the individual investor, especially if the rating is solicited and the rated entity also makes available reserved information. Unlike for other information providers, in almost all markets (even in those with strict laws to avoid information asymmetry) the information collected for the rating process can be disclosed only to the raters (e.g. Jorion, Liu, and Shi, 2005). The service provided by the agencies can thus increase the amount of information available in the market and the prices of instruments traded in financial markets will be more consistent with the real risk–return profile of the issuer and issue.

The usefulness of a new rating may be higher for firms that use mostly the financial markets to cover their financial needs, with respect to other firms that frequently use financial intermediaries. The existence of lenders financing a firm implicitly signals the firm's creditworthiness to the market, whereas firms that mostly use the financial markets need external evaluators to provide objective evaluations of their risk–return profiles and to give a certification signal to the market about firm creditworthiness (Nayar and Rozeff, 1994).

The effect of a new rating issue is affected by the existence of ratings issued by other agencies and the coherence of the new rating, or lack thereof, with respect to existing ones. In the event of a dual bond rating for the same issue or issuer, investors perceive the investment as less risky due to the larger information set available and the fact that the cost of capital of the firm can decrease significantly (by several basis points) if rating judgments agree (Hsueh and Kidwell, 1972).

The effectiveness of a new rating issue for a firm already rated by another agency is normally affected by the size and reputation of the original issuer: The smaller the rated entity and the lower its reputation, the greater the advantages related to the new rating issued (He, Qian, and Strahan, 2012).

Solicited and unsolicited rating issues can have different impacts on the stock market. Normally, unsolicited rating issues have a worse impact on financial market dynamics (Behr and Guttler, 2008). Their negative and (sometimes) significant impact on the market may be partially explained by the smaller set of information used for the analysis, which frequently leads to a lower rating issue than those already on the market.

2.3 THE IMPACT OF RATING CHANGES ON ISSUERS AND ISSUES

The impact of a rating change on price market dynamics depends on the characteristics of the rating change. Market reactions are different for positive and negative news: The impact of a downgrade is normally more relevant than upgrades (Holthausen and Leftwich, 1986). The greater relevance of downgrades with respect to upgrades may be explained on the basis of the following:

*   The impact on market participant expectations
*   The effect on the cost of capital for the rated entity
*   The capability of the market to anticipate the rating change.

The information provided by the raters will have an impact on market performance due to the effect on market expectations and the market reaction is frequently independent with respect to the judgment provided. The impact on the market is mainly driven by the rater's reputation, which is normally considered by investors as one of the more affordable sources of information (Goh and Ederington, 1999).

A rating downgrade impacts directly on the cost of lending due to the high capital requirements related to the bank's lending exposure and/or the higher risk assumed by the bondholders or stockholders. The market reacts to a downgrade by anticipating the negative effects on capital collection capability and costs, such that normally the firm's stock and/or bond prices significantly decrease immediately after a downgrade (Jorion, Liu, and Shi, 2005). If the rating changed is an issue rating, the effect on the cost of capital is related to the role of the specific funding source with respect to the overall capital collected: The greater the role of the specific financing source, the greater the change in the cost of capital after the issue rating change (Chandy, Hsueh, and Liu, 1993).

Companies voluntarily release good news to the market but are reluctant to release unfavorable information, creating a bias toward negative information content (Matolcsy and Lianto, 1995). Normally, upgrades are expected by the market, while downgrades are less anticipated by the market; therefore, market reactions to negative news are significantly greater than market reactions to good news (Ederington and Goh, 1998).

Normally, the effect of any rating change is lower when the issuer or issue rating is under review (i.e. put on Creditwatch) by the rater. The lower impact of positive or negative changes anticipated by a credit watch can be ascribed to the capability of the financial markets to incorporate the Creditwatch issued by the rater into stock and bond prices. Therefore, the impact of anticipated rating revisions is normally significantly lower than that of unanticipated ones (Creighton, Gower, and Richards, 2007).

The impact of the rating change is affected by the characteristics of the rated entity. Certain sectors are characterized by higher stock market price sensitivity to new information. The higher (lower) sensitivity may be explained by a higher (lower) degree of market competition or a lower (higher) frequency of new evaluations made by a rater on the same issuer or issues offered by the same issuer (Pinches and Singleton, 1978). Moreover, the size of the firm can affect market reactions. Normally, bigger firms suffer a greater increase in systematic risk exposure in the event of a downgrade than smaller firms (Impson, Karafiath, and Glascock, 1992).

The effect of rating changes on the stock or bond market is also affected by the relation between the initial and final ratings. The impact is more significant when, independently of the size of the change, the rated entity drops from investment grade to non-investment grade (Goh and Ederington, 1999). The difference in market reactions may be ascribed to the larger effect on the firm's cost of capital for debt financing opportunities (Caton and Goh, 2003) and the lower probability of becoming a takeover target is even lower for companies with non-investment-grade bonds, which adversely affects equity value (Billett, 1996).

If the issue or issuer is evaluated by more than one rating agency, the effect of a rating change is related to the ratings assigned by all other raters. In the event of misalignment between ratings assigned (i.e. split ratings), the impact of financial market dynamics could be different, depending on the rating procedure adopted (Ederington, 1974) and the rater's reputation (Baker and Mansi, 2002), the scheduling of the rating changes, and the complexity of the evaluation procedure for the rated entity (Morgan, 2002). A greater difference in the ratings assigned normally implies a bigger reaction from the market due to the increase in the issuer's opaqueness (Livingston, Naranjo, and Zhou, 2010).

The effect of a rating downgrade or upgrade may affect not only the entity rated but also all firms in the same sector/area. The reason for this systemic effect is related to market uncertainty where a downgrade may affect not only the evaluated firm but also all its rivals, which may then be perceived by investors as being exposed to the same risk of downgrade (Caton and Goh, 2003).

2.4 REGULATION IN THE RATING SECTOR

When regulators linked the minimum capital requirement, for example, of a bank's loan to the issuer's rating, as done in the Basel II Accord, they implicitly made agencies systemically relevant (Posch, 2011). Due to this regulatory activity, the correlation identified between ratings and financial instrument performance can also be considered a causal relation in which, due to external constraints (the law), ratings are able to drive the market (West, 1973).

The role of regulation in the rating sector may be related to the number of players authorized/recognized to work in a market and/or to a constraint applied to the rating activity to increase the quality and objectivity of the service provided.

The main instrument used to control the rating market is the recognition process, and all the main regulators define their accreditation processes for the rating agencies. The two main recognition processes are the SEC (for nationally recognized statistical rating organizations, or NRSROs, as in Box 2.1) or the BIS (for external credit assessment institutions, or ECAIs, as in Box 2.2).

The approaches adopted by the Basel Committee and the SEC are quite different because the purpose of each supervisory authority is different, but there are some features that are important for both of them. The main aspects considered by the evaluator are:

- Objectivity
- Information access
- Transparency
- Human resources
- Reputation
- Independence.

The relevance of the rating service for financial markets depends on the objectivity of the evaluation and the agency's reputation (Partnoy, 1999). To offer high-quality service, the evaluator must collect sufficiently detailed time series data and invest in software to construct objective evaluation procedures. These requirements are normally more easily satisfied by the biggest players, which are able to collect this information over many years and apply the standard economy-of-scale principles in order to minimize the relation to each service provided (Weber and Darbellay, 2008).

To reduce the information asymmetry characterizing the market, a rating agency has to make its judgment available to all interested counterparties. To satisfy this requirement, a minimum amount of information (such as the judgment and the summary report) must be distributed to all investors, while some of these investors may be interested in subscribing to a more complete and detailed service. To achieve economic equilibrium, these extra details are normally offered for a fee (Frost, 2007).

The transparency of the evaluation methodology allows users to understand the meaning of the alphanumeric rating. Rating agencies are aware of transparency, because the more details that are provided, the higher the probability

BOX 2.1 Recognition Criteria for NRSROs

US Securities and Exchange Commission nationally recognized statistical rating organizations

The term "nationally recognized statistical rating organization" means a credit rating agency that:

1. has been in business as a credit rating agency for at least the 3 consecutive years immediately preceding the date of its application for registration under section 15E;
2. issues credit ratings certified by qualified institutional buyers, in accordance with section 15E(a)(1)(B)(ix), with respect to:
   a. financial institutions, brokers, or dealers;
   b. insurance companies;
   c. corporate issuers;
   d. issuers of asset-backed securities (as that term is defined in section 1101(c) of part 229 of title 17, Code of Federal Regulations, as in effect on the date of enactment of this paragraph);
   e. issuers of government securities, municipal securities, or securities issued by a foreign government; or
   f. a combination of one or more categories of obligors described in any of clauses (i) through (v); and
3. is registered under section 15E.

Section 15E: Information requirements

An application for registration under this section shall contain information regarding:

1. Credit ratings performance measurement statistics over short-term, mid-term, and long-term periods (as applicable) of the applicant.
2. The procedures and methodologies that the applicant uses in determining credit ratings.
3. Policies or procedures adopted and implemented by the applicant to prevent the misuse, in violation of this title (or the rules and regulations hereunder), of material, nonpublic information.
4. The organizational structure of the applicant.
5. Whether or not the applicant has in effect a code of ethics, and if not, the reasons therefore.
6. Any conflict of interest relating to the issuance of credit ratings by the applicant.
7. The categories described in any of clauses (i) through (v) of section 3(a)(62)(B) with respect to which the applicant intends to apply for registration under this section.
8. On a confidential basis, a list of the 20 largest issuers and subscribers that use the credit rating services of the applicant, by amount of net revenues received therefrom in the fiscal year immediately preceding the date of submission of the application.
9. On a confidential basis, as to each applicable category of obligor described in any of clauses (i) through (v) of section 3(a)(62)(B), written certifications described in subparagraph (C), except as provided in subparagraph (D).
10. Any other information and documents concerning the applicant and any person associated with such applicant as the Commission, by rule, may prescribe as necessary or appropriate in the public interest or for the protection of investors.

Source: Credit Rating Agency Reform Act of 2006.

that a competitor will learn and duplicate the methodology. Moreover, the risks associated with transparency are also important for the market and supervisory authorities, because the higher the risk, the lower the investment in the innovation and development of evaluation methodologies. Supervisory authorities

BOX 2.2 Recognition Criteria for ECAIs

External Credit Assessment Institution

National supervisors are responsible for determining whether an external credit assessment institution (ECAI) meets the criteria and the assessments of ECAIs may be recognized on a limited basis, e.g. by type of claims or by jurisdiction.

An ECAI must satisfy each of the following six criteria.

Objectivity: The methodology for assigning credit assessments must be rigorous, systematic, and subject to some form of validation based on historical experience. Moreover, assessments must be subject to ongoing review and responsive to changes in financial condition. Before being recognized by supervisors, an assessment methodology for each market segment, including rigorous backtesting, must have been established for at least one year and preferably three.

Independence: An ECAI should be independent and should not be subject to political or economic pressures that may influence the rating. The assessment process should be as free as possible from any constraints that could arise in situations where the composition of the board of directors or the shareholder structure of the assessment institution may be seen as creating a conflict of interest.

International access/Transparency: The individual assessments should be available to both domestic and foreign institutions with legitimate interests and at equivalent terms. In addition, the general methodology used by the ECAI should be publicly available.

Disclosure: An ECAI should disclose qualitative and quantitative information as set forth below. Disclosures by ECAIs have been designed to ensure that the ratings that banks employ in the allocation of risk weightings are compiled by reputable institutions. An absence of transparency in this context could lead to banks assessment shopping for institutions that may give more favorable assessments, leading to misleading indicators of risk exposures and the potential for inadequate capital requirements. Furthermore, such disclosures will underpin the comparability of disclosures across banks. Qualitative disclosures enable users to compare assessment methods and put quantitative information into context. Thus information such as the definition of default, the time horizon, and the target of the assessment are all required. Quantitative disclosures present information on the actual default rates experienced in each assessment category and information on assessment transitions, i.e. the likelihood of an AAA credit transiting to AA over time. The disclosure of certain aspects of ECAI's methodologies and definitions is important where differences in methodologies present the opportunity for exploitation by individual banks. The information that needs to be disclosed is presented in more detail in Annex 1. The Committee will be carrying out further work on how to make disclosures by ECAIs comparable.

Resources: An ECAI should have sufficient resources to carry out high-quality credit assessments. These resources should allow for substantial ongoing contact with senior and operational levels within the entities assessed in order to add value to the credit assessments. Such assessments should be based on methodologies combining qualitative and quantitative approaches.

Credibility: To some extent, credibility is derived from the criteria above. In addition, the reliance on an ECAI's external credit assessments by independent parties (investors, insurers, trading partners) is evidence of the credibility of the assessments of an ECAI. The credibility of an ECAI is also underpinned by the existence of internal procedures to prevent the misuse of confidential information. In order to be eligible for recognition, an ECAI does not have to assess firms in more than one country.

Source: Basel Committee on Banking Supervision (2006), *International Convergence of Capital Measurement and Capital Standards.*

no longer explicitly state the level of transparency that satisfies the needs of the entities evaluated, users, and evaluators (Shiren and Crosignani, 2009). Nowadays rating agencies are obliged to publish their rating criteria and disclose the main items considered in their evaluations without giving any details about the weights assigned and they must inform the market of any changes in their evaluation procedures (Rousseau, 2006).

In a low-competition market such as the rating sector, incentives for providing high-quality goods or services may be insufficient (Admati and Pfleiderer, 1986). In this context, for example, reduced investments in human resources can negatively affect the quality of service for an overall portfolio or for certain (residual) sectors (Galil, 2002). For international rating agencies, any analysis of the quality of resources available for the rating process must consider the volume of information available for each country and its adequacy in the correct evaluation of counterparties working in different countries. Empirical evidence demonstrates that due to the inadequacy of resources available, the bigger players may also offer lower-quality service to countries that do not represent their core business (Ferri, 2004).

The rating service is intangible, however, and the user thus faces difficulties evaluating the characteristics and value of the service bought. An agency can signal the quality of the service it offers only through its reputation and must therefore consider the impact of any mistakes or collusion with the evaluated entity on expected profits in upcoming years (Kreps and Wilson, 1982). Reputation is not easy to measure (especially for small agencies), because it depends on word of mouth and market perception of the accuracy of evaluations.

Independence concerns, especially in the relationship between an evaluator and its customers, involve preventing any main customer from influencing rating agency activity (Gibilaro and Mattarocci, 2011a). Moreover, independence analysis must also consider the ownership of the firm, its internal control structure, and the existence of firewalls inside the firm to ensure the independence of the evaluation committee (Committee of European Banking Supervisor, hereinafter CEBS, 2006). The analysis also examines economic and organizational features to determine any feature that can negatively affect the objectivity of judgments.

2.5 THE GREAT FINANCIAL CRISIS AND THE ROLE OF RATING AGENCIES

Failures in the rating industry are not a new issue and the most famous failures prior to the great financial crisis were associated with Enron and Worldcom. Raters were unable to identify the crisis signals in advance and in both cases the firms were downgraded from investment-grade to junk bonds only days before their default. Such scandals increase regulatory attention and the Sarbanes–Oxley Act was the first regulatory intervention in the sector to avoid the same scenario (Hill, 2002).

The development of the great financial crisis is ascribed to the real estate bubble and the excessive use of structured finance products, which increased systemic risk and created the framework for the crisis. The rating agencies failed to act as gatekeeper (Sinclair, 2005) and many of the ratings issued before the crisis were overestimated due to the availability of limited information on issues or issuers under evaluation (Diamond and Rajan, 2009).

The main failures registered during the crisis consisted of large financial institutions that went from investment-grade ratings to default within a few days (e.g. Bear Stearns) and immediately thereafter went out of business through an acquisition or bankruptcy. The literature demonstrates that the lack of variability (especially among top-level ratings) is not always explained by market information available because during the crisis even an increase of the disclosure in the risk of default of an issue or issuer did not imply an immediate change in the rating assigned (Mulligan, 2009).

The next two subsections, using a representative set of worldwide raters, provide a detailed analysis of the behavior of raters before and during the crisis. The analysis considers both aggregate data and data by rater (Section 2.5.1). Given the current academic debate on the supervisory framework's reform, a description of the main proposals currently evaluated by European and US authorities for reorganizing the rating sector is presented (Section 2.5.2).

2.5.1 Rating Actions During the Crisis and Different Rater Behaviors

The analysis of rating actions released by different rating agencies before and during the crisis allows the identification of changes in rater attitudes among the two sub-periods. To obtain a representative sample of the overall market, the study uses data on the number of ratings issued for each customer from each rating agency listed in the Bloomberg database from 2001 to 2012 (Table 2.1).

The changes in rater attitudes are examined by comparing the relative frequencies of upgrades, downgrades, and rating confirmations during the period considered. Table 2.2 presents statistics on the overall market useful in identifying the existence of any changes in the numbers of ratings withdrawn and revisions.

During the period considered the number of rating actions released each year increases over time, and the numbers of changes and new ratings issued in 2012 are more than 2.6 times the number of those registered in 2001. The results are significantly affected by the number of rated entities, which increases significantly, causing higher probabilities of rating changes.

The number of ratings withdrawn also significantly decreases over time and the percentage withdrawn with respect to all rating actions decreases from more than 6% in 2001 to around only 1% in 2012.

Regarding the percentage of downgrades with respect to the percentage of upgrades, from 2003 to 2007 the percentage of upgrades is always significantly higher, while since 2008 (excluding 2010) downgrades are more frequent.

Table 2.1 Sample Description

A.M. Best Company Inc.	Korea Ratings Corporation
Austin Rating	Malaysian Rating Corporation Berhad
BRC Investor Services S.A.	Mikuni & Co. Ltd.
Canadian Bond Rating Service	Moody's Investors Service
Capital Intelligence Ltd.	National Information & Credit Evaluation Inc.
Chengxin International Credit Rating Co. Ltd.	P.T. PEFINDO Credit Rating Indonesia
Credit Analysis & Research Ltd.	Philippine Rating Services Corp.
CRISIL Ltd.	RAM Rating Services Berha
Dagong Global Credit Rating Co. Ltd.	Rating and Investment Information Inc.
Dominion Bond Rating Service	Rus Ratings
European Rating Agency	Shanghai Brilliance Credit Rating & Investors Service Co. Ltd.
Fitch Ratings Ltd.	Standard & Poor's
Global Credit Rating Co.	TCR Kurumsal Yonetimve Kredi Derecelendirme Hizmetleri A.S.
Investment Information and Credit Rating Agency	Thai Rating and Information Services Co. Ltd.
Japan Credit Rating Agency Ltd.	Xinhua Finance

Source: Bloomberg data processed by the author.

During a financial crisis raters tend to be more cautious in upgrading existing ratings and, due to bad economic conditions (current and expected), rating downgrades are more frequent.

If one considers the behavior of each agency separately, a ranking of the frequency of upgrades and downgrades can be constructed to verify if during the crisis the behavior of some raters changes more than that of others (Table 2.3).

The policy normally adopted by raters is to try to confirm the previous rating assigned. Changes of at least one class are less frequent with respect to changes of only a few notches. During the crisis the number of changes (on average) decreases with respect to that in previous years (from 31% to 29%). Normally upgrade revisions are more frequent with respect to downgrade revisions, even if the differences are (on average) only a few percentage points.

Considering each agency separately, only around 47% of raters show a decrease in the number of upratings released after the crisis with respect to pre-crisis years and more than 63% of raters show an increase in the number of downgrades. Only eight rating agencies show both a decrease in upgrades and an increase in downgrades and, among them, only few are big players in the rating industry (Dominion Bond Rating Service, Japan Credit Rating Agency, and Moody's Investor Service).

Table 2.2 Rating Actions During 2001–2012

Year	Rated Entities	Rating Actions During the Year	Rating Withdrawn	Rating Unchanged	Upratings of At Least One Class	Downratings of At Least One Class
2001	26,959	56,509	6.14%	73.40%	8.59%	11.88%
2002	27,995	61,209	6.26%	74.09%	7.58%	12.07%
2003	28,764	64,708	6.98%	78.02%	6.58%	8.41%
2004	32,334	68,016	4.18%	85.25%	5.78%	4.79%
2005	35,876	76,072	3.73%	84.95%	6.51%	4.81%
2006	39,619	85,486	3.42%	85.87%	6.34%	4.37%
2007	42,910	98,546	3.31%	84.58%	7.44%	4.67%
2008	44,754	108,449	2.07%	85.97%	4.80%	7.16%
2009	46,610	114,515	2.69%	80.59%	6.58%	10.14%
2010	50,333	121,250	1.92%	89.56%	4.48%	4.04%
2011	52,563	133,885	1.54%	87.11%	5.45%	5.90%
2012	55,979	147,798	1.12%	89.24%	4.25%	5.39%

Source: Bloomberg data processed by the author.

2.5.2 Perspectives of the New Regulation

A number of critics have argued that the agencies should be subject to some type of liability for their ratings. The argument is straightforward: If raters are liable for negligent ratings, they will be less likely to be negligent and will improve the quality of their credit ratings. The main problem with applying this simple rule is the huge difference in the amount of revenues related to fees paid and the potentially enormous effect that any mistake in evaluation can cause, if a rater is found guilty, instant bankruptcy for the agency. Thus, placing unlimited liability on credit rating agencies may simply terminate the credit ratings business, with potentially deleterious effects for the financial system and the information disclosure (Listokin and Taibleson, 2010).

To avoid the assumption of such risky regulatory choices, supervisors have tried to define new rules to improve the expected quality of services offered by raters. The main issues considered are the following:

- Procyclicality
- The evaluation of complex issues and issuers
- Information quality disclosure
- Corporate governance
- The proposal of a new type of supervisor
- The public liability of the raters
- Payment upon results
- The role of a public-owned rater.

Table 2.3 Rating Agency Actions from 2001 to 2012, by Rater

	Stable Rating		Upratings		Downratings	
	2001–2006	2007–2012	2001–2006	2007–2012	2001–2007	2007–2012
A.M. Best Company Inc.	93.26%	87.98%	4.17%	7.06%	2.57%	4.96%
Austin Rating	88.75%	46.67%	6.25%	40.83%	5.00%	12.50%
BRC Investor Services S.A.	92.58%	96.93%	3.71%	0.88%	3.70%	2.19%
Canadian Bond Rating Service	100%	100%	0.00%	0.00%	0.00%	0.00%
Capital Intelligence Ltd.	100%	41.98%	0.00%	12.42%	0.00%	45.59%
Chengxin International Credit Rating Co. Ltd.	100%	76.35%	0.00%	23.27%	0.00%	0.38%
Credit Analysis & Research Ltd.	52.79%	65.32%	15.14%	3.60%	32.07%	31.09%
CRISIL Ltd.	67.52%	77.90%	18.54%	9.50%	13.94%	12.59%
Dagong Global Credit Rating Co. Ltd.	100%	61.13%	0.00%	24.78%	0.00%	14.10%
Dominion Bond Rating Service	76.14%	76.54%	9.07%	5.84%	14.80%	17.62%
European Rating Agency	100%	100%	0.00%	0.00%	0.00%	0.00%
Fitch Ratings Ltd.	61.07%	63.72%	19.58%	24.63%	19.34%	11.65%
Global Credit Rating Co.	72.73%	65.86%	27.27%	10.65%	0.00%	23.48%
Investment Information and Credit Rating Agency	50.23%	50.65%	15.30%	19.91%	34.46%	29.45%
Japan Credit Rating Agency Ltd.	70.73%	68.62%	17.13%	15.13%	12.14%	16.25%
Korea Ratings Corporation	61.62%	47.76%	33.94%	41.28%	4.43%	10.96%
Malaysian Rating Corporation Berhad	75.29%	86.62%	18.58%	2.20%	6.13%	11.18%
Mikuni & Co. Ltd.	0.00%	100%	66.67%	0.00%	33.33%	0.00%
Moody's Investors Service	41.46%	40.61%	30.78%	24.77%	27.77%	34.62%
National Information & Credit Evaluation Inc.	58.49%	51.73%	27.10%	29.32%	14.41%	18.95%
P.T. PEFINDO Credit Rating Indonesia	47.24%	60.01%	26.89%	30.15%	25.87%	9.84%
Philippine Rating Services Corp.	10.00%	86.43%	42.50%	5.71%	47.50%	7.86%
RAM Rating Services Berha	57.54%	91.69%	25.29%	4.60%	17.16%	3.71%
Rating and Investment Information Inc.	91.93%	92.69%	4.33%	2.71%	3.74%	4.61%
Rus Ratings	100%	66.53%	0.00%	28.61%	0.00%	4.86%
Shanghai Brilliance Credit Rating & Investors Service Co. Ltd.	100%	76.73%	0.00%	18.27%	0.00%	5.00%
Standard & Poor's	66.61%	67.48%	13.36%	13.96%	20.03%	18.57%
TCR Kurumsal Yonetimve Kredi Derecelendirme Hizmetleri A.S.	54.63%	68.28%	33.88%	17.20%	11.49%	14.52%
Thai Rating and Information Services Co. Ltd.	63.99%	56.94%	31.90%	30.10%	4.11%	12.96%
Xinhua Finance	21.77%	61.54%	14.47%	26.92%	63.76%	11.54%

Source: Bloomberg data processed by the author.

The evaluations made by raters are affected by the overall trend of the economy and, normally, rising (decreasing) economies are characterized by a higher frequency of upratings (downratings). During the last financial crisis the negative effects of procyclicality on the capital requirements for financial intermediaries and the shortage in the supply of credit were exacerbated (Goodhart, 2008). The new regulatory framework therefore stresses the importance of creating a through-the-cycle evaluation model for raters to avoid the risk of unnecessary downgrades of issuers and issues due to just downturns in the economy.

The development of the financial crisis is ascribed to the inaccuracy of the ratings assigned to more complex transactions (structured finance) due to the raters' insufficient skills and available knowledge. To avoid the same mistakes, rating agencies now invest more in collecting the information necessary to evaluate such complex instruments and invest their money directly into constructing more complex and detailed procedures to increase the quality and usefulness of their private certification (Schwarz, 2008).

The quality of a rating service can be measured on the basis of the historical probability of default of the issuer or issues classified on the basis of the rating assigned and the migration matrix among rating classes. The new regulatory approach requires recognized raters to periodically disclose detailed statistics on the quality of services provided and to provide this information without charge on their websites (Darbellay and Partnoy, 2012).

To ensure the quality of the service provided, the new regulatory approach adopted by the main supervisors tries to control the rating procedure adopted by raters and the quality and amount of resources (both human and real capital) used. The information requirements for the accreditation process are significantly increased, even if all these data are frequently disclosed only to the supervisor and investors cannot directly access them (Kotecha et al., 2013).

A less market-oriented solution proposed is the creation of a new type of supervisor specializing only in the rating sector who can more effectively control the raters. The new regulator must be independent of both the financial markets and politicians. The value of the service provided is then strictly related to the quality of the specific knowledge available in the rating sector (Levine, 2012).

Ratings are opinions on the risk of an issuer or issue, defined on the basis of the information available and/or collected by the rater. In the event of an inaccurate evaluation, the evaluator is not liable. One of the revisions currently proposed is to assign a liability when ratings are not accurate assessments of the risk inherent in the investment, where the cost for the rater is proportional to the losses suffered by the financial system due to the misspecification of the risk (e.g. Ellis, Fairchild, and D'Souza, 2012).

To create an incentive for raters' correct risk evaluations, the solution proposed is to construct a new remuneration mechanism that considers the historical fitness of the evaluation procedure to define the amount of fees paid for each evaluation. This idea allows rating agencies to be rewarded for the quality of service provided and increases the value of the reputation acquired by the rater, which is useful not only to acquire new customers but also to increase the revenues related to each service provided (Alcubilla and Del Pozo, 2012).

To increase the level of competition, since 2010 European countries have been evaluating the opportunity to implement public rating agencies. These public agencies would compete with existing private rating agencies to avoid an increase in the sovereign default risk caused by downgrades realized by raters in the last years. The role of public raters would be to increase market competition, creating an incentive for existing raters to increase the quality of the service they provide and avoiding the risk of collusion among privately owned raters (Voorhees, 2012).

2.6 CONCLUSIONS

Issuer and issue ratings can significantly affect market demand and thus the cost of capital for the evaluated firm. The impact differs on the basis of the existence and type of ratings available. Normally the impact is always higher when the information is unexpected and not coherent with available information provided by other raters.

The current financial crisis demonstrates the limits of the service provided by raters in evaluating the risk of issuers and issues in a distressed scenario. In 2007 and 2008 the number of rating downgrades was double that during the pre-crisis period and sometimes the change registered was significant. In the comparison of different raters, large players did not show behavior coherent with expectations in the crisis period and normally the numbers of relevant upgrades and downgrades are not as relevant as the stability of the ratings issued.

The biggest failures registered in the 1990s (e.g. Enron) are normally ascribed to a lack of competition in the rating market that failed to create incentives to properly evaluate risk profiles (Hill, 2002). To understand the reasons behind the current financial crisis, a detailed analysis of the current rating market structure is necessary to determine if the limits and failures registered during this crisis can be ascribed to a lack of competition.

Chapter three

The Rating Market

3.1 INTRODUCTION

Even if a rating service began in the late nineteenth century, the main development of the market is normally ascribed to the development of the financial markets in the main markets, which has caused a significant increase in the demand for the service (Partnoy, 2006). The development of the market was not independent with respect to the type of issue or issuer and during the twentieth century the supply of different types of ratings was characterized by different cycles (e.g. Gaillard, 2012).

The current market scenario is characterized by the existence of a few main players that control the market and several smaller rating agencies (Smith and Walter, 2001). The market competition is not very relevant owing to the small number of players (Cantor and Parker, 1995) and the non-exclusivity of the customer relationship, which has created an incentive for customers to adopt a "multi-rating" solution (Mattarocci, 2005).

Empirical evidence in the literature demonstrates that currently the top three rating agencies (Fitch Rating, Moody's Investor Service, and Standard & Poor's) publish the ratings for more than 90% of the value of all issues rated worldwide (El-Shagi, 2010). They therefore have, at the very least, a competitive advantage with respect to the other, smaller players. No detailed analysis of market concentration over time is available and there is still little evidence on the differences between rating agencies, especially those not among the top three.

This chapter analyzes the rating market and presents a detailed, updated analysis of the market shares of different types of agencies. Sections 3.2 and 3.3 present and outline the main events related to the birth and development of the industry and the reasons behind the low competition in the market. Section 3.4 presents a detailed outlook of the worldwide market, pointing out the current level of competition and the role of strategic alliances in the development of the small rating agencies. Section 3.5 studies the development of rating market concentration during the last decade and presents some data on the concentration and the role of multi-rating. Section 1.6 summarizes the chapter and concludes with some policy implications.

The Independence of Credit Rating Agencies.
© 2014 Elsevier Inc. All rights reserved.

3.2 HISTORY OF THE RATING INDUSTRY

The origin of the rating agency industry can be ascribed to the first credit reporting institution in 1841, the so-called Mercantile agency. It was started as a solution to reduce the information asymmetry that characterized the market, using a network of agents to gather information on operating statistics, business standing and creditworthiness, and to define a judgment on the commercial risk exposure of counterparties on the basis of the information available and the wholesaler's experience (White, 2010).

The modern rating industry began in the early 1900s due to a radical change in capital market demand, driven by the development of the corporate sector and the decrease in public financial aid. During the 1800s, especially in the USA, there was a huge development of corporates in the railroad sector to develop new construction projects not directly funded by government. This growth opportunity of the US market generated a huge demand for funding opportunities. In the beginning, financing sources were prevalently (exclusively) related to the banking sector, but in the second half of the century corporations sought alternative sources of capital and focused on opportunities related to the bond market. Since its beginning, the bond market has been characterized by the prevalence of government-issued instruments whose investors are not normally exposed to the risk of default due to the strength and power of the sovereign issuers. Investors can thus subscribe to these financial instruments without considering or evaluating the risk of default relating to the contract. Once corporates came on to the market, the risk of instruments traded increased significantly and there was a huge demand for credit risk evaluation services not previously requested (Sylla, 2002).

In the first half of the 1900s, all the current biggest players of the present rating industry began and developed a different model for entering into the market and acquiring in a short time a relevant market share (Box 3.1).

In the beginning the growth of the market was very slow and the value added offered by the rating agencies was essentially related to the opportunity to collect information unavailable to other investors due to the low disclosure of the issuer market. Once rating services were recognized as a criterion for ensuring the quality of issues and issuers (e.g. the SEC rules on NRSRO in 1975), the market began to grow rapidly and in the 1980s and 1990s there was a significant increase in the number of rating agencies in all markets worldwide (Table 3.1).[1]

During the 1980s and 1990s the growth of the market was so significant that in each of the two decades the number of rating agencies at least doubled. Comparing the market size at the end of the 1970s and at the end of the 1990s, in less than 20 years the number of rating agencies was more than six times greater. The significant increase registered in the number of players starting

---

[1] Due to the availability of data we consider only the rating agencies that still exist and we are unable to control for the problem of survivorship bias.

BOX 3.1 The Origins of the Three Main Rating Agencies

Fitch Ratings

Fitch Ratings was founded as the Fitch Publishing Company on December 24, 1913, by John Knowles Fitch. Located in the heart of the financial district in New York City, the Fitch Publishing Company began as a publisher of financial statistics. In 1924, the Fitch Publishing Company issued the first rating.

Moody's Investor Service

John Moody & Company was founded in 1900 by John Moody to serve the needs of the investment community. The first output was the publication of *Moody's Manual of Industrial and Miscellaneous Securities*, a collection of information and statistics on stock and bonds. After its bankruptcy, in 1909 John Moody decided his company would get into the business of analyzing the stock and bonds of America's railroads, publishing *Moody's Analyses of Railroad Investments*. It described for readers the analytic principles that Moody used to assess a railroad's operations, management, and financing. The new manual used letter rating symbols adopted from the mercantile and credit rating system, which had been used by credit-reporting firms since the late 1800s, and the manual quickly found a place in investor hands.

Standard & Poor's

In 1860 Henry Varnum Poor published *History of the Railroads and Canals of the United States*, the first major attempt to compile a comprehensive account of both the financial and operational details of US railroads. In 1873 Henry William Poor created the Poor and Co., an insurance and brokerage firm, and in 1906 Luther Lee Blake created the Standard Statistics Bureau (renamed in 1914 to Standard Statistics Inc.). In 1919 Poor and Co. merged with Moody's Manual Co. and changed the name to Poor's Publishing. In 1922 it began rating corporate bonds and municipal services. Standard Statistics Inc. issued its first ratings in 1923 and in 1941 it merged with Poor's Publishing, creating the Standard & Poor's Corporation.

Source: Information collected from rating agency websites.

from the 1980s could be explained by the development of the asset-backed securities that normally represent the more profitable business for the rater due to the higher fees applied to the customers (Partnoy, 2006).

Looking at the geographical areas of the rating agencies, some difference in the time patterns of the different geographical areas could be identified. The USA was the country with the highest number of new rating agencies created before the 1970s and during the last 40 years the number of new agencies created has usually been lower with respect to other countries, and only in the 1980s was the number of new players entering into the market significant with respect to the worldwide market.

In the 1970s Japan supported the initiation and the development of local rating agencies in order to reduce the opaqueness of the financial market and increase the amount of resources invested by both domestic and foreign investors.

Starting from the 1980s, the more significant growth of the rating market was in developing economies in which the government decided to support the development of both private and public rating agencies (e.g. Ferri and Lacitignola, 2010) in order to increase the transparency of the market and support foreign capital investment into the country.

Table 3.1 Number of New Rating Agencies Created Each Decade, by Country of Origin

	Before 1970	1970s	1980s	1990s	2000s
Overall	4	4	13	34	17
Africa	0	0	0	2	0
Asia	0	2	8	16	13
Australia and New Zealand	0	0	0	1	0
Europe	1	0	1	1	1
North America	3	2	3	2	1
Central and South America	0	0	1	12	2
Country with the highest number of new rating agencies created in the decade	USA	Japan	USA and South Korea	Peru	Turkey

Source: <www.defaultrisk.com> data processed by the author.

3.3 ENTRY BARRIERS FOR NEWCOMERS

Even if the market has grown significantly during the last century, the number of agencies is still quite small due to the existence of some entry barriers in the market. The lack of competition can be ascribed to the characteristics of the production process and the usefulness of the marketing mix instrument.

The analysis of the production process of the rating service demonstrates that the main entry barrier is represented by the scale economies in the market (Williamson, 1969) that characterize the service offered to existing customers. In fact, the issue of a new rating for an existing customer is normally lower with respect to the cost of evaluation of a new customer. Savings are essentially related to the information collection process and theoretically the price applied to the service offered could be lowered in order to increase customer satisfaction (Butler and Rodgers, 2003). In this scenario a newcomer could not partake in price competition with existing rating agencies in order to increase its market share because, ceteris paribus, the profit margin will be lower for the new agencies with respect to existing ones. Moreover, normally the older rating agencies have increased their size over time due to merger and acquisition activity (Sylla, 2002), and so existing raters are normally more able to take greater advantage of the economies of scale.

If one considers the opportunity of a newcomer to start activity in a market trying to serve customers not served by other rating agencies, some other entry barriers could justify the low number of agencies available in the market.

Considering the marketing mix, the main instrument used to increase the market share is related to the quality of the product because the rating represents an immaterial service for which the value depends on the credibility of the rater and the usefulness of the rating judgment for potentially interested users. A newcomer normally does not have the reputation necessary to compete in the market with existing raters (Partnoy, 2001) and needs a lot of time in order to be recognized by the market as a good and trustworthy information provider. Looking at the instruments that may be used in order to compete, the rating industry does not allow modifications of the quality and/or price of the service offered in order to increase the rater's market share. Regarding the quality of the service offered, the agency that adopts a less selective evaluation process can increase customer satisfaction due to the better evaluation assigned to each rated entity. This solution may be reasonable only until the market discovers the less strict standards adopted for the evaluation because later the reputation of the agency will be lower, causing its exit from the market. Considering price competition, the choice to modify the price may be risky because, due to the high relevance of fixed costs in the evaluation procedure, any decrease in price not followed by an increase in demand will impact negatively on profit margins and can impact negatively on the survivorship of the firm (Mukhopadhyay, 2009).

3.4 THE CURRENT RATING MARKET

Rating agencies' features impose a level of acceptable competition that does not create incentives to lower the quality of the evaluation process to increase market share (White, 1981). The current scenario shows only a small number of players (less than 80), which implies a low-competition environment for the rating sector (see Table 3.2).

The rating agency started in the USA, and even today the USA is the most represented nation in that it is the country of residence of the most evaluators (nine agencies). In the last decades, some Asian countries have grown significantly, and China, India, and Turkey are now the most represented countries after the USA, with nine, five, and five agencies respectively.

The competition is even lower than that shown in the previous market outlook, because agreements to reduce competition are frequently made by the main international players with the small rating agencies (see Table 3.3).

As stated in the literature (Ferri and Lacitignola, 2010), strategic affiliations are frequently adopted by Asian agencies (70% of the affiliations listed) to offer services comparable with those of the best international players. The leading agencies with such agreements are normally the three market leaders (Fitch Ratings, Moody's Investors Service, and Standard & Poor's), but some smaller agencies (such as the European Rating Agency and Japan Credit Rating Agency) have also started to use alliances to increase their market share in Eastern Europe and Asia.

Such alliances may be just marketing agreements to use the leading company's brand, a method to obtain technical support to develop and refine evaluation models, or even equity capital agreements (Todhanakasem, 2001). Excluding rating agencies engaged in strategic alliances, the number of independent rating agencies in the market is lower than 50.

Table 3.2 Rating Agency Market at the End of 2012

Rating Agency	Country	Rating Agency	Country
A.M. Best Company Inc.	USA	Islamic International Rating Agency B.S.C.	Bahrain
Agusto & Co. Ltd.	Nigeria	Istanbul International Rating Services Inc.	Turkey
Ahbor Rating	Uzbekistan	Japan Credit Rating Agency Ltd.	Japan
Apoyo & Asociados Internacionales S.A.C.	Peru	JCR Avrasya Derecelendime A.S.	Turkey
Bank Watch Ratings S.A.	Ecuador	JCR-VIS Credit Rating Co. Ltd.	Pakistan
BRC Investor Services S.A.	Colombia	Kobirate	Turkey
Calificadora de Riesgo, PCA	Uruguay	Korea Investors Service Inc.	South Korea
Capital Intelligence Ltd.	Cyprus	Korea Ratings Corporation	South Korea
Capital Standards	Kuwait	Kroll Bond Rating Agency Inc.	USA
Caribbean Information & Credit Rating Services Ltd.	Trinidad and Tobago	Lanka Rating Agency Ltd.	Sri Lanka
Central European Rating Agency	Poland	Malaysian Rating Corporation Berhad	Malaysia
Chengxin International Credit Rating Co. Ltd.	China	Mikuni & Co. Ltd.	Japan
China Lianhe Credit Rating Co. Ltd.	China	Moody's Investors Service	USA
Clasificadora de Riesgo Humphreys Ltd.	Chile	National Information & Credit Evaluation Inc.	South Korea
Class y Asociados S.A. Clasificadora de Riesgo	Peru	ONICRA Credit Rating Agency of India Ltd.	India
CMC International Ltd.	Nigeria	P.T. PEFINDO Credit Rating Indonesia	Indonesia
Companhia Portuguesa de Rating SA	Portugal	Pacific Credit Rating	Peru
Credit Analysis & Research Ltd.	India	Pakistan Credit Rating Agency Ltd.	Pakistan
"Credit-Rating": A Ukrainian rating agency	Ukraine	Philippine Rating Services Corp.	Philippines
Credit Rating Agency of Bangladesh Ltd.	Bangladesh	RAM Rating Services Berha	Malaysia
Credit Rating Information and Services Ltd.	Bangladesh	Rapid Ratings International Inc.	Australia
CRISIL Ltd.	India	Rating and Investment Information Inc.	Japan

(Continued...)

Table 3.2 Rating Agency Market at the End of 2012 (continued)

Rating Agency	Country	Rating Agency	Country
Dagong Global Credit Rating Co. Ltd.	China	Realpoint, LLC	USA
Demotech Inc.	USA	Rus Ratings	Russia
Dominion Bond Rating Service	Canada	Saha Kurumsal Yönetimve Kredi Derecelendirme Hizmetleri A.Ş.	Turkey
Duff&Phelps de Colombia, S.A., S.C.V.	Colombia	Seoul Credit Rating & Information Inc.	South Korea
Ecuability, SA	Ecuador	Shanghai Credit Information Services Co. Ltd.	China
Egan-Jones Rating Company	USA	SME Rating Agency of India Limited	India
Emerging Credit Rating	Bangladesh	Sociedad Calificadora de Riesgo Centroamericana, S.A.	Costa Rica
Equilibrium Clasificadora de Riesgo	Peru	SR rating	Brazil
European Rating Agency	UK	Standard & Poor's	USA
Feller Rate Clasificadora de Riesgo	Chile	Taiwan Ratings Corp.	Taiwan
Fitch Ratings Ltd.	UK	TCR Kurumsal Yonetimve Kredi Derecelendirme Hizmetleri A.Ş.	Turkey
Global Credit Rating Co.	South Africa	Thai Rating and Information Services Co. Ltd.	Thailand
HR Ratings de Mexico, S.A. de C.V.	Mexico	Veribanc Inc.	USA
Interfax Rating Agency	Russia	Weiss Ratings Inc.	USA
Investment Information and Credit Rating Agency	India	Xinhua Finance	China

Source: <www.defaultrisk.com> (accessed 03.01.2013).
From the list available on the website Slovak Rating Agency, a.s. and Kasnic Credit Rating Indonesia are excluded due to acquisitions made by other rating agencies (respectively from European Rating Agency P.T. and Moody's).

3.5 THE EVOLUTION OF COMPETITION IN THE RATING MARKET

To evaluate the degree of competition in the rating market, it is not sufficient to count the number of agencies; it is also necessary to construct proxies of their economic relevance in the market on the basis of the number of ratings offered and/or the number of customers served.

To measure the level of concentration in the world rating market, the attention is focused only on rating agencies listed in the Bloomberg database, for which it is possible to collect data about the number of ratings issued for each customer served from 2001 to 2012 (Table 3.4).

Table 3.3 Strategic Alliances in the Rating Sector

Affiliated Entity	Leading Agency
Apoyo & Asociados Internacionales S.A.C.[*]	Fitch Ratings Ltd.
Bank Watch Ratings S.A.	Fitch Ratings Ltd.
Central European Rating Agency	Fitch Ratings Ltd.
Chengxin International Credit Rating Co. Ltd.	Moody's Investors Service
Clasificadora de Riesgo Humphreys Ltda.	Moody's Investors Service
CRISIL Ltd.	Standard & Poor's
Duff&Phelps de Colombia, S.A., S.C.V	Fitch Ratings Ltd.
Equilibrium Clasificadora de Riesgo	Moody's Investors Service
Feller Rate Clasificadora de Riesgo	Standard & Poor's
JCR Avrasya Derecelendime A.S.	Japan Credit Rating Agency Ltd.
JCR-VIS Credit Rating Co. Ltd.	Japan Credit Rating Agency Ltd.
Korea Investors Service Inc.	Moody's Investors Service
Korea Ratings Corporation	Fitch Ratings Ltd.
Lanka Rating Agency Ltd.[†]	Standard & Poor's
Malaysian Rating Corporation Berhad	Fitch Ratings Ltd.
P.T. Kasnic Credit Rating Indonesia	Moody's Investors Service
Pakistan Credit Rating Agency Ltd.	Fitch Ratings Ltd.
RAM Rating Services Berhad	Standard & Poor's
Seoul Credit Rating & Information Inc.	Japan Credit Rating Agency Ltd.
Slovak Rating Agency, a.s.	European Rating Agency
Taiwan Ratings Corp.	Standard & Poor's

Source: <www.defaultrisk.com> (accessed 03.01.2013).
[*]*Apoyo & Asociados Internacionales S.A.C. is not only affiliated with Fitch Rating but it is also included in the financial group that owns Fitch Ratings (FIMALAC).*
[†]*Lanka Rating Agency Ltd. is controlled by RAM Rating Services Berha and so the strategic affiliation with Standard & Poor's is only indirect.*

To evaluate the rating market, some concentration measures are constructed for both the number of customers served and the number of ratings issued:

$$\% Ratings_{it} = \frac{No.\ of\ ratings_{it}}{\sum_{k=1}^{n} No.\ of\ ratings_{kt}} \tag{3.1}$$

$$\% Customers_{it} = \frac{No.\ of\ customers_{it}}{\sum_{k=1}^{n} No.\ of\ customers_{kt}} \tag{3.2}$$

Table 3.4 Sample Description

A.M. Best Company Inc.	Japan Credit Rating Agency Ltd.
Austin Rating	Korea Ratings Corporation
BRC Investor Services S.A.	Malaysian Rating Corporation Berhad
Canadian Bond Rating Service	Mikuni & Co. Ltd.
Capital Intelligence Ltd.	Moody's Investors Service
Chengxin International Credit Rating Co. Ltd.	National Information & Credit Evaluation Inc.
China Lianhe Credit Rating Co. Ltd.	P.T. PEFINDO Credit Rating Indonesia
Credit Analysis & Research Ltd.	Philippine Rating Services Corp.
CRISIL Ltd.	RAM Rating Services Berha
Dagong Global Credit Rating Co. Ltd.	Rating and Investment Information Inc.
Dominion Bond Rating Service	Rus Ratings
European Rating Agency	Shanghai Brilliance Credit Rating & Investors Service Co. Ltd.
Fitch Ratings Ltd.	Standard & Poor's
Global Credit Rating Co.	Thai Rating and Information Services Co. Ltd.
Investment Information and Credit Rating Agency	Xinhua Finance

Source: Bloomberg data processed by the author.

$$HHRatings_{it} = \sum_{i=1}^{m}(\%Ratings_{it})^2 \qquad (3.3)$$

$$HHCustomers_{it} = \sum_{i=1}^{m}(\%Customers_{it})^2, \qquad (3.4)$$

where *No. of ratings$_{it}$* is the number of ratings issued by rating agency *i* in year *t* and *No. of customers$_{it}$* is the number of firms with at least one rating issued by rating agency *i* in year *t*. Equations (3.1) and (3.2) represent the relevance of the agency on the basis of, respectively, the rating issuer and the number of customers, while equations (3.3) and (3.4) are the standard Herfindahl–Hirschman index (Hirschman, 1945; Herfindahl, 1950) measures constructed based on equations (3.1) and (3.2).

An analysis of the top five rating agencies on the basis of the number of customers and the number of ratings allows one to identify distinctive features of the rating market (Table 3.5).

The main rating agencies (Moody's Investor Services, Standard & Poor's, and Fitch Ratings) always issue more that 60% of all the ratings available and evaluate more than 73% of the customers, even if the role of these agencies

Table 3.5 The Role of the Top Five Agencies in the Rating Market

	Top 1		Top 2		Top 3		Top 4		Top 5	
Percentage of Ratings Issued by the Agency With Respect to the Overall Market										
2001	Moody's	34.68%	S&P	30.71%	Fitch	14.19%	R&I	3.72%	JCR	3.34%
2002	Moody's	35.51%	S&P	28.87%	Fitch	14.63%	JCR	3.50%	R&I	3.41%
2003	Moody's	36.57%	S&P	25.94%	Fitch	15.17%	JCR	3.49%	R&I	3.14%
2004	Moody's	33.97%	S&P	23.53%	Fitch	15.30%	AM Best	5.31%	JCR	3.36%
2005	Moody's	32.68%	S&P	21.77%	Fitch	16.66%	AM Best	6.69%	DBRS	3.25%
2006	Moody's	31.91%	S&P	22.39%	Fitch	16.07%	AM Best	6.61%	DBRS	3.85%
2007	Moody's	31.46%	S&P	20.90%	Fitch	15.65%	AM Best	7.48%	DBRS	4.72%
2008	Moody's	31.15%	S&P	20.16%	Fitch	15.04%	AM Best	7.41%	DBRS	4.62%
2009	Moody's	30.94%	S&P	19.01%	Fitch	14.40%	AM Best	6.98%	DBRS	4.49%
2010	Moody's	30.08%	S&P	18.04%	Fitch	14.33%	AM Best	6.42%	CRIS	4.45%
2011	Moody's	30.08%	S&P	17.79%	Fitch	14.22%	AM Best	6.00%	CRIS	4.51%
2012	Moody's	29.60%	S&P	17.47%	Fitch	13.79%	AM Best	5.85%	CRIS	5.25%

Percentage of Customers Served by the Agency With Respect to the Overall Market

2001	Moody's	35.75%	S&P	34.09%	Fitch	16.48%	R&I	2.29%	JCR	2.22%
2002	Moody's	36.72%	S&P	32.04%	Fitch	17.25%	JCR	2.30%	R&I	2.09%
2003	Moody's	37.99%	S&P	29.30%	Fitch	17.89%	JCR	2.38%	DBRS	2.06%
2004	Moody's	37.20%	S&P	26.90%	Fitch	17.83%	AM Best	3.64%	JCR	2.28%
2005	Moody's	35.86%	S&P	24.87%	Fitch	20.10%	AM Best	4.24%	DBRS	2.73%
2006	Moody's	35.33%	S&P	26.34%	Fitch	19.01%	AM Best	3.99%	DBRS	3.15%
2007	Moody's	36.09%	S&P	24.50%	Fitch	18.42%	AM Best	4.30%	DBRS	4.14%
2008	Moody's	35.96%	S&P	23.61%	Fitch	17.88%	AM Best	4.21%	DBRS	4.14%
2009	Moody's	36.17%	S&P	22.27%	Fitch	17.11%	DBRS	4.13%	AM Best	3.92%
2010	Moody's	35.90%	S&P	21.07%	Fitch	17.05%	DBRS	4.10%	AM Best	3.57%
2011	Moody's	35.93%	S&P	21.01%	Fitch	17.09%	DBRS	4.23%	AM Best	3.27%
2012	Moody's	35.80%	S&P	20.25%	Fitch	16.05%	AM Best	4.64%	DBRS	4.04%

Source: Bloomberg data processed by the author.
AM Best = A.M. Best Company; Fitch = Fitch Ratings; JCR = Japan Credit Rating Agency; Moody's = Moody's Investor Services; R&I = Rating and Investment Information; DBRS = Dominion Bond Rating Service; S&P = Standard & Poor's.

has decreased significantly. The market share (in terms of both the number of customers and the number of ratings) of the strongest of the top three rating agencies is never higher than one and a half times that of the third strongest. However, the role of smaller agencies is increasing over time: In fact, the data show that the number of ratings issued by the top three raters decreased from 79% to 61% from 2001 to 2012 and the number of customers decreased from 86% to 72% in the same time period.

To measure the rating market concentration, for each year the value of the Herfindahl–Hirschman index is compared with the theoretical value for a market with perfect competition:

$$\left(HH_{\text{Theoretical}} = n \times \left(\frac{1}{n}\right)^2 = \frac{1}{n} \right).$$

The results do not point to significant differences with respect to the analysis of the top players and support the hypothesis that the market is highly concentrated between a few raters, even if the value of the concentration measures is far from their maximum values (Table 3.6).

Regardless of whether the focus is on the number of ratings or customers, the level of market concentration is always lower than 30%, far from that to support the hypothesis of perfect market competition. However, time trends show a significant decrease in concentration for both the number of ratings and the number of customers (decreases of more than 8% and 6% respectively). The concentration measures constructed on the number of ratings are never less than 3% higher than those constructed on the number of customers, because the number of services requested by each customer is higher for the larger rating agencies (on average).

The concentration in each local market is significantly different with respect to the figures relating to the worldwide market due to the existence of many raters specialized in only a few countries. Therefore, the degree of competition may be significantly lower for those markets that do not appeal to a high number of raters (Table 3.7).

Regarding the number of countries served by each rating agency, on average, more than 30% of rating agencies have a customer portfolio concentrated in no more than four countries and more than 50% of raters serve at least 10 countries. The role of the more internationalized rating agencies has increased over time and the number of rating agencies serving more than 30 countries has doubled from 2001 to 2012. In fact, given the relation between the number of customers and the number of markets served, the mean number of customers served has increased for the more internationalized rating agencies.

To evaluate market competition, it is necessary to consider that the rating market is not characterized by exclusivity of the relationship between the rater and the rated entity; therefore, customers frequently take the opportunity to request the same service from more than one rating agency (Ellis, 1998).

Table 3.6 Herfindahl–Hirschman Index on the Basis of the Number of Ratings and Customers

	$HH_{Theoretical}$	$HH_{Customer}$	$HH_{Ratings}$
2001	4.00%	24.41%	27.65%
2002	3.57%	24.18%	27.37%
2003	3.57%	23.69%	27.03%
2004	3.45%	21.04%	25.25%
2005	3.33%	20.13%	24.27%
2006	3.13%	19.93%	24.37%
2007	3.13%	19.16%	23.96%
2008	3.13%	18.58%	23.38%
2009	3.13%	17.85%	22.75%
2010	3.13%	16.96%	22.02%
2011	3.13%	16.87%	22.02%
2012	3.13%	16.35%	21.24%

Source: Bloomberg data processed by the author.

Few issuers or issues in the industry are evaluated by only one rater (Boot, Milbourn, and Schmeits, 2006) and multi-rating is a solution frequently adopted by all the main players. The data show that the number of rating agencies that serve customers that never had a relationship with another rating agency has decreased over time and currently there are no agencies with no customers evaluated by another rating agency (Table 3.8).

Market development during recent years has significantly increased the number of multi-rated customers and in 2012 75% of raters had a customer portfolio served by more than 10 other rating agencies (with respect to 2001, the percentage more than doubled). The percentage of rating agencies that have a portfolio of customers served by no more than five other raters has decreased from around 26% to less than 6% on the overall time horizon and the percentage of rating agencies with customers served by at least six and no more than 10 raters has decreased by around 10%.

Given the mean percentage of multi-rated customers for rating agencies classified on the basis of the number of raters that evaluate their customers' portfolios, there is no clear relation between the number of raters and the average number of multi-rated customers. The average number of multi-rated customers is always lower when more than 10 other rating agencies are interested in evaluating the customers served by one rater. If one compares rating agencies whose customers are served by fewer than five raters with those whose customers are served by six to 10 rating agencies, the increase in the number

Table 3.7 Rating Agencies Classified on the Basis of the Number of Countries Served

	2001	2002	2003	2004	2005	2006	2007	2008	2009	2010	2011	2012
Number of Rating Agencies, Classified by the Number of Countries Served												
≥50 countries	11.11%	10.00%	10.00%	16.13%	15.15%	20.00%	20.00%	19.44%	19.44%	22.22%	22.22%	22.22%
30 ≤ countries < 50	7.41%	6.67%	13.33%	12.90%	12.12%	8.57%	8.57%	11.11%	13.89%	16.67%	16.67%	16.67%
20 ≤ countries < 30	7.41%	6.67%	0.00%	12.90%	15.15%	11.43%	14.29%	13.89%	11.11%	11.11%	11.11%	13.89%
10 ≤ countries < 20	29.63%	26.67%	30.00%	35.48%	33.33%	31.43%	28.57%	25.00%	25.00%	22.22%	22.22%	19.44%
5 ≤ countries < 10	0.00%	0.00%	0.00%	0.00%	0.00%	0.00%	0.00%	0.00%	0.00%	0.00%	0.00%	0.00%
3 ≤ countries < 5	22.22%	20.00%	20.00%	9.68%	9.09%	8.57%	8.57%	8.33%	8.33%	11.11%	11.11%	11.11%
2 countries	14.81%	13.33%	16.67%	0.00%	0.00%	0.00%	5.71%	8.33%	8.33%	5.56%	8.33%	11.11%
Only 1 country	7.41%	16.67%	10.00%	12.90%	15.15%	20.00%	14.29%	13.89%	13.89%	11.11%	8.33%	5.56%
Mean Number of Customers Served by Rating Agencies Classified on the Basis of the Number of Countries Served												
≥50 countries	6011.33	6806.33	7198.00	7448.67	7559.67	5279.40	5885.00	5046.14	5454.86	5611.00	5704.14	5304.25
≥30 countries	3945.60	4460.40	4703.60	4861.60	3624.86	3331.89	3710.89	3729.50	4036.10	3790.36	3599.92	3449.29
≥20 countries	3301.50	3731.17	3410.00	3536.14	3624.86	2559.58	2480.07	2750.50	2784.40	2709.94	2775.94	2752.33
≥10 countries	2501.38	2581.11	2735.00	2837.33	2634.80	1552.24	1731.57	1757.22	1901.39	1984.04	2057.74	2145.13
≥5 countries	1614.54	1643.27	1740.47	1807.27	1855.13	1422.74	1521.25	1688.29	1826.88	1906.08	1978.46	2059.84
≥3 countries	1251.24	1384.44	1466.72	1523.89	1416.40	1267.12	1360.85	1509.44	1633.00	1703.67	1768.37	1848.61
≥2 countries	1136.58	1264.65	1285.14	1335.43	1314.09	1220.96	1313.18	1456.50	1575.75	1643.93	1706.43	1737.13
All	1079.85	1021.72	1085.04	1129.36	1081.04	1220.96	1313.18	1456.50	1479.43	1498.32	1561.06	1641.09

Source: Bloomberg data processed by the author.

Table 3.8 The Relevance of Multi-Rating in the World Market

	2001	2002	2003	2004	2005	2006	2007	2008	2009	2010	2011	2012
Rating Agencies Classified on the Basis of the Number of Other Agencies that Evaluate at Least One of Their Customers												
Not multi-rated	11.11%	10.00%	10.00%	9.68%	15.15%	0.00%	0.00%	0.00%	0.00%	0.00%	0.00%	0.00%
From 2 to 5 rating agencies	25.93%	30.00%	20.00%	9.68%	3.03%	17.14%	14.29%	8.33%	5.56%	5.56%	5.56%	5.56%
From 6 to 10 rating agencies	29.63%	30.00%	33.33%	6.45%	12.12%	11.43%	14.29%	19.44%	16.67%	19.44%	19.44%	19.44%
More than 10 agencies	33.33%	30.00%	36.67%	74.19%	69.70%	71.43%	71.43%	72.22%	77.78%	75.00%	75.00%	75.00%
Mean Percentage of Multi-Rated Customers for Rating Agencies Classified on the Basis of the Number of Other Agencies that Evaluate Their Customers												
Not multi-rated	–	–	–	–	–	–	–	–	–	–	–	–
From 2 to 5 rating agencies	18.09%	14.56%	18.47%	29.31%	7.35%	13.00%	19.19%	10.06%	12.50%	12.12%	18.52%	13.89%
From 6 to 10 rating agencies	16.72%	16.14%	14.39%	33.79%	19.53%	17.45%	13.32%	13.45%	20.12%	22.26%	21.15%	19.25%
More than 10 agencies	6.91%	6.58%	7.63%	7.84%	9.05%	8.20%	7.90%	7.13%	6.42%	6.29%	6.26%	6.27%
Mean Percentage of Coverage of the Rating Agency's Customers by the Most Representative Competitor for Rating Agencies Classified on the Basis of the Number of Other Agencies that Evaluate Their Customers												
Not multi-rated	–	–	–	–	–	–	–	–	–	–	–	–
From 2 to 5 rating agencies	20.00%	24.07%	24.14%	31.72%	37.05%	42.37%	45.69%	40.32%	56.25%	59.09%	66.67%	62.50%
From 6 to 10 rating agencies	47.03%	46.02%	40.74%	77.23%	45.74%	41.36%	31.76%	45.87%	45.08%	45.16%	44.37%	41.99%
More than 10 agencies	40.25%	40.69%	42.96%	41.53%	43.47%	41.46%	41.29%	39.41%	37.66%	39.45%	39.55%	39.73%

Source: Bloomberg data processed by the author.

of raters involved does not always cause an increase in the share of multi-rated customers. The results obtained demonstrate that the attention given by the rating agencies to each customer is not always the same and only a few customers are interested in the multi-rating solution independent of the number of rating agencies involved.

The average coverage ensured by the main competitor of a rating agency, among rating agencies with customers rated by no more than five other raters during the overall time horizon, has increased significantly over time (from 20% in 2001 to more than 62% in 2012). For all the other rating agencies there is not such significant change over time, but the main competitor always evaluates at least 30% of customers' portfolios.

3.6 CONCLUSION

Rating market development in recent decades has increased the number of players, even if the existence of significant entry barriers (such as reputation) did not allow the development of a competitive market characterized by comparable market shares owned by each rater. Independent of the criterion adopted (number of ratings or number of customers), the three main players always have a market share that is significantly higher than that of any other rater.

The degree of concentration in recent years has been decreasing due to the growth of the smaller rating agencies, but until now the market share of these smaller players has never been comparable to that of the top three agencies. The number of more internationalized rating agencies has been increasing, even if the choice to go abroad is always more convenient for the bigger raters with respect to the smaller ones. An analysis of the number of relationships established by each customer demonstrates that the rating market is always characterized by the multi-rating phenomenon, even if the role of multi-rated customers in a rating agency's portfolio is unrelated to its size and/or relevance.

Once the existence of a difference in the roles of the top three rating agencies with respect to all the other raters is demonstrated, a comparison of economic rationales for the different raters can allow one to test if the higher market share allows revenue maximization or if it is insufficient for the top three agencies to obtain a clear advantage over their competitors. The next chapter presents a detailed analysis of the balance sheet, income statement, and cash flow statement for a representative sample of rating agencies.

Chapter | four

Economic and Financial Equilibrium of Rating Agencies

4.1 INTRODUCTION

Rating agencies are (public or private) firms created from a market demand for an information service that is not directly satisfied by the public authorities. As firms, rating agencies must respect the standard functioning mechanism of creating value for stakeholders (White, 2002).

The main instrument for evaluating firm performance is the annual report (balance sheet, income statement, and cash flow report), which notes the features of a firm at the end of each fiscal year and the economic and financial flows generated that year (Cavalieri and Ranalli, 1995). The information available in these documents can change, depending on the firm's country of residence and its laws. Even if some differences always exist, a minimum harmonization of the data available is assumed, due to the fact that International Financial Reporting Standards are currently adopted in the main world markets (Rodgers, 2007).

This chapter analyzes the rating agencies' balance sheets to determine the main characteristics of their investments and liabilities, income drivers, and cash flow dynamics. Due to the sector's lack of transparency, it is impossible to study all the market participants and attention must be focused on only a small (but representative) set of agencies for which information is available. Data for nine rating agencies are collected through Compustat over a time horizon of 10 years (see Table 4.1).

To compare the annual report values for different rating agencies, all the data are translated to equivalent US dollars using the exchange rate at the end of the year. As far as the balance sheet analysis is concerned, a set of firms (a benchmark) needs to be identified that can be considered comparable to the rating sector. The control sample is constructed from all 44 firms included in the credit report service category (Standard Industrial Classification code

47

The Independence of Credit Rating Agencies.
© 2014 Elsevier Inc. All rights reserved.

Table 4.1 The Sample

Name	Years Available										
	2001	2002	2003	2004	2005	2006	2007	2008	2009	2010	2011
CRISIL	☐	☑	☑	☑	☑	☑	☑	☑	☑	☑	☑
Duff & Phelps	☐	☐	☐	☑	☑	☑	☑	☑	☑	☑	☑
Fitch Ratings	☑	☑	☑	☑	☑	☑	☑	☑	☑	☑	☑
ICRA	☐	☐	☑	☑	☑	☑	☑	☑	☑	☑	☑
Korea Ratings	☐	☐	☑	☑	☑	☑	☑	☑	☑	☑	☑
Moody's Investors Service	☑	☑	☑	☑	☑	☑	☑	☑	☑	☑	☑
Realpoint LLC	☑	☑	☑	☑	☑	☑	☑	☑	☑	☑	☑
NICE	☑	☑	☑	☑	☑	☑	☑	☑	☑	☑	☑
Seoul Credit Rating Information	☐	☐	☐	☐	☑	☑	☑	☑	☑	☑	☑

Source: Compustat data processed by the author.

7323) defined by Compustat.[1] The median values of the two samples are used to perform a nonparametric test on the differences between the two distributions (Arbuthnott, 1710).

The next sections analyze each document of the annual report separately: Section 4.2 discusses the characteristics of the balance sheet, Section 4.3 examines the income statement, and Section 4.4 discusses the characteristics of the cash flow statement. Section 4.5 summarizes the results and presents the conclusions and implications of the analysis.

4.2 BALANCE SHEET

The balance sheet notes the features of a firm at an established date (normally the end of the year) and presents its assets and liabilities separately. The value of each item is defined on the basis of its economic residual value (Ranalli, 2005). To increase the information content of the balance sheet, the activities and the liabilities are aggregated on the basis of criteria the evaluator considers useful for the firm's business analysis. The standard reclassification procedure distinguishes assets and liabilities on the basis of their duration in current and non-current assets and liabilities, using the year as a time threshold (Poddighe, 2004). This classification allows one to determine the existence of any mismatch between the deadlines of assets and liabilities that can impact negatively on the firm due to the need to redefine pricing conditions in the market and with financial intermediaries (Ferrero et al., 2006).

Due to the significant differences in the sizes of the firms analyzed, a comparison of their balance sheets can be performed only after standardizing the data and considering the ratio of each item with respect to its firm's overall assets or liabilities instead of the value presented in the balance sheet. The asset side of the balance sheet of the rating agencies and the benchmark is presented in Table 4.2.

Rating agencies show a higher relevance of current assets compared to the other credit report agencies, with median values of 75% and 25% respectively. Analysis of the time trend shows that the relevance is increasing over time, and during the last six years the hypothesis of equality of the two subsamples is excluded with a confidence level of over 90%. In current assets, the main items are liquidity (over 43%) and receivables (around 23%), and the main distinctive feature of the rating agency sector is liquidity, which in the last four years shows significant differences from the benchmark, with a threshold of 99%.

Analysis of the liabilities identifies specific characteristics of rating agencies with respect to other information providers that can affect their business model and riskiness (see Table 4.3).

Analysis of the financing sources used by the rating agencies reveals a preponderance of medium- and long-term liabilities (more that 80%) and, more specifically, that the main financing source is represented by shareholder capital (more than 76%) issued as common equity.

---

[1] For further details about the control sample composition, see Table A.3 in the Appendix.

Table 4.2 Rating Agencies' Balance Sheet, Asset Side

		2001	2002	2003	2004	2005	2006	2007	2008	2009	2010	2011
Cash and ST investments	Rating	37.84%	52.68%	61.82%	64.26%	51.33%	39.03%	51.12%	51.83%	44.00%	34.35%	38.34%
	Bmk	2.59%	6.01%	6.24%	7.86%	9.31%	11.11%	11.69%	12.12%	14.45%	11.08%	15.13%
	Prob	0.54	0.74	0.13	0.13	0.31	0.07	0.00	0.00	0.00	0.01	0.00
Receivables (net)	Rating	34.41%	17.47%	20.42%	19.99%	25.19%	24.35%	18.94%	20.47%	21.37%	20.30%	19.59%
	Bmk	14.31%	12.09%	14.51%	11.32%	13.07%	13.20%	13.33%	13.00%	12.95%	12.66%	16.79
	Prob	0.69	0.62	0.65	0.65	0.39	0.40	1.00	0.31	0.85	0.26	0.20
Total inventories	Rating	3.68%	0.00%	0.00%	0.00%	0.00%	0.00%	0.00%	0.00%	0.00%	0.00%	0.00%
	Bmk	0.00%	0.00%	0.00%	0.00%	0.00%	0.00%	0.00%	0.00%	0.00%	0.00%	0.00%
	Prob	0.39	0.41	0.26	0.26	0.21	0.12	0.12	0.12	0.09	0.43	0.40
Other current assets	Rating	2.91%	4.84%	4.61%	3.93%	2.91%	1.59%	2.60%	4.22%	3.13%	2.25%	1.00%
	Bmk	0.08%	0.71%	0.77%	0.74%	0.53%	0.68%	0.99%	0.93%	2.00%	4.33%	0.02%
	Prob	0.52	0.74	0.51	0.64	0.83	0.37	1.00	0.85	0.83	0.35	0.30
Current assets	Rating	78.84%	74.99%	86.85%	88.18%	79.43%	64.97%	72.66%	76.52%	68.50%	56.90%	52.85%
	Bmk	16.98%	18.81%	21.52%	19.92%	22.91%	24.99%	26.01%	26.05%	29.40%	28.07%	37.94%
	Prob	0.47	1.00	0.39	0.39	0.01	0.01	0.01	0.01	0.01	0.07	0.01
Non-current assets	Rating	21.17%	25.00%	13.14%	11.81%	20.57%	35.02%	27.34%	23.48%	31.50%	43.10%	47.15%
	Bmk	83.02%	81.19%	78.48%	80.09%	77.10%	75.01%	73.99%	73.95%	70.61%	70.09%	62.16%
	Prob	0.11	0.15	0.03	0.03	0.01	0.02	0.02	0.01	0.01	0.07	0.01

Source: Compustat data processed by the author.

Table 4.3 Rating Agencies' Balance Sheet, Liability Side

		2001	2002	2003	2004	2005	2006	2007	2008	2009	2010	2011
Accounts payable	Rating	4.57%	6.93%	8.26%	5.69%	4.07%	2.82%	1.91%	1.09%	1.43%	1.33%	0.27%
	Bmk	8.63%	14.14%	18.45%	16.17%	18.95%	14.15%	12.82%	10.46%	11.60%	16.91%	12.00%
	Prob	0.52	0.62	0.62	0.62	0.74	0.15	0.09	0.07	0.02	0.08	0.10
ST debt and current LT debt	Rating	0.59%	0.24%	0.00%	0.00%	0.00%	0.00%	0.15%	0.12%	0.00%	0.00%	0.00%
	Bmk	0.00%	0.00%	0.00%	0.10%	0.00%	3.50%	3.64%	1.86%	0.80%	0.71%	0.02%
	Prob	0.74	0.56	0.17	0.13	0.01	0.01	0.17	0.23	0.31	0.04	0.03
Other current liabilities	Rating	9.47%	10.00%	15.15%	14.44%	14.05%	14.79%	16.83%	14.87%	14.89%	17.14%	8.26%
	Bmk	59.94%	70.18%	64.12%	66.92%	70.39%	61.33%	67.79%	67.35%	62.16%	55.17%	78.00%
	Prob	0.18	0.56	0.36	0.62	0.13	0.65	0.65	0.51	0.47	0.43	0.65
Current liabilities	Rating	26.34%	17.76%	25.06%	20.42%	19.12%	17.91%	19.32%	15.48%	16.32%	18.47%	21.94%
	Bmk	68.57%	84.32%	82.57%	91.58%	91.68%	92.12%	94.01%	93.97%	93.67%	92.07%	80.09%
	Prob	0.43	0.03	0.07	0.01	0.00	0.01	0.06	0.06	0.02	0.11	0.02
Long-term debt	Rating	25.99%	10.13%	0.02%	0.00%	0.00%	0.06%	0.00%	0.00%	0.00%	0.00%	0.00%
	Bmk	0.00%	0.00%	0.00%	0.03%	0.00%	0.00%	0.00%	0.18%	0.00%	0.00%	2.08%
	Prob	0.54	0.74	0.24	0.03	0.08	0.08	0.12	0.08	0.01	0.11	0.10
Other liabilities	Rating	0.00%	0.00%	0.00%	0.00%	0.00%	0.00%	0.00%	1.04%	1.17%	0.84%	0.00%
	Bmk	22.55%	12.63%	13.46%	5.98%	6.41%	5.01%	3.65%	3.78%	3.49%	2.51%	3.60%
	Prob	0.55	0.73	0.18	0.26	0.49	0.49	0.49	1.00	0.49	0.48	0.49

(Continued...)

Table 4.3 Rating Agencies' Balance Sheet, Liability Side (continued)

		2001	2002	2003	2004	2005	2006	2007	2008	2009	2010	2011
Minority interest	Rating	2.03%	0.00%	0.00%	0.00%	0.00%	0.00%	0.00%	0.00%	0.21%	0.10%	0.00%
	Bmk	0.00%	0.00%	0.00%	0.00%	0.00%	0.03%	0.00%	0.07%	0.78%	0.61%	0.05%
	Prob	0.71	0.78	0.30	0.30	0.17	0.16	0.35	0.35	1.00	0.46	0.35
Preferred stock	Rating	0.00%	0.00%	0.00%	0.00%	0.00%	0.00%	0.00%	0.00%	0.00%	0.00%	0.00%
	Bmk	3.67%	3.05%	3.98%	2.41%	1.91%	2.84%	2.33%	2.00%	2.06%	1.12%	0.00%
	Prob	0.09	0.01	0.01	0.01	0.03	0.05	0.03	0.03	0.03	0.01	0.03
Common equity	Rating	39.38%	65.64%	76.60%	68.93%	83.59%	81.71%	76.84%	80.88%	70.68%	76.54%	71.40%
	Bmk	0.00%	0.00%	0.00%	0.00%	0.00%	0.00%	0.00%	0.00%	0.00%	3.70%	13.31%
	Prob	0.55	0.63	0.14	0.02	0.01	0.08	0.34	0.07	0.01	0.07	0.01
Retained earnings	Rating	6.26%	6.46%	−1.68%	10.65%	−2.71%	0.32%	3.83%	2.61%	11.62%	4.04%	0.00%
	Bmk	5.21%	0.00%	0.00%	0.00%	0.00%	0.00%	0.00%	0.00%	0.00%	0.00%	0.00%
	Prob	0.54	1.00	1.00	1.00	0.73	1.00	0.72	1.00	1.00	1.00	1.00
Non-current liabilities	Rating	73.66%	82.23%	74.94%	79.58%	80.88%	82.09%	80.67%	84.53%	83.68%	81.52%	78.06%
	Bmk	31.43%	15.68%	17.43%	8.42%	8.32%	7.88%	5.99%	6.03%	6.33%	7.93%	19.91%
	Prob	0.06	0.13	0.49	0.88	1.00	1.00	1.00	1.00	1.00	1.00	1.00

Source: Compustat data processed by the author.

At the beginning of the sample period, the debt was used for medium- and long-term financial needs, but starting from 2003 it has become a residual financing source. Trade debt is not very relevant for most information providers (always lower than 4%), and the net trade exposure is always positive because the trade credit is always higher than the liability exposure. The test for the median comparison shows that a significant difference exists between the two macro categories of short-term debt and medium- and long-term debt. As shown by the single items of the balance sheet, the main changes in the last five years relate to short-term debt and trade debt policy.

To analyze more deeply the characteristics of the rating agencies with respect to other information providers, some ratios are computed on both the asset and liability sides of the balance sheet (see Table 4.4).

The ratio between current assets and liabilities measures the coherence of the time horizon of the investments released with the financing sources used and index values lower than 1 identify riskier firms, which may be obliged to sell fixed assets to refund lenders (Brearley et al., 2010). The index computed for the rating agencies is significantly high (never lower than 2.99) due to the low relevance of short-term liabilities. The value is also significantly higher than the ratio computed for the information providers, even if these firms always have an index greater than 1. Excluding from the ratio inventories that represent less liquid current assets, the results remain the same because the inventory policy is irrelevant for all information providers.

The coverage of non-current assets is examined by comparing their worth with the different types of long-term financing solutions available. Indexes lower than 1 indicate a scenario in which the refinancing risk is not very relevant to the firm because long-term or open-ended financing solutions are used to finance short-term investments (Pavarani, 2002). Not considering the year 2001, rating agencies cover financial needs related to fixed investments using mostly shareholder capital (the median ratio varies from 0.15 to 0.53). Indexes computed for the credit registers are always higher than those computed for the rating agencies, and in some years they are even greater than 1 (2006–2009).

A clearer idea about the sustainability of a financing choice can be obtained by comparing overall debt and shareholder capital: The higher the value of leverage index, the lower the flexibility of the liability structure and thus the riskier the firm (Massari, 1990). In the rating sector, the role of debt is always marginal and, in addition, the index decreases over time, while for other information providers the index is always over 45%, indicating greater risk exposure for these types of firms.

4.3 INCOME STATEMENT

The income statement summarizes the firm's activities and the results during an established time horizon (normally one year), comparing the costs and revenues of different business areas (Cavalieri and Ferraris, 2005). The document can be reclassified on the basis of the evaluator's needs, and one of the main

Table 4.4 Balance Sheet Indexes

		2001	2002	2003	2004	2005	2006	2007	2008	2009	2010	2011
Current assets/current liabilities	Rating	2.99	4.22	3.47	4.32	4.15	3.63	3.76	4.94	4.20	3.08	1.82
	Bmk	1.03	1.17	1.37	1.18	1.51	0.93	0.81	1.11	1.09	1.39	1.89
	Prob	0.09	0.39	0.72	1.00	0.87	0.65	0.33	0.09	0.08	0.37	0.08
Current assets – inventories/current liabilities	Rating	2.85	4.22	3.47	4.32	4.15	3.63	3.76	4.94	4.20	3.08	1.81
	Bmk	1.03	1.17	1.37	1.18	1.51	0.93	0.80	1.11	1.02	1.39	1.71
	Prob	0.09	0.39	0.72	1.00	0.87	0.88	0.33	0.40	0.38	0.37	0.09
Non-current assets/shareholders' equity	Rating	0.44	0.35	0.18	0.15	0.25	0.43	0.34	0.28	0.38	0.53	0.66
	Bmk	0.68	0.91	0.72	0.63	0.82	1.07	1.09	1.72	1.33	0.94	1.22
	Prob	0.01	0.40	0.40	0.13	0.41	0.42	0.11	0.41	0.40	1.00	1.00
Non-current assets/non-current debt and shareholders' equity	Rating	0.29	0.30	0.18	0.15	0.25	0.43	0.34	0.28	0.38	0.53	0.64
	Bmk	0.93	0.90	0.84	0.94	0.90	1.08	1.09	0.92	0.89	0.79	0.79
	Prob	0.02	0.13	0.49	0.13	0.41	0.02	0.11	0.10	0.10	0.01	0.01
Total debt/total debt and shareholders' equity	Rating	0.27	0.10	0.00	0.00	0.00	0.00	0.00	0.00	0.00	0.00	0.00
	Bmk	0.46	0.69	0.69	0.68	0.60	0.55	0.53	0.57	0.53	0.56	0.11
	Prob	0.07	0.49	0.88	0.13	1.00	1.00	0.42	1.00	1.00	1.00	0.07

Source: Compustat data processed by the author.

Table 4.5 Rating Agency Operating Activities

CRISIL	Income from Operating Activities			Other Income	Ratio Income from Operating Activities/ Overall
	Rating Service	Advisory Service	Research Service		
2001	233,709,088 Rs	107,351,638 Rs	48,722,557 Rs	16,859,687 Rs	95.85%
2002	426,028,875 Rs	119,641,021 Rs	53,784,087 Rs	25,209,025 Rs	95.96%
2003	455,728,693 Rs	153,783,869 Rs	60,394,579 Rs	48,653,432 Rs	93.23%
2004	486,251,917 Rs	133,926,235 Rs	79,263,858 Rs	43,130,897 Rs	94.19%
2005	521,389,229 Rs	193,755,589 Rs	114,451,283 Rs	26,536,671 Rs	96.90%
2006	905,505,064 Rs	362,319,735 Rs	199,633,644 Rs	67,048,588 Rs	95.63%
2007	1,300,783,882 Rs	1,066,968,793 Rs	1,639,731,807 Rs	91,602,304 Rs	97.77%
2008	1,887,753,462 Rs	996,253,081 Rs	2,194,752,914 Rs	216,242,520 Rs	95.92%
2009	2,389,016,014 Rs	–	2,027,218,436 Rs	228,320,849 Rs	95.08%
2010	2,840,877,156 Rs	–	2,446,243,703 Rs	736,222,592 Rs	87.78%
2011	3,260,130,484 Rs	573,059,524 Rs	4,236,503,863 Rs	428,177,309 Rs	94.96%

Source: Rating agency annual report data processed by the author.

methods distinguishes between operating activities and other business areas. This allows the relevance of the firm's core business to be evaluated when determining yearly performance, and thus the results achieved are not extemporaneous and can be replicated in coming years (Caramiello, Di Lazzaro, and Fiori, 2003).

In the rating sector, core business identification is not unique, but a more widespread definition includes within the core business the rating evaluation, the advisory service, and the research service. These activities represent the main source of revenues from operating activities (the mean ratio is around 95%), even if the ratio varies over time (see Table 4.5).

Once the rating agency's core business is identified, the reclassified income statement can be constructed using the same approach adopted for the other types of firms. Due to the heterogeneity of the sample, the analysis of the income statement does not consider the value of each item but, instead, computes a standardized ratio that allows a comparison that is not affected by the different firm sizes (see Table 4.6).

Yearly sales are quite relevant for rating value, because they represent between 66% and 101% of total assets and, excluding the year 2010, the median value is always higher than that of the information providers (by at least 8%), even if the difference is not statistically significant. The value of the ratio is variable over time and there is no clear time trend.

Table 4.6 Rating Agency Income Statements

		2001	2002	2003	2004	2005	2006	2007	2008	2009	2010	2011
Net sales or revenues/ total assets	Rating	80.68%	76.28%	69.90%	66.58%	85.19%	94.67%	99.10%	101.04%	86.11%	68.74%	71.18%
	Bmk	65.68%	56.72%	61.59%	55.34%	59.11%	75.01%	64.45%	68.67%	51.39%	79.99%	45.00%
	Prob	1.00	0.63	0.66	0.88	1.00	1.00	0.42	1.00	1.00	1.00	1.00
Cost of goods sold/sales	Rating	29.32%	25.78%	22.97%	31.08%	34.90%	40.38%	39.91%	35.00%	37.79%	49.30%	66.12%
	Bmk	37.45%	40.95%	37.37%	31.06%	33.53%	35.40%	30.74%	30.63%	30.49%	30.70%	30.49%
	Prob	0.36	0.74	0.78	0.66	0.67	0.77	0.67	0.78	0.78	0.80	0.82
Depreciation, depletion and amortization/sales	Rating	5.45%	3.66%	3.50%	2.81%	2.34%	2.40%	2.33%	2.54%	1.87%	2.16%	2.44%
	Bmk	2.26%	3.61%	2.76%	2.63%	3.23%	2.18%	2.57%	3.71%	4.09%	4.03%	1.78%
	Prob	0.62	0.49	0.79	1.00	1.00	0.87	0.87	0.85	1.00	1.00	1.00
Selling, gen. and admin. expenses/sales	Rating	55.44%	64.61%	63.65%	56.66%	50.42%	41.76%	41.51%	44.01%	41.65%	29.03%	29.14%
	Bmk	41.87%	42.68%	39.83%	43.60%	39.11%	43.99%	44.95%	43.53%	41.48%	41.06%	10.08%
	Prob	0.83	0.62	0.65	1.00	0.31	0.88	1.00	0.31	1.00	0.83	0.80
Operating income/sales	Rating	9.79%	5.94%	9.87%	9.44%	12.35%	15.47%	16.26%	18.44%	18.70%	23.93%	19.59%
	Bmk	18.43%	12.75%	20.04%	22.71%	24.13%	18.43%	21.74%	22.14%	23.94%	24.21%	23.36%
	Prob	0.54	0.48	0.29	0.52	0.14	0.15	0.15	0.11	0.10	0.09	0.11

Non-operating income/operating income	Rating	120.09%	13.67%	40.69%	18.64%	6.88%	5.55%	4.51%	0.10%	2.34%	−3.23%	8.69%
	Bmk	6.58%	−3.85%	−1.01%	0.00%	−1.62%	5.31%	1.15%	−1.38%	−6.48%	−7.02%	1.20%
	Prob	1.00	0.62	0.17	0.05	0.00	0.09	0.01	0.06	0.00	0.00	0.06
EBIT/operating income	Rating	217.67%	112.61%	138.61%	117.59%	86.61%	91.29%	88.90%	79.30%	95.34%	98.94%	111.12%
	Bmk	106.58%	93.47%	98.82%	100.00%	95.86%	103.96%	100.08%	97.02%	90.30%	89.61%	96.08%
	Prob	0.83	0.04	0.06	0.00	0.02	0.02	0.02	0.01	0.01	0.00	0.01
Interests and other capital charges/EBIT	Rating	6.41%	20.90%	0.72%	1.47%	0.00%	1.18%	0.18%	9.23%	12.28%	7.55%	0.00%
	Bmk	0.00%	4.27%	2.39%	2.15%	0.00%	0.64%	4.35%	7.96%	8.64%	14.38%	0.40%
	Prob	0.63	0.24	0.05	0.06	0.09	0.01	0.01	0.01	0.00	0.00	0.00
Taxes/EBIT	Rating	34.46%	34.93%	29.72%	28.49%	30.83%	28.06%	34.99%	30.40%	30.56%	28.38%	26.32%
	Bmk	39.03%	37.12%	28.69%	34.98%	36.43%	32.49%	35.14%	35.07%	31.40%	37.23%	29.13%
	Prob	0.55	0.57	0.02	0.03	0.00	0.13	0.00	0.02	0.40	0.07	0.02
Net income/EBIT	Rating	59.13%	44.17%	69.56%	70.04%	69.17%	70.76%	64.83%	60.37%	57.17%	64.08%	73.12%
	Bmk	60.97%	67.16%	73.69%	67.16%	63.57%	68.15%	69.21%	72.88%	77.24%	77.15%	70.63%
	Prob	0.24	0.12	0.02	0.03	0.01	0.02	0.11	0.10	0.01	0.01	0.01

Source: Compustat data processed by the author.

Costs related to the service offered are high, as is the case for all information providers, and in one year firms can absorb around 50% of revenues. On the basis of the characteristics of the rating service, amortization is not very relevant (always less than 5.5%) and there are no differences from the benchmark considered. The costs of the service are mostly common and general expenses that can represent from 29% to 64% of total revenues.

The median operating income for the rating agencies varies from 6% to 24% of yearly sales and is normally lower than that for the other information providers. The value of the difference is variable over time but since 2005 the difference has always been significant at a level of 85%.

To compute earnings before interest and taxes (EBIT), the results achieved by non-operating activities must be taken into account. The analysis of the rating agencies reveals some differences with respect to information providers overall. The role of non-operative activities significantly decreases over time but is normally higher than the benchmark because they normally contribute negatively for the other information providers. Since 2004 the difference has always been significant at more than 90%.

The yearly net income for the rating sector represents from 44% to 70% of EBIT, and the difference is mainly related to the impact of taxes with respect to the impact of interest. The ratio for the rating agencies is normally lower than the benchmark, and the difference is always significant at a 75% confidence level.

To compare the profitability achieved by the rating agencies with respect to the information service market, some standard indexes are computed using information from the income statement combined with data from the balance sheet (see Table 4.7).

Return on equity (ROE) is the yield of the return for shareholders, and the higher its value, the higher shareholder satisfaction and retention (Mella, 1998). For the rating agencies, as shown in the balance sheet analysis, shareholder equity is the main source of capital, and a high rate of return had to be offered to satisfy the needs of their main capital providers. The ratio is normally higher than the benchmark, but this assumption may be violated and the difference is not statistically significant in all years.

A more complete index of performance is the return on assets (ROA), which considers the overall results produced in the year with respect to the overall value of investments released (Dallocchio and Salvi, 2005). For the rating agencies, the ROA is more stable over time than the ROE and, except for the years 2001 and 2009, the performance achieved is better than the benchmark, even if the difference is not statistically significant.

If only operating activities are considered, performance can be measured using the return on capital invested (ROI), a measure that summarizes production (return on sales) and distributive (turnover) efficiency (Rossignoli, 1991). Excluding the year 2009, the median ROI of the rating sector is always higher than 10%, and the performance is better than that of the other information providers, even if the difference is not statistically significant. If one considers the

Table 4.7 Income Statement Indexes

		2001	2002	2003	2004	2005	2006	2007	2008	2009	2010	2011
ROE	Rating	4.56%	10.65%	10.86%	11.31%	19.12%	11.92%	12.41%	10.45%	−3.64%	14.46%	15.59%
	Bmk	11.81%	2.13%	6.16%	6.49%	6.95%	0.78%	1.64%	1.12%	1.56%	2.93%	16.27%
	Prob	0.11	0.45	0.88	0.33	0.10	0.02	0.11	0.10	0.40	1.00	0.10
ROA	Rating	7.92%	8.97%	9.66%	9.64%	12.60%	9.83%	10.43%	9.97%	5.61%	12.43%	15.51%
	Bmk	8.61%	4.00%	7.51%	7.11%	8.50%	6.40%	5.15%	4.87%	5.79%	7.54%	9.62%
	Prob	0.48	0.40	0.88	0.88	0.10	0.02	0.42	0.10	0.40	1.00	1.00
ROI	Rating	10.32%	11.57%	11.30%	13.29%	19.32%	11.04%	11.79%	11.59%	6.75%	14.71%	13.54%
	Bmk	10.68%	5.83%	7.70%	7.76%	11.95%	8.10%	8.89%	7.28%	7.33%	12.58%	11.27%
	Prob	0.48	0.40	0.88	0.32	0.41	0.02	0.11	0.10	0.40	1.00	1.00
ROS	Rating	14.33%	10.23%	15.35%	16.99%	21.38%	13.70%	18.12%	18.35%	6.00%	15.40%	19.59%
	Bmk	10.76%	5.46%	13.18%	14.55%	16.08%	9.34%	9.89%	11.27%	11.64%	12.59%	23.36%
	Prob	0.48	0.40	0.88	0.88	0.41	0.11	0.42	0.41	1.00	1.00	1.00
Turnover	Rating	0.82	1.14	1.35	1.47	1.30	1.37	1.22	1.23	1.13	0.95	1.42
	Bmk	1.19	1.03	1.02	1.16	1.27	1.37	1.21	1.47	1.11	0.98	1.93
	Prob	0.48	1.00	0.88	0.88	0.41	1.00	1.00	1.00	1.00	1.00	1.00

Source: Compustat data processed by the author.

ROI components, the main advantage for the rating agencies is related to operative efficiency (ROS), because the turnover is always close to 1 and the difference from the benchmark is very small for almost all years.

4.4 CASH FLOW STATEMENT

The financial equilibrium of the rating agencies is defined on the basis of the differences between costs and revenues that have monetary implications for the firm in the period considered (normally one year). The analysis distinguishes cash flows by the business areas that generate them to evaluate the role of operating activities with respect to all other extraordinary or accessory areas (Bhattacharyya, 2010). The standard approach normally distinguishes operating activities from investment and financing and, if necessary, other accessory areas. To compare cash flows generated by heterogeneous firms, a standard reclassification is carried out using total assets as a benchmark.

The analysis of the operating activities starts from EBIT and defines the items that generate cash flow in the same years. It then revises the data for certain accounting practices (e.g. amortization) and includes some extra positive or external cash flows not considered in EBIT (see Table 4.8).

The EBIT (increased by the amount amortizing expenditure) is normally translated into cash flows, and the role of taxes and extraordinary items is residual. The cash flows available for other information providers are less driven by EBIT and more affected by such components as taxes and residual activities. Looking at the statistical significance of the median comparison test, the other cash flows are always positive and relevant for the information service while they are frequently negative for rating agencies and the difference is statistically significant at the 99% level.

Analysis of cash flow allocation must consider opportunities to use available cash flows to make new investments or to sell assets to overcome a lack of financial resources for planned investments (see Table 4.9).

For the rating agencies, the investment area contributes positively to the cash flow during the sample period through the disinvestment of activities that, if they occur, can have a significant impact on overall cash flows (from 0% to 35% on the basis of the year considered). In addition, the information provider sector is characterized by a comparable trend in the disinvestment of activities, but the overall effect is lower because this decrease is balanced by an increase in new assets purchased. Other statistically significant differences between the two samples pertain to capital expenditures and residual items, which are more relevant for the rating agency sector. The difference is statistically significant for almost all the years, with a level of significance greater than 99%.

Cash flows can also be generated by new financing issues or absorbed by a capital refunding policy. Every choice in this area affects the firm's independence from its lenders (see Table 4.10).

Rating agencies are not overly leveraged and thus the impact of any change in the financing policy on overall cash flows is limited. The main item in the

Table 4.8 Rating Agencies' Cash Flow Statement: Operating Activities

		2001	2002	2003	2004	2005	2006	2007	2008	2009	2010	2011
EBIT/TA	Rating	12.43%	5.61%	9.97%	10.43%	11.67%	15.05%	11.67%	11.51%	12.66%	12.79%	15.51%
	Bmk	14.40%	5.77%	11.51%	11.68%	13.59%	7.65%	5.42%	6.85%	7.70%	10.91%	8.74%
	Prob	0.81	0.27	1.00	0.81	0.35	1.00	1.00	0.80	0.75	1.00	1.00
Depreciation, depletion and amortization/TA	Rating	4.44%	4.20%	4.56%	4.07%	2.42%	2.82%	2.69%	3.23%	2.59%	2.30%	2.44%
	Bmk	-0.76%	-1.08%	-0.89%	-0.48%	0.00%	-0.43%	-0.74%	-0.90%	-0.78%	-1.20%	0.42%
	Prob	0.14	0.03	0.31	0.31	0.26	0.01	0.07	0.04	0.22	0.03	0.21
Deferred taxes/TA	Rating	0.18%	-0.15%	-0.02%	0.00%	0.00%	-0.31%	-0.20%	0.18%	0.00%	0.01%	0.00%
	Bmk	6.87%	7.42%	11.72%	12.17%	13.26%	7.67%	7.11%	6.76%	6.03%	10.55%	0.00%
	Prob	1.00	0.43	0.75	0.75	0.43	0.61	0.12	0.75	0.76	0.48	0.00
Other cash flows/TA	Rating	-6.66%	3.31%	3.33%	4.43%	1.71%	-3.89%	-0.37%	0.64%	-0.43%	1.22%	-1.66%
	Bmk	6.60%	2.88%	3.46%	2.48%	2.54%	2.45%	2.16%	4.17%	2.06%	2.78%	0.00%
	Prob	0.00	0.00	0.00	0.00	0.00	0.00	0.00	0.00	0.00	0.00	0.00
Extraordinary items/TA	Rating	0.00%	0.00%	0.00%	0.00%	0.00%	0.00%	0.00%	0.00%	0.00%	0.00%	0.00%
	Bmk	0.00%	0.00%	0.00%	0.00%	0.00%	0.00%	0.00%	0.00%	0.00%	0.00%	0.00%
	Prob	0.57	0.79	0.01	0.01	0.88	0.30	0.62	0.32	0.92	0.45	0.00
Funds from/for other operating activities/TA	Rating	1.74%	6.27%	0.92%	-0.30%	-0.94%	-0.85%	-0.05%	-1.06%	0.24%	-0.54%	1.65%
	Bmk	0.00%	0.00%	0.00%	0.00%	0.00%	0.00%	0.00%	0.00%	0.00%	0.00%	0.13%
	Prob	0.58	1.00	1.00	1.00	0.52	1.00	1.00	0.52	1.00	1.00	1.00
Net cash flow from operating activities/TA	Rating	12.13%	19.24%	18.76%	18.63%	14.86%	12.82%	13.74%	14.50%	15.06%	15.78%	14.73%
	Bmk	27.11%	14.99%	25.80%	25.85%	29.39%	17.34%	13.95%	16.88%	15.01%	23.04%	12.42%
	Prob	0.88	0.25	0.89	0.89	0.089	0.42	0.42	0.41	1.00	1.00	1.00

Source: Compustat data processed by the author.

Table 4.9 Rating Agencies' Cash Flow Statement: Investment Activities

		2001	2002	2003	2004	2005	2006	2007	2008	2009	2010	2011
Capital expenditures/TA	Rating	2.93%	3.92%	2.43%	1.55%	2.80%	2.78%	3.78%	4.31%	1.71%	2.02%	1.53%
	Bmk	0.76%	1.08%	0.89%	0.48%	0.00%	0.43%	0.74%	0.90%	0.78%	1.20%	0.69%
	Prob	0.02	0.00	0.00	0.00	0.01	0.00	0.00	0.01	0.00	0.01	0.01
Net assets from acquisitions/TA	Rating	0.00%	0.00%	0.00%	0.00%	0.00%	0.00%	0.00%	0.00%	0.00%	0.94%	0.00%
	Bmk	6.87%	7.42%	11.72%	12.17%	13.26%	7.67%	7.11%	6.76%	6.03%	10.55%	0.00%
	Prob	0.71	0.59	0.54	0.83	0.16	0.80	0.48	0.13	0.07	0.83	0.00
Decrease in investments/TA	Rating	0.01%	2.78%	30.45%	26.78%	21.26%	25.31%	12.45%	3.50%	11.39%	10.72%	1.78%
	Bmk	6.60%	2.88%	3.46%	2.48%	2.54%	2.45%	2.16%	4.17%	2.06%	2.78%	0.06%
	Prob	0.57	0.51	0.01	0.13	0.02	0.00	0.00	0.02	0.00	0.00	0.00
Other/TA	Rating	0.21%	1.04%	2.67%	2.31%	2.80%	0.26%	0.09%	0.66%	0.99%	0.88%	0.00%
	Bmk	0.00%	0.00%	0.00%	0.00%	0.00%	0.00%	0.00%	0.00%	0.00%	0.00%	0.00%
	Prob	0.77	0.00	0.00	0.00	0.00	0.00	0.02	0.00	0.00	0.37	0.00
Net cash flow from investing activities/TA	Rating	−4.32%	23.72%	1.82%	9.37%	10.32%	7.99%	12.37%	17.56%	4.42%	7.11%	−9.53%
	Bmk	−6.87%	−2.98%	−7.58%	−2.27%	−4.23%	−0.20%	−3.21%	0.00%	−1.11%	−5.80%	−5.36%
	Prob	0.91	0.64	0.16	0.64	0.26	0.83	0.04	0.83	0.83	0.26	0.91

Source: Compustat data processed by the author.

Table 4.10 Rating Agencies' Cash Flow Statement: Financing Activities

		2001	2002	2003	2004	2005	2006	2007	2008	2009	2010	2011
Debt consolidation and others/TA	Rating	−0.57%	−0.03%	0.00%	0.00%	0.00%	−0.20%	−0.05%	−0.40%	0.00%	−1.07%	0.00%
	Bmk	0.00%	0.00%	0.00%	0.00%	0.00%	0.00%	0.00%	0.00%	0.00%	0.00%	0.00%
	Prob	0.23	0.03	1.00	0.01	0.80	0.80	0.47	0.80	0.80	0.25	0.00
Δ Long-term borrowings/TA	Rating	−4.08%	−0.46%	0.00%	−0.09%	0.00%	−0.16%	0.00%	−0.12%	−0.24%	0.00%	0.00%
	Bmk	−1.13%	−1.93%	−0.94%	−1.06%	−0.95%	−0.83%	−1.24%	−2.21%	−0.80%	−1.82%	0.00%
	Prob	0.27	0.06	0.38	0.02	0.30	0.06	0.58	0.06	0.04	0.86	0.00
Δ ST borrowings/TA	Rating	0.36%	0.00%	0.00%	0.00%	0.00%	0.00%	0.00%	0.00%	0.00%	0.00%	0.00%
	Bmk	0.00%	0.00%	0.00%	0.00%	0.28%	0.04%	0.00%	0.00%	0.00%	0.00%	0.00%
	Prob	0.23	0.04	0.81	0.01	0.62	0.62	0.13	0.62	0.62	0.20	0.00
Cash dividends paid/TA	Rating	−1.43%	−2.69%	−2.85%	−3.26%	−4.14%	−2.94%	−2.83%	−2.75%	−3.22%	−4.19%	−1.47%
	Bmk	−1.08%	−3.92%	−5.08%	−1.91%	−4.03%	−3.07%	−9.63%	−14.26%	−5.48%	−0.02%	−3.98%
	Prob	0.19	0.02	1.00	0.20	0.81	0.20	0.43	0.20	0.20	0.81	0.20
Other/TA	Rating	−0.02%	0.00%	0.00%	0.00%	−0.11%	−0.01%	−1.52%	−0.13%	−0.36%	−0.25%	0.00%
	Bmk	0.00%	0.00%	0.00%	0.00%	0.00%	0.00%	0.00%	0.00%	0.00%	0.00%	0.00%
	Prob	0.19	0.01	0.76	0.01	0.59	0.01	0.11	0.01	0.01	0.59	0.00
Net cash flow from financing/TA	Rating	−9.01%	−2.48%	−3.50%	−6.93%	−2.66%	−4.59%	0.00%	−3.93%	−4.57%	−5.84%	−2.67%
	Bmk	0.00%	0.00%	0.04%	0.00%	−2.18%	−2.92%	−0.04%	−0.48%	−0.02%	−0.90%	−3.47%
	Prob	00.19	0.01	0.59	0.11	0.75	0.01	0.17	0.07	0.07	0.46	0.07

Source: Compustat data processed by the author.

Table 4.11 Cash Flow Statement Indexes

		2001	2002	2003	2004	2005	2006	2007	2008	2009	2010	2011
CFO/debito	Rating	6.10%	34.96%	65.53%	52.09%	57.34%	63.44%	49.86%	56.80%	53.80%	40.92%	41.67%
	Bmk	3.94%	4.30%	7.55%	6.61%	6.37%	−0.78%	2.54%	8.65%	5.71%	−1.67%	45.26%
	Prob	0.00	0.00	0.01	0.00	0.01	0.03	0.09	0.01	0.05	0.12	0.00
CFO/ passivocorrente	Rating	11.00%	72.47%	78.78%	62.08%	61.78%	74.45%	72.93%	65.30%	62.94%	56.20%	57.54%
	Bmk	32.97%	36.08%	47.82%	37.50%	59.16%	37.26%	33.50%	38.80%	49.86%	39.09%	60.14%
	Prob	0.04	0.39	1.00	1.00	0.87	0.07	0.88	0.40	0.39	1.00	0.00
CFO/vendite	Rating	7.94%	28.06%	21.29%	19.73%	16.25%	22.22%	20.99%	13.46%	20.08%	23.30%	23.09%
	Bmk	16.59%	16.71%	11.46%	18.93%	19.50%	15.01%	17.43%	21.44%	22.71%	16.85%	23.76%
	Prob	0.01	0.49	0.88	0.88	1.00	1.00	0.42	1.00	1.00	0.37	0.00
CFO per share	Rating	0.48	3.38	8.74	9.35	4.84	12.15	20.53	36.11	45.64	35.47	67.40%
	Bmk	0.00	0.00	0.00	0.00	0.00	0.00	0.01	0.01	0.01	0.00	79.25%
	Prob	0.11	0.67	0.07	0.07	0.01	0.00	0.00	0.00	0.00	0.00	0.00
Earnings quality	Rating	0.75	1.32	1.11	1.30	1.17	1.11	1.19	1.21	1.23	1.21	1.20
	Bmk	0.84	1.27	1.10	1.05	1.07	1.14	1.12	1.42	1.61	1.30	1.40
	Prob	0.37	0.49	0.49	0.88	1.00	1.00	0.42	0.41	1.00	1.00	1.00

Source: Compustat data processed by the author.

financing area involves cash dividends paid; these are normally higher for information providers than for rating agencies, even if this relationship is not satisfied every year.

To evaluate the financial stability of the rating agencies some indexes are constructed to compare the cash flows generated by operating activities and the main items of the balance sheet with the firm's income statement (see Table 4.11).

A preliminary analysis of debt sustainability on the basis of cash flows generated by operating activities can be carried out by constructing the ratio between these and total debt (Arnold, 2002). Due to the low relevance of leverage for rating agencies, the yearly cash flow is normally half the overall debt, while its relevance is always significantly lower for other information providers.

The same index can be constructed considering only debt that expires in one year to focus only on debt that is more exposed to the risk of renewal (White, Sondhi, and Fried, 2003). The results do not change significantly because rating agencies have even less debt exposure in the short term, but the difference with respect to the benchmark is not always statistically significant.

The comparison between cash flows from operating activities and sales allows one to measure the capability of a firm to transform revenues into positive cash flows (Woelfel, 1994). For rating agencies, the ratio is quite low, due to the high costs related to the service offered, and the results are not significantly different from those achieved by other information providers.

An index of the monetary value created for each shareholder can be computed by comparing the cash flow from operating activities to the overall number of shares available (Raiborn, 2010). The value of the index varies from zero to US $45 per share, significantly higher than for the information service sector, probably due to the lower number of shares issued by rating agencies.

A measure of earnings quality can be defined by considering annual performance, interest costs and taxes, and comparing cash flow data and the economic values reported in the income statement (Stolowy and Lebas, 2006). Except for the year 2001, the index is always greater than 1 and thus the accounting data are not useful in evaluating firms' financial conditions because they underestimate inflows and/or overestimate outflows. There are no significant differences between rating agencies and other information providers.

4.5 CONCLUSIONS

Rating agency balance sheet analysis shows a high degree of liquidity of the investments released and low investment in trade credit. Given the financing sources available, rating agencies prefer to raise capital by issuing shares and debt is prevalently used for short-term financial needs. The net income achieved by a rating agency is driven by its operating income, with other areas frequently contributing negatively to overall performance. The income statement indexes show that the ROE is quite high, to remunerate shareholders for large investments in the agency, and the ROI is driven by the productive efficiency and not by the distributive efficiency.

The cash flow analysis demonstrates the agency is quite capable of creating cash flow through its operating activities, and a comparison of cash flows with the income statement and balance sheet data demonstrates low liquidity exposure. The main role assumed by the operating activities of rating agencies demonstrates the need to focus on the activities of rating evaluations, advisory services, and research services, which are the main drivers of their revenue. In a low-competition market such as the rating industry, better evaluations of business characteristics are necessary to focus on the agencies' pricing policies. In such a scenario, price is not defined by the market and a firm can select any pricing model that best fits its economic purpose.

Chapter five

Rating Agencies' Pricing Policies

5.1 INTRODUCTION

Ratings are used to rank investment/financing opportunities on the basis of their default risk (Pinches and Mingo, 1973), and thus the availability of a judgment can create advantages for both the investor and the evaluated entity. Investors can combine this information with other available data to make a more complete evaluation of possible investments (Hill, 2004). The evaluated entity may reduce the cost of capital, signaling to the market the quality of the issuer or issue, with the cost savings representing an indirect advantage of the reduction in information asymmetry (Wessendorf, 2008).

Pricing policies adopted by rating agencies are quite heterogeneous, and normally different services are established for the new evaluations and to monitor existing ratings (Rosner, 2009). Users do not always have to pay for the service, and frequently the rating agencies obtain the fee directly from the evaluated entity (OICV-IOSCO, 2003). The issuer fee model is frequently criticized and is identified as one of the main causes of some of the financial disasters of the last century, such as Enron (Coffee, 2004). Even if the issuer fee model is not the only solution available, the alternative method (a user fee) represents only a choice not frequently adopted due to the high risk of free-riding.

Section 5.2 first identifies the main characteristics of information providers that affect their pricing policy and then focuses on the choices made by rating agencies. The analysis considers the advantages and risks related to issuer and user fee modes in Section 5.3 and the fee structures requested by the main rating agencies in Section 5.4, and Section 5.5 summarizes the main results and presents the implications of the results achieved.

The Independence of Credit Rating Agencies.
© 2014 Elsevier Inc. All rights reserved.

5.2 PRICING POLICIES FOR INFORMATION PROVIDERS AND RATING AGENCIES

Information is a public good with specific characteristics that makes it unique with respect to the standard definition of any other good or commodity (Bates, 1990). Its distinctive features are:

- The lack of an objective and measurable value
- Scale economies
- Exposure to the risk of free-riding.

The information value is affected by the user's perception of coherence between expectations and the good's real characteristics. Its value can be approximated even before its use on the basis of the reputation of the evaluated entity and word of mouth in the market (Westbrook, 1987). The information provider usually has to build a reputation, especially if it if deficient, through an increase of expenditures in information collection and database development.

The information production process is characterized by high costs associated with the realization of the first unit of service, and variable but minimal costs for any new units. The provider can maximize profits using standard principles of economies of scale and maximizing the number of services sold (Lowe, 1999).

Users of information services are not easily excluded, and there is always a high risk of free-riding that can significantly reduce profits for the information provider (Shapiro and Varian, 1998). The selling strategy for such goods can be either:

- A price competition or
- A quality competition.

In a price competition, to minimize prices and production costs, the information provider offers a standardized product that is subscribed to by a high number of users. The free-riding risk is then minimal, because the replication cost is equal to (or greater than) the price of the good offered (Gallaugher, Augerb, and BarNirc, 2001). Normally this strategy is adopted when the cost of the service is low (e.g. newsletters, newspapers) and the information can be used as an instrument for cross-selling opportunities: The information provider then tries to maximize the number of customers and sell advertisement opportunities, for example to sponsors interested in contacting them.

A quality competition assumes the information provider has distinctive/unique skills that allow it to offer a unique service. The service is non-standardized and customized to the specific needs of the user (an ex novo good or a standardized good packaged according to user requests); the pricing of the service is not based on the production cost but rather on the value created for the user. The information provider can maximize profits by adopting a price discrimination policy that defines different prices for each customer on the basis of their specific reserve prices.

To maximize overall profits, the information provider can also bundle policies, defining prices for sets of services instead of individually. This method is generally used to increase customer retention and can prevent customers from adopting a cherry-picking approach where they subscribe only to low-priced services (Geng, Stinchcombe, and Whinston, 2005).

Depending on the information, the user can use it only once or several times. In the former case, a fee for the service is paid for each request of information, while in the latter case a fixed fee, independent of the number of services requested, is usually paid (Varian, 2000).

Rating services are highly complex information services that do not conform to a standardized procedure or, therefore, a price competition approach. Standardization can affect only the service's production process, and the most relevant costs are fixed and unrelated to the number of requests for a given rating.

The low competition that characterizes the rating market allows agencies to adopt bundling strategies in which the evaluator rates not only the issuer but also all issues made within an established time horizon. Moreover, for rating agencies affiliated with groups, there are opportunities for cross-selling goods and services offered by the other group members.[1]

The pricing methodologies adopted by rating agencies are normally heterogeneous and generally apply both one-time and pay-as-you-go fees for their different services. The lack of an objective procedure to measure the value of services and the low competition in the market allow agencies to define the prices of their services on the basis of the expected value created for the subscriber.

5.3 RATING AGENCY FEES

The rating process can be divided into two different phases: the initial evaluation of the issuer or issue and the post-judgment monitoring process. Rating agencies normally could set different fees for the two phases: a one-off fee for the initial evaluation procedure that will cover the costs related to the new evaluation and a periodic (normally annual) fee for the monitoring service (Rosner, 2009).

For the initial evaluation, rating agencies normally adopt different pricing procedures according to the entity evaluated and generally distinguish between an issue fee and an issuer fee. The policy can be summarized as follows:

$$\text{Issuer rating} \qquad Fee_{it} = Issuer\,fee_{it} \qquad\qquad (5.1)$$

$$\text{Issue rating} \qquad Fee_{it} = Issue\,fee_{it}\,(Issue\,amount_{it}). \qquad (5.2)$$

For issuer ratings, agencies define a fixed fee that is higher for more complex firms due to the greater time and costs associated with the evaluation process. The definition of the level of complexity is ambiguous, and normally a rating agency, in order to apply fewer subjective procedures, uses mathematical formulas based on firm size proxies. The more frequently used proxies are the firm's book value, market value and turnover, and the computational rule is normally clearly stated in the advertising documentation produced by the rating agency.

---

[1] For further details on cross-selling opportunities, see Section 6.5.

The underlying hypothesis behind the relation between the size of a firm and its fees is that the larger the firm, the higher the advantages related to the service offered. A rating agency tries to maximize its profits by applying the highest fees to the largest companies likely to pay higher fees.

For issue ratings, agencies can charge a fee dependent on the characteristics of the issue and proportional to its value, assuming that the number of advantages associated with the judgment increase with the size of the issue.

The more profitable services for rating agencies are those of higher value financial instruments, since they allow the fee applied to each unit of value of the issue to be maximized. To increase customer satisfaction, a rating agency can also apply discounts for larger issues, using progressive fees that decrease when the amount is beyond a defined threshold. Progressive fees reduce firm profits, because when the size of an issue increases, the customer will sustain a lower cost for the service (Covitz and Harrison, 2003). The loss of profits for a rating agency associated with such a discount policy is, however, normally justified by retention purposes.

Aside from size, other features of the issue can affect fees, and normally the higher the complexity of the instrument evaluated, the higher the price of the rating service. Within the standard sector division adopted, structured finance is normally the most profitable area for agencies because the fees applied per unit of issue are significantly higher than for other sectors.

Issuer and issue fees are frequently related, because the evaluated entity cannot request an issue rating if the issuer rating is not available. Therefore, the rating agency frequently sells the two services jointly (Sufi, 2009).

Once a (issue or issuer) rating is published, the agency requests a periodic fee for monitoring and updates. The fee is normally fixed and defined for the overall services requested:

Issuer rating   *Surveillance fee* $= \alpha \times$ *Issuer fee$_{it}$*   (5.3)

Issue rating   *Surveillance fee* $= \alpha \times$ *Issue fee$_{it}$* $\times$ *Remaining issue size$_{it}$*
(5.4)

where α varies from 0 to 1 and each rater can define different α for different types of rating service. The fee is generally paid annually and the amount increases with any increase in the complexity of the evaluated entity due to the lower standardization and the higher costs the agency must sustain to monitor them.

The rater can also define a unique fee that includes both the surveillance and the initial fee (for both issue and issuer ratings) previously identified, and this solution is frequently adopted by rating agencies that have a high customer turnover.

5.4 ISSUER AND USER FEE MODELS

Rating agency fee models can be classified into two macro categories: user fee models and issuer fee models. The choice of model has direct implications

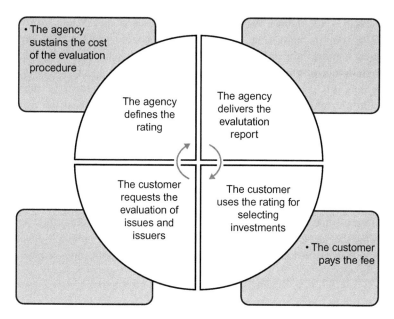

FIGURE 5.1 User fee model.

for the business model, and the agency must evaluate the advantages and risks of each method. After presenting the two models and their characteristics, the next section analyzes the choices made by rating agencies worldwide.

5.4.1 User Fee Model

Rating agencies that adopt the user fee model request fees for the initial evaluation and the monitoring process directly from the user. They produce a detailed report on the issuer or issue's features and render a synthetic judgment on its risk (White, 2002). The customer then uses the information collected to select the best available investment (see Figure 5.1).

The rating service is a standard consultancy service in which the agency uses its distinctive skills to express a judgment and the customer accepts paying it a fee because of its informational advantage in evaluating the issue or issuer (Hill, 2010). The user fee approach is suitable for a rating agency only if the customer is able to pay fees sufficiently high to cover all expenses sustained by the agency to produce the evaluation report and make a profit. This model can have a negative effect on rating agencies due to the low mark-up that may be applied to the rating price. Due to the high cost of monitoring and to achieve their economic and financial goals, agencies are thus incentivized to provide cautious ratings, since the ratings will then be biased upward, even if not updated promptly (Manns, 2009).

At the beginning of the rating market, the first agencies requested fees from their customers. They have since grown and increased their market share through a supervisory approach that forces investors and financial intermediaries to request their services (Richardson and White, 2009). In the 1970s, due to innovations in information technology, the free-riding risk increased significantly and rating agencies had to change their approach to avoid going out of business (Gudzowski, 2010). Rating agencies that wanted to continue this pricing model had to consider that the number of subscribers could be significantly lower due to free-riding, and thus that the mark-up applied to each service should be higher.

An excessive increase in prices, however, can have a negative impact on the number of customers and cause an agency to go out of business. Since the free-riding issuer cannot be solved in an open market scenario (Richardson and White, 2009), external monitoring became necessary. The method proposed in the literature assigns to a public authority the role of collecting compulsory fees from all market investors and paying back the fee to the rating agencies that offer the service (Listokin and Taibleson, 2010). This method ensures a high number of customers and allows agencies to significantly reduce their customer fees.

5.4.2 Issuer Fee Model

In the issuer fee model, the evaluated entity selects the rating agency and establishes a commercial relationship with it. Rating fees are paid by the issuer once the agency presents a report on the risk of the issuer or issue. The customer then has the choice to make the information publicly available (see Figure 5.2).

The issuer fee model was used for the first time in the 1970s, by Moody's. Due to its advantages, it became the most widespread method adopted in the market (Wessendorf, 2008). Customer surveys for these types of rating agencies identify the main reasons for the issuer fee model (Bond Market Association, 2006):

- Access to new national or international financial markets
- Reduction of the cost of capital
- Increased market reputation
- Value of the internal process efficiency
- Better relationships with shareholders or the market
- Better relationships with suppliers.

The issuer requesting the rating service can use agency reputation to signal its qualities to the market (Ferri and Liu, 2003). Empirical evidence shows that for investment-grade issues (Baker and Mansi, 2002) and low-liquidity financial markets (Kumar, Chuppe, and Perttunen, 1997), firms are obliged to hire a rating agency in order to collect money also from main institutional investors (Dale and Thomas, 1991).

Rating availability can affect the cost of capital for firms throughout the market or financial intermediaries. The return requested by lenders is related to the risk of the investment, and the better the rating assigned, the lower the overall cost of capital (Liu, Seyyed, and Smith, 1999).

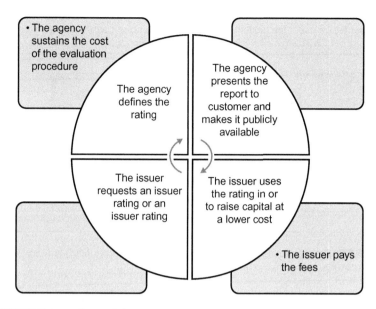

FIGURE 5.2 Issuer fee model.

A rating agency certifies the quality of an issuer or issue with its judgment, and the usefulness of the rating approach is greater when the firm is young and/or suffers from a low reputation in the financial markets. Hiring an agency of high standing can have a significant impact on such a firm's relationship with the capital markets, facilitating the raising of capital (Mathis, McAndrews, and Rochet, 2009).

Internal procedures are not frequently given a value by the market, and firms that adopt more efficient methods can use rating agencies to signal to the market the expected advantages related to the more efficient internal procedure. An agency rating can valorize the investment in the qualitative component of the evaluation procedure (Baker and Mansi, 2002).

The market always needs new information about a firm, and the rater must also periodically confirm the quality of the information available. In some market scenarios, the firm has the convenience of asking for other ratings issued by different firms (multi-rating). The quality of the information previously available can thus be confirmed by the new ratings (Thompson and Vaz, 1990).

Commercial transactions are not usually paid in cash, and there is always a lag between the delivery of goods and services and payment (Carretta, 1982). The length and cost of the payment delay depend on the relationship between the firm and its suppliers, sector standards, and the firm's reputation (Cheng and Pike, 2003). Firms can use a rating agency judgment to demonstrate to suppliers their creditworthiness and thus obtain trade credits.

The issuer fee model is a useful approach for a firm unless the cost of services (fees) is higher than the expected benefits associated with the availability of the judgment. The intangibility of the benefits and the lack of transparency

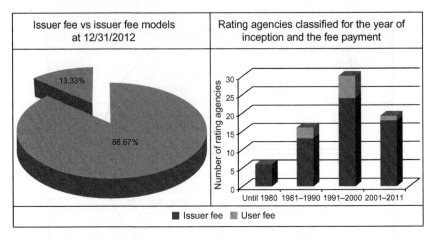

Issuer fee vs issuer fee models at 12/31/2012	Rating agencies classified for the year of inception and the fee payment

FIGURE 5.3 Rating agencies classified by pricing model. *Source*: Rating agencies websites (accessed 03.01.2013).

of the fees applied prevent the advantages relating to a firm's rating request from being empirically measured.

5.4.3 Rating Agency Choices and their Implications for the Business Models

Rating agency websites publish pricing policy information, declaring whether they obtain fees from the entities evaluated (issuer fee model) or from their users (user fee model). An analysis of this information determines the relevance of the two pricing models in the worldwide market[2] (see Figure 5.3).

In more than 86% of cases, agencies charge fees mostly or exclusively to the issuer. Surveys of the chief executive officers of the main rating agencies demonstrate that the choice is explained by the economic unsustainability of the other models (Fridson, 2010). The user fee model is adopted by only 13% of players, mostly those working in the USA or Asia.

After the radical change made in the 1970s by Moody's with the introduction of the issuer fee payment model, new development of the user fee model occurred during the 1980s and 1990s, while in the 2000s only one new user fee rating agency was created. Even if no new players started business in the 2000s using the user fee model, on December 21, 2007, for the first time, a user fee rating agency (Egan-Jones) was recognized by a supervisory authority (the SEC in the USA).

User fee rating agencies present themselves as the only agencies that can ensure economic independence with respect to the entity evaluated due to their total economic independence with respect to the evaluated entities (see Box 5.1).

---

[2]For further details about the pricing policy adopted by each rating agency, see Table A.1 in the Appendix.

BOX 5.1 Business Declarations of Rating Agencies that Adopt the User Fee Model

Egan-Jones Ratings Company

Unlike all previously recognized NRSRO rating firms, Egan-Jones is not paid by issuers but is paid solely by institutional investors. Since issuer interests are often not aligned with investor interests, a rating firm representing investors is a welcome change.

[...] To protect investors and increase returns, hedge funds, fiduciaries, and large commercial lenders would be well-served to review ratings issued by non-conflicted rating firms.

Weiss Ratings

We are proud to offer a complete line of products designed to direct consumers and business professionals alike toward safe banking and insurance options while avoiding unnecessary risks that could lead to financial losses.

We don't accept compensation from the companies we rate for issuing the rating. Nor do we give the companies an opportunity to preview the ratings or suppress their publication if they're unfavorable. We are totally independent and unbiased because our loyalty is to you—the customer.

Source: Rating agencies websites (accessed 03.01.2013).

The user fee model normally implies less detailed information, including public data. The rating models adopted by user fee agencies generally involve pure quantitative procedures that reduce the cost and time of processing information; the main value of the service offered thus relates to the agency's ability to construct a successful model (Smith and Walter, 2001). The choice of pricing model can also affect the characteristics of the rating service and thus its usefulness to users. Empirical evidence shows that rating agencies that adopt the user fee model are more sensitive to new market conditions and update their ratings more frequently (Saunders and Allen, 2010). Moreover, these agencies normally revise their ratings before issuer fee agencies revise theirs (Beaver, Shakespeare, and Soliman, 2006), and especially if there is an increase in the default risk of the evaluated entity, they normally make more relevant downgrades (Johnson, 2003).

5.5 PRICING POLICIES FOR ISSUER AND USER FEE MODELS

The choice to adopt the issuer fee model versus the fee model implies a change in the number of customers served by the rater. In the first case the customers are restricted to the issuers, while in the second case more customers can request an evaluation for the same issuer or issue. The rater has to define different pricing policies for the two pricing models because in the issuer fee model the revenues relating to an evaluation (issue or issuer rating) are paid by only one customer, while (potentially) in the user fee model the overall revenues relating to an evaluation depend on the sum of payments made by all customers interested in the rating issued.

The next two subsections (Sections 5.5.1 and 5.5.2) present a brief analysis of the pricing policies adopted by a set of rating agencies.[3]

5.5.1 Fee Policy for Issuer Fee Rating Models

Rating agencies that adopt the user fee model normally present a detailed fee schedule that distinguishes the price of the service by type of evaluation (issuer versus issue rating) and the stage of the rating issuing procedure (new rating or existing rating).

Regarding issuer ratings, there are significant differences in the pricing policies adopted by different rating agencies and normally the fee is also affected by the complexity of the issuer evaluated (Table 5.1).

Some of the raters disclose only certain general principles used to define the fee applied to each issuer for the initial rating and/or existing ratings. The main issuer features considered on the basis of the declaration provided are the size and complexity of the firms.

If one examines the fees requested for the first rating issued, in only one case is a fixed fee defined independently with respect to issuer characteristics (A.M. Best Company), but this anomaly is related to the degree of specialization of the rater that evaluates only issuers that work in a specific sector (insurance). All other raters define a range of possible fees and the differences between the minimum and maximum values are significant, with maximum fees always at least double the minimum fees.

The number of rating agencies that provide information on the surveillance fee is lower with respect to those that disclose initial rating fees; sometimes the rater provides only general information on the relation between the new rating and existing rating fees (Agusto & Co.) or only the general guidelines used to define the fee applied (Malaysian Rating Corporation Berhad). As expected, the surveillance fee is always lower than the fee requested for a first issuing, but the difference between the two fees can be more or less relevant on the basis of the fee policy adopted by the rater.

Fees applied for an initial issue rating are normally linked to the value of the title issued, while the surveillance fee is normally linked to the remaining value of the title (if the title is amortized over time; Table 5.2).

The fee mechanism used for the initial issue rating normally defines a link with the value of the issue and sometimes the rater defines a minimum threshold for the amount that has to be paid, independent of the size of the issue, or a maximum threshold. Only in a few cases (Emerging Credit Rating Ltd. and Fitch Ratings Ltd.) is the fee applied not computed directly as a percentage of the issue value.

---

[3]The sample construction is affected by data availability. Even if fee disclosure is expected of all rating agencies, around 75% of raters declare that the fee definition is based on one-on-one negotiation, with no further information provided. For further details about rating agencies that disclose their fee policy, see Table A.4 in the Appendix.

Table 5.1 Fee Policy for Issuer Fee Rating Agencies

	New Rating	Surveillance
A.M. Best Company Inc.	US $500,000	From US $5000 to US $25,000
Agusto & Co. Ltd.	Define using different basis points on the basis of the size and complexity of the transaction involved, with a minimum threshold	A relatively smaller fee for annual rating reviews
Capital Intelligence Ltd.	Fee varies in accordance with the size and complexity of the entity	n.a.
Caribbean Information & Credit Rating Services Ltd.	n.a.	n.a.
Companhia Portuguesa de Rating, SA	Fee varies in accordance with the size and complexity of the entity	n.a.
Credit Rating Agency of Bangladesh Ltd.	From 2.00 to 5.50 Lac TK	From 1.50 to 4.00 Lac TK
CRISIL Ltd.	Fee varies in accordance with the size and complexity of the entity	n.a.
Ecuability, SA	From US $5000 to US $25,000	
Emerging Credit Rating Ltd.	From US $475,000 to US $800,000	From US $375,000 to US $700,000
Fitch Ratings Ltd.	From US $1000 to US $750,000	n.a.
JCR-VIS Credit Rating Co. Ltd.	From US $350,000 to US $1,000,000	From US $300,000 to US $950,000
Malaysian Rating Corporation Berhad	Fee varies in accordance with the size and complexity of the entity	Fee varies in accordance with the size and complexity of the entity
Moody's Investors Service	From US $1500 to US $2,500,000	n.a.
Pakistan Credit Rating Agency Ltd.	From PKR 350,000 to PKR 1,000,000	n.a.
SME Rating Agency of India Limited	From Rs 9100 to Rs 67,400	n.a.
Standard & Poor's	From US $45,000 to US $200,000	n.a.

Source: Rating agencies websites (accessed 03.01.2013).

Only a few raters (A.M. Best Company Inc. and Emerging Credit Rating Ltd.) define surveillance fees as a fixed amount to be paid every year; the solution more frequently adopted is to link the fee to the value (or remaining value) of the issue. Comparing annual fees related to new and existing issues, one finds the difference to be limited to no more than 5 basis points and in one case (JCR-VIS Credit Rating Co. Ltd.) there are no differences in the fees applied.

Table 5.2 Fee Policy for Issue Fee Rating Agencies

	New Rating	Surveillance
A.M. Best Company Inc.	From 0.6% to 1.0% of the issue size or up to US $120,000 per issue	From US $5000 to US $25,000
Agusto & Co. Ltd.	Fee varies in accordance with the size and complexity of the type of rating being assigned, with a minimum threshold	A relatively smaller fee for annual rating reviews
Capital Intelligence Ltd.	Fee varies in accordance with the size and complexity of the type of rating being assigned	n.a.
Caribbean Information & Credit Rating Services Ltd.	0.10% of the issue size of the rated instrument, with a floor of US $20,000	0.05% of the remaining issue size of the rated instrument, with a floor of US $10,000
Companhia Portuguesa de Rating, SA	Fee varies in accordance with the size and complexity of the type of rating being assigned	n.a.
Credit Rating Agency of Bangladesh Ltd.	0.08% of the issue size	0.06% of the remaining issue size of the rated instrument
CRISIL Ltd.	Fee varies in accordance with the size and complexity of the type of rating being assigned	n.a.
Ecuability, SA	0.01% of the issue size, with a floor of US $5000 and a cap of US $25,000	n.a.
Emerging Credit Rating Ltd.	From US $450,000 to US $700,000	From US $350,000 to US $500,000
Fitch Ratings Ltd.	From US $1000 to US $750,000	n.a.
JCR-VIS Credit Rating Co. Ltd.	From 0.075% to 0.10%	From 0.075% to 0.10%
Malaysian Rating Corporation Berhad	From 0.6%, with a floor of 150,000 RM per issue	From 0.4%, with a floor of 100,000 RM per issue
Moody's Investors Service	From $1500 to $2,500,000	n.a.
Pakistan Credit Rating Agency Ltd.	From 0.075% to 0.10%, with minimum threshold from PKR 300,000 to PKR 3,600,000 depending on the issue size	n.a.
SME Rating Agency of India Limited	n.a.	n.a.
Standard & Poor's	Up to 1.2% of the issue value	n.a.

Source: Rating agencies websites (accessed 03.01.2013).

Table 5.3 Fee Policy for User Fee Rating Agencies

	Global Credit Rating Co.	Shanghai Credit Information Services Co. Ltd.	Veribanc Inc.	Weiss Ratings Inc.
Subscription of single rating	–	$30	From $5 to $95, depending on the type of rating	–
Subscription of a set of ratings	From $3500 to $5000 for one sector	–	From $40 to $120, depending on the sector	From $249 to $499 for four quarterly full reports, depending on the type of rating
Discount policy	From 10% to 30% in the case of a multiple-sector request	–	–	10% of discount in the case of a multiple-year subscription

Source: Rating agencies websites (accessed 03.01.2013).

Raters can define for both issuer and issue ratings a discounting policy to apply lower fees to customers that require a higher number of services. Normally the discount policy is based on a one-on-one negotiation.

5.5.2 Fee Policy for User Fee Rating Models

Raters that use the user fee model define a fee that has to cover all the expenses related to the evaluation (both initial and surveillance costs). The fee applied is normally more standardized than that of raters that adopt the issuer fee model.

Given the fee policies disclosed on the rating agency websites, it is possible to identify common features of pricing policies adopted by raters applying the user fee model (Table 5.3).

Regarding raters that offer the opportunity to subscribe for a single rating (Global Credit Rating and Veribanc Inc.), there is no unique consensus on the procedure adopted for defining the fee: Global Credit Rating Co. adopts higher standardized solutions with a fixed fee, while Veribanc Inc. defines different prices on the basis of the complexity of the issue or issuer. In the case of multiple fees defined by the rater, normally the more expensive evaluation services relate to the financial sector and/or structured finance.

To apply some economies of scale in standardizing the product offered to all customers, raters can decide to offer a subscription to a package of products instead of only one rating evaluation. Normally the rater offers an opportunity to subscribe to a full report that includes all the evaluations related to a specific sector and the price of the service offered may increase with an increase in the complexity of the evaluation made. If one compares the fees requested for one rating with those related to the subscription to a set of ratings, normally the difference in fees is not too relevant, especially when complex rated entities are taken into account.

To establish long-term relationships with customers, raters can offer a discount to customers that request a multiple-sector subscription (Global Credit Rating Co.) or a multi-year service (Weiss Rating Inc.).

5.6 CONCLUSIONS

The prices of rating services differ according to the type of service requested, and normally the fee charged is defined by the customer's expected benefits. With regard to initial ratings, the issuer fee is defined on the basis of various proxies of firm size, whereas the issue fee is defined on the basis of the size and complexity of the financial instrument evaluated. Monitoring services are normally paid annually, and the fee is defined by the number of outstanding ratings and/or the remaining value of the issues.

Rating agencies can charge fees to the issuer or to the user but, due to the high risk of free-riding, the issuer fee model is the prevalent model. The user fee model is used by smaller rating agencies, which use their independence as a marketing instrument to increase their market share. The relevance of different types of raters is not comparable and, even if in the 1980s and 1990s many new user fee raters started to work, the main market players adopt the issuer fee model.

Comparing fees applied by raters that apply the user or the issuer fee model, there are huge differences in the prices applied due to the different numbers of customers that will pay for each evaluation. In the user fee model the rater defines low prices in order to maximize the number of possible interested subscribers while in the issuer fee model the fee is defined in order to maximize the revenues related to selling the service to only one customer.

The choice of pricing model can affect a firm's independence, since the issuer fee model increases the risk of collusion. Raters that adopt the issuer fee model can ensure the quality and objectivity of the information service provided only if certain organizational and economic methods are applied to ensure their independence. The next two chapters analyze the best practices adopted by agencies to ensure independence and the usefulness of the marketing measures used for monitoring customer dependence.

Chapter six

Organizational Structure and Rating Agency Independence

6.1 INTRODUCTION

A firm's organizational structure is based on its business model and purpose, and the features that must be taken into consideration in order to identify the best model are therefore quite heterogeneous (Daft, 2008). Rating agencies are private firms in the information service industry, and their success is related to their reputation in the market and the perceived value of their service (Rom, 2009). Due to the role of reputation in market success, rating agencies can be classified as professional service firms, where the price of the service offered is strictly affected by the value of the brand. The core value of these firms is always related to the human capital available, and their organizational structure must aim to maximize the value of this unique asset (Greenwood et al., 2005).

To achieve their business goals, a firm must establish contracts and rules to motivate and monitor its employees and stakeholders to create value for all stakeholders (Williamson, 2002). In the rating sector the main stakeholders are the employees (inside and outside the evaluation committee), shareholders, public authorities, and (if the firm is affiliated to a group) the other group members.

Section 6.2 identifies the main characteristics of employee ethical codes. Section 6.3 then examines the relationship between the rating evaluation team and other agency business areas. The implications of the firm's legal status are discussed in Section 6.4, the effects of group affiliation in Section 6.5, and the impact of public support or ownership in Section 6.6. Section 6.7 summarizes the results and presents some conclusions and implications.

6.2 ETHICAL CODES

Excluding unsolicited ratings, the rating process always implies interaction between the rating committee and the entity evaluated to collect all the information necessary to define the issue or issuer rating (De Laurentis, 2001).

The Independence of Credit Rating Agencies.
© 2014 Elsevier Inc. All rights reserved.

Independent of the pricing model (issuer fee or user fee), contact between a rating agency employee and an evaluated entity leads to the risk of corruption. Employees may consider the agency's reputation as being less important than bribes from the customer in exchange for a better evaluation (Hunt, 2009).

An ethical code is the method normally adopted by firms to define the minimum rules of conduct for all employees and to reduce conflicts of interest. The main purpose of the code is to reduce the firm's legal risk relating to employee misconduct (Stevens, 1994). Rating agencies adopt the same approach in managing conflicts of interest and reducing the risk of reputation loss (see Box 6.1).

The main aspects considered in all ethical codes pertain to:

- The relationship between the evaluation committee and the rated entity
- Gift policies
- Constraints on the use of the information collected during the evaluation process.

Rating agencies' employees are forbidden to work for, serve as an independent contractor to, or serve on the board of directors of any entity rated, and the same constraint is applied to their relatives (Bai, 2010). The reason for this constraint is to prevent rating committee members from offering more favorable ratings to rated entities for personal economic advantage. If the rating agency discovers such a conflict of interest, the employee can be fired.

In commercial relationships, employees and managers often exchange gifts and firms must thus define rules and objective criteria to prevent this policy from negatively affecting stakeholder goals (Bird, 1989). Employees and their immediate family members are forbidden from soliciting and/or accepting high-value gifts from rated entities, clients, and prospective clients or any third party representing these entities. Normally the threshold value is very low and such gifts do not impact negatively on the objectivity of the rating judgment (Coskun, 2008).

One of the main reasons for hiring a rating agency is the opportunity to signal to the market some private information that can positively impact their economic perspective without divulging it (Goh and Ederington, 1993). Rating agencies are forbidden to disclose these data and must define rules that prevent rating committee members from using this inside information for personal benefits (insider trading). The efficacy of these constraints is one of the main features considered in the accreditation procedure defined by the main supervisory authorities (White, 2007).

6.3 INFORMATION FLOWS AND MONITORING METHODS

Any information provider can obtain the benefits related to a long-term relationship with customers that allows them to maximize the value of the information collected on the quality and features of the evaluated entity. The principle of the economics of the information creates an incentive to transfer information inside the firm in order to identify any revenue opportunity related to the customers' features (Demski et al., 1999). In large firms, information flow can create conflicts of interest among different employees and negatively

BOX 6.1 Example of a Rating Agency's Ethical Code

LACE Financial Corp

Gift Policy. LACE employees and their immediate family members are forbidden from soliciting and/or accepting money, gifts, favors and benefits from rated entities, clients and prospective clients or any third party representing those entities. Employees must notify the Compliance Officer upon receipt of any prohibited item and the Compliance Officer will determine if it should be returned to the sender.

Outside Activity Policy. LACE employees and related personnel may not: (1) work for, serve as an independent contractor to or serve on the board of directors of any entity rated by LACE or any entity affiliated with an entity rated by LACE; (2) hold an elected or appointed government office that may create a conflict of interest or the appearance of a conflict of interest; (3) serve on any government or public agency, authority, commission, or regulatory body that may create a conflict of interest or the appearance of a conflict of interest; (4) serve on any self-regulatory body that performs oversight of any entity that LACE rates that may create a conflict of interest or the appearance of a conflict of interest; (5) serve in any capacity for any trade or professional organization or association that may create a conflict of interest or the appearance of a conflict of interest; (6) serve in any capacity for any broker or dealer engaged in underwriting securities or money market instruments. [...]

Personal Trading Policy. LACE requires that: (1) Employees may not buy or trade securities or money market instruments during the "rating season" for any given class of ratings. (2) If an employee of LACE Financial is involved in the rating process, he or she is prohibited from owning securities or money market instruments of any institution covered by that rating process. (3) All LACE employees and contractors are required to disclose any brokerage accounts that they directly own or have a beneficial interest. (5) All brokerage statements for LACE's employees and related personnel must be disclosed and statements for the accounts must be sent to, and reviewed by, the Compliance Officer. (6) LACE Financial's employees must seek and receive approval from the Compliance Officer before engaging in securities trades. (7) No LACE employee may trade in any security or recommend the purchase or sale of a security while in possession of material, non-public information regarding that security.

"Look Back" Policy. LACE's Compliance Officer will conduct a review for every former employee that had input into the ratings process while at LACE to ensure that the ratings decisions for the former employee were not biased toward that person's next employer. [...].

Prohibited Acts and Practices. LACE and its employees are prohibited from engaging in any of the following unfair, coercive, or abusive practices: (1) Conditioning or threatening to condition the issuance of a credit rating on the purchase by an obligor or issuer, or an affiliate of the obligor or issuer, of any other services or products, including pre-credit rating assessment products, of LACE or any person associated with LACE. (2) Issuing, or offering or threatening to issue, a credit rating that is not determined in accordance with LACE's established procedures and methodologies for determining credit ratings, based on whether the rated person, or an affiliate of the rated person, purchases or will purchase the credit rating or any other service or product of LACE or any person associated with LACE. (3) Modifying, or offering or threatening to modify, a credit rating in a manner that is contrary to LACE's established procedures and methodologies for modifying credit ratings based on whether the rated person, or an affiliate of the rated person, purchases or will purchase the credit rating or any other service or product of LACE or any person associated with LACE. (4) Issuing or threatening to issue a lower credit rating, lowering or threatening to lower an existing credit rating, refusing to issue a credit rating, or withdrawing or threatening to withdraw a credit rating, with respect to securities or money market instruments issued by an asset pool or as part of any asset-backed or mortgage-backed securities transaction, unless all or a portion of the assets within such pool or part of such transaction also are rated by LACE, where such practice is engaged in by LACE for an anticompetitive purpose.

Source: LACE Financial Corp.'s Exhibit 8—NRSRO application form 2010.

affect firm performance. In such cases, the firm creates internal firewalls to restrict information flow to certain business areas (Grandori, 1991).

For rating agencies the main problem is related to contact between the marketing area and the evaluation committee, which can have a negative impact on the objectivity of the judgment issued. To ensure the quality of the service provided, supervisory authorities impose firewalls to avoid any exchange of information between the evaluating committee and any counterparties that can influence their decisions (IOSCO, 2004). To ensure the independence of the rating committee with respect to all the other employees, rating agencies use a "Chinese box" solution (De Meijer and Saaf, 2008): Rating committee members are evaluated and controlled only by the firm's top management and any information flow is prohibited from all other employees (see Figure 6.1).

The evaluation and the rating committees are normally totally independent with respect to all other business areas, but to be effective the separation must not only be between employees but also within the information system. The method adopted is consistent with US and European supervisory approaches that consider such firewalls useful in avoiding conflicts of interest for the evaluation and rating committees (Leyens, 2011) (see Box 6.2).

Moreover, a rating agency must identify employees within the rating and evaluation committee who will supervise activities, and their number must be defined relative to the yearly volume of activities (Mulligan, 2009). Normally, to identify supervisors, top management considers their skills and experience and tries to create an internal control structure that allows the best use of the skills of all employees (see Box 6.3).

To identify the volume of activity for the rating and evaluation committee, the most widespread proxy is the number of outstanding ratings. The number of supervisors must be defined by considering the number of analysts and mean number of judgments issued by each evaluator[1] (see Table 6.1).

Due to the high number of evaluated entities, the three main agencies—Fitch, Moody's, and Standard & Poor's—hire the highest numbers of employees (analysts and supervisors). According to the overall sample, the mean number of analysts that can be monitored by a supervisor is around three, and for the majority of rating agencies this number is slightly lower. There is no clear relation between the number of analysts and supervisors and the number of ratings issued. This anomaly can be explained by examining the business practices adopted by rating agencies that normally define the number of employees on the basis of the complexity of the evaluated entity: The easier the evaluation, the lower the number of employees engaged (Rona-Tas and Hiss, 2010). The lack of further details about the type and number of ratings and the size of the evaluation committee prevents a verification of this hypothesis.

---

[1] Data about the internal organizations of firms are not available from their annual reports, and such information can only be collected by considering the rating agencies subject to SEC supervision. Exhibit 8 requested by the supervisory authority allows information to be collected about any employees directly engaged in the evaluation process.

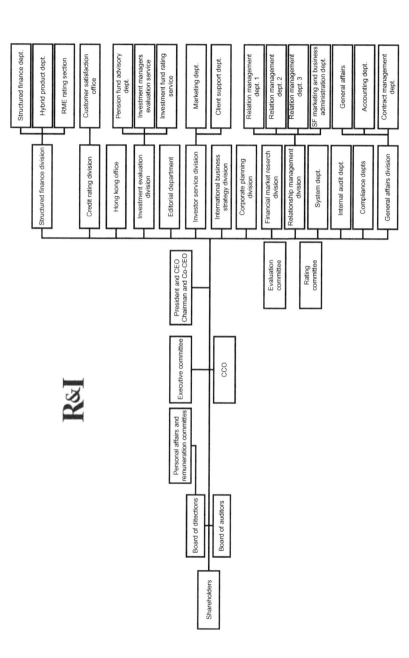

FIGURE 6.1 Example of a rating agency's internal organization. *Source*: Rating & Investment Information Inc., Exhibit 4—NRSRO application form 2010.

BOX 6.2 Example of Methods Adopted to Ensure Rating Independence

Moody's Investors Service

Moody's Investors Service Commercial Group is operationally segregated from any analytical line of business and any involvement in Credit Rating activities and analysts are required to refrain from participating in fee or payment discussions with issuers or their agents. [...]

Records of contractual relationships with issuers, along with exchanges with issuers related to commercial and fee information, are handled by the Commercial Group that is segregated from the analytical teams. Those records that relate to contracts, commercial or fee information are electronically filed in a separate retention system from the records filed as part of the analytical process.

Source: Moody's European Union Transparency report 2010.

BOX 6.3 Example of an Internal Control Structure

A.M. Best Company Inc.

Financial Analysts (FAs) and Senior Financial Analysts (SFAs) are responsible for the primary oversight and analysis of a specified portfolio of credit rating. SFAs are typically more experienced credit analysts that follow larger, more complex portfolios and contribute regularly to A.M. Best industry research, statistical studies, and internal projects. FAs and SFAs typically report to a Managing Senior Financial Analyst (MSFA), an Assistant General Manager (AGM) or an Assistant Vice President (AVP).

Each MSFA, AGM, GM, and AVP supervises a team of analysts, providing oversight, guidance and support to the credit analysts on their team. AGMs, GMs, and AVPs are typically more experienced, have broader supervisory responsibilities, and regularly contribute to oversee A.M. Best research, statistical studies, and internal projects. MSFAs, AGMs, and AVPs generally report to a GM or a Vice President. VPs and GMs typically report to a Group Vice President (GVP).

GVPs and certain VPs are responsible for the oversight and management of the credit analysts for an entire industry segment. GMs are responsible for the oversight and management of the credit analyst within our subsidiary offices and work with a responsible GVP. The GVP or VP is ultimately responsible for the credit ratings, research, and project management for all activities related to their respective industry segment. This includes responsibility for the consistent execution of corporate rating procedures and policies. The GVPs serve as Chair of the Rating Committee for their industry segment. GVPs, one VP, and one GM report to the Senior Vice President (SVP).

The Senior Vice President—Global Ratings is the head of the A.M. Best Rating Division and as such is responsible for the operations of the division.

Source: Exhibit 8—NRSRO application form of A.M. Best Inc. 2010.

To ensure the independence of the rating and evaluation committee, the last aspects that must be taken into account pertain to the wages and premiums offered to employees and employee turnover.

To avoid creating misleading incentives, the rating agency cannot define premiums on the basis of revenues created due to their rating activities. Surveys of the main rating agencies note that the remuneration mechanism is generally consistent with these requirements because wages are based prevalently on experience and skills, and premiums are defined on the basis of the efficiency of the employee in the rating process and the firm's overall yearly performance (Leonard, 2009).

Table 6.1 Analysts and Supervisors in Rating Agencies Recognized as NSRSOs

		A.M. Best	DBRS	Egan-Jones	Fitch Ratings	JCR	LACE Financial Corp.	M	Morningstar	Standard & Poor's
Outstanding ratings	2008	8882	2365	911	962,920	899	18,414	386,500	10,235	1,245,900
	2009	8776	43,260	934	671,947	872	20,400	1,112,317	9200	1,255,000
	2010	7667	42,930	1007	511,735	822	18,384	1,081,841	8856	1,231,600
	2011	6792	51,570	1136	348,536	722	17,278	998,878	16,070	1,170,600
Analysts	2008	–	–	–	–	–	–	–	–	–
	2009	144	62	12	1.057	59	8	1124	15	1081
	2010	134	67	5	1.035	61	7	1096	15	1019
	2011	82	84	2	758	24	22	1124	26	1172
Supervisors	2008	–	–	–	–	–	–	–	–	–
	2009	50	24	3	305	23	4	126	7	228
	2010	42	20	3	345	27	4	143	7	223
	2011	41	34	3	338	33	6	128	10	244
Average number of ratings for analyst	2008	–	–	–	–	–	–	–	–	–
	2009	60.94	697.74	77.83	635.71	14.78	2550.00	989.61	613.33	1160.96
	2010	57.22	640.75	201.40	494.43	13.48	2626.29	987.08	590.40	1208.64
	2011	82.83	613.93	568.00	459.81	30.08	785.36	888.68	618.08	998.81
Average number of analysts for supervisor	2008	–	–	–	–	–	–	–	–	–
	2009	2.88	2.58	4.00	3.47	2.57	2.00	8.92	2.14	4.74
	2010	3.19	3.35	1.67	3.00	2.26	1.75	7.66	2.14	4.57
	2011	2.00	2.47	0.67	2.24	0.73	3.67	8.78	2.60	4.80

Source: SEC data processed by the author.

BOX 6.4 Example of a Rating Agency's Employee Turnover Rules

Standard & Poor's

- Primary Analysts (a) must not be involved in Credit Rating Activities for an Issuer for a period exceeding four years and (b) must wait for at least two years before being involved again in any Credit Rating Activities for that Issuer.
- Employees in an Analytical Role who are involved in making Rating Decisions with respect to an Issuer (a) must not be involved in Rating Activities for that Issuer for a period exceeding five years and (b) must wait for at least two years before being involved again in any Credit Rating Activities for that Issuer. For these purposes, being involved in making Rating Decisions requires voting in relevant Rating Committees and regularly attending routine management meetings.
- Rating Committee chairpersons—the individuals who approve the Rating Decision or determination of the Rating Committee with respect to an Issuer—(a) must not be involved in Credit Rating Activities for that Issuer for a period exceeding seven years and (b) must wait for at least two years before being involved again in any Credit Rating Activities for that Issuer.

Source: Standard & Poor's European Union Transparency report 2010.

For firms that offer (intangible) services, an employee can increase the perceived service value for a customer due to the relationship established. Generally the impact is more significant for long-duration and high-frequency contacts (Gwinner, Gremler, and Bitner, 1998). This can lead to the risk of collusion when an information provider tries to satisfy the needs of the customer, and agencies must therefore try to mitigate this risk. One method is to turn over the employees who interact directly with the evaluated entity; however, this works only if the agency has a sufficient number of employees (McVea, 2010). Normally, rating agencies define different turnover policies according to the role of the employees in the evaluation process, and the constraint tends to be more severe for those in more frequent contact with the issuer (see Box 6.4).

6.4 LEGAL STATUS AND OWNERSHIP CONCENTRATION

Rating agencies, like all other firms, are exposed to the risk of going out of business, and the ownership and management define the firm's legal status to reduce their personal risk exposure with respect to firm performance. Analysis of the worldwide market demonstrates that normally rating agencies adopt the legal status of a public or limited liability company to separate their assets and liabilities with respect to top management and the owners[2] (see Figure 6.2).

Although most agencies are public companies (more than 50% of the agencies considered), they normally do not have to be listed. This evidence is not consistent with the standard assumption that one of the main reasons for the

---

[2] For further details about the legal status adopted by each rating agency, see Table A.2 in the Appendix.

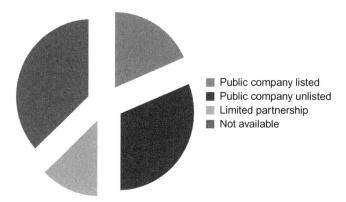

FIGURE 6.2 Legal status adopted by rating agencies. *Source*: Rating agency websites (accessed 03.01.2013).

limited liability structure is the opportunity to significantly increase the number of shareholders, and thus available capital (Hicks, 1982). Lack of interest in going public is also related to the effect of the listing choice, which normally implies lower levels of control in the firm due to the higher number of owners and regulatory constraints on ownership (Mikkelson, Partch, and Shah, 1997).

For smaller rating agencies, this anomaly can be explained by examining the role assumed by the owners inside the firm. Frequently these owners are also the top managers, and thus the requirement criteria for listed companies are not satisfied due to the high concentration of ownership and the unavailability of professional managers capable of running the firm and making decisions independently of the shareholders (see Table 6.2).

This scenario can be risky for agencies, because studies on firms in similar businesses (the auditing sector) show that this can lead to a lower quality of service offered. The lack of separation between management and ownership can lead to excessive attention to customer needs, and the resulting impact of extra profits on the value of the firm's shares can become even more important than its reputation (DeAngelo, 1981). For larger rating agencies, ownership is more widespread and the owners can be either individuals or firms (see Table 6.3).

The main shareholders of the bigger rating agencies are banks and investment companies, but sometimes other rating agencies have established commercial agreements or joint ventures. The involvement of users in the agency's equity capital (investor-owned credit rating agencies) raises the risk, if not scrutinized by the public authorities, of defining the rating in order to maximize the benefits related to using the information produced (Grundfest and Hochenberg, 2009). On the basis of current supervisory authorities, raters cannot give judgments on direct owners (Ederington and Yawitz, 1987), but for indirect shareholders general principles only suggest that the rating agency avoid the evaluation if there is any risk of lack of objectivity (IOSCO, 2004).

Table 6.2 Examples of Shareholder Composition for Small Rating Agencies

SAHA		Kobirate	
Ownership Structure			
Shareholder	**% Ownership**	**Shareholder**	**% Ownership**
Selim Suhan Seçkin	25.00%	Hasan Tüzün	25.00%
Abbas Yüksel	25.00%	Burhan Taştan	25.00%
Ali Perşembe	25.00%	Can Tekin	24.50%
Mehmet İnhan	12.50%	Veli Candar	24.50%
Hıfzı Deveci	10.00%	Hayrettin Keskin	1.00%
Demet Deveci	2.50%		
Role of the Owners in the Rating Agency			
Name	**Role**	**Name**	**Role**
Selim Suhan Seçkin	Chairman Board of Directors	Hasan Tüzün	Chairman Board of Directors
Abbas Yüksel	–	Burhan Taştan	Member Board of Directors— CEO
Ali Perşembe	Vice Chairman Board of Directors	Can Tekin	Member Board of Directors— Executive Vice President
Mehmet İnhan	Member Board of Directors	Veli Candar	Member Board of Directors
Hıfzı Deveci	Member Board of Directors	Hayrettin Keskin	Member Board of Directors
Demet Deveci	–		

Source: Rating agencies website (accessed 03.01.2013).

6.5 GROUP AFFILIATION

A group is an organization form wherein ownership is separated from control over a set of legally independent entities and affiliated entities operate in different sectors and/or geographical areas by flexibly exploiting the possible synergies existing among its members (Vander Vennet, 2002).

Rating agencies can be affiliated with a group to obtain the advantages related to certain synergies or economies of scale or scope (Csikos, 2005). Such a tactic has been adopted by a large number of rating agencies, especially the biggest market players. Group affiliation is not a constraint for a rating agency, and many select independence for developing their business (BIS, 2000). Data show that more than 45% of all agencies are affiliated with a group, and the number of reference groups is quite low because groups can include up to nine rating agencies (see Figure 6.3).

Regarding the rating agency groups, those that include more than one rating agency are those that include the three main players (Fimalac, McGraw-Hill, and Moody's) and the three groups that work only in the rating sector

Table 6.3 Examples of Shareholder Composition for Medium to Large Rating Agencies: RAM

Shareholder	%	Shareholder	%
Affin Bank Berhad	3.60%	Fitch Ratings Limited	4.90%
Affin Investment Bank Berhad	2.00%	Hong Leong Bank Berhad	4.00%
Alliance Bank Malaysia Berhad	3.20%	HSBC Bank Malaysia Berhad	3.50%
Alliance Investment Bank Berhad	2.00%	J.P. Morgan Chase Bank Berhad	1.30%
Am Bank (M) Berhad	3.30%	KewanganBersatuBerhad	0.70%
Am Investment Bank Berhad	3.50%	Malayan Banking Berhad	6.90%
Asian Development Bank	4.90%	OCBC Bank (Malaysia) Berhad	3.50%
Bangkok Bank Berhad	0.80%	Public Bank Berhad	5.33%
Bank of America Malaysia Berhad	2.10%	RHB Bank Berhad	8.85%
Bank of Tokyo-Mitsubishi UFJ (Malaysia) Berhad	2.10%	RHB Bank Berhad (RMBB Assets)	1.20%
Boon Siew Credit Berhad	0.30%	SIBB BERHAD	1.20%
CIMB Bank Berhad	14.43%	Standard Chartered Bank Malaysia Berhad	3.50%
Citibank Berhad	3.50%	The Bank of Nova Scotia Berhad	1.30%
Deutsche Bank (Malaysia) Berhad	0.80%	The Royal Bank of Scotland Berhad	1.30%
EON Bank Berhad	1.80%	United Overseas Bank (Malaysia) Berhad	4.20%
Affin Bank Berhad	3.60%	Fitch Ratings Limited	4.90%
Affin Investment Bank Berhad	2.00%	Hong Leong Bank Berhad	4.00%

Source: Rating agencies website (accessed 03.01.2013).

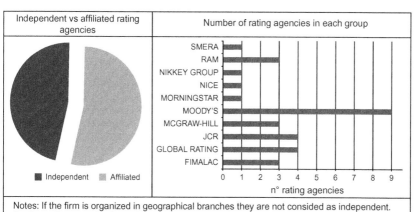

Notes: If the firm is organized in geographical branches they are not consided as independent. For four rating agencies it was impossible to collect information about the group affiliation

FIGURE 6.3 Group affiliation in the rating sector. *Source*: Rating agency websites (accessed 03.01.2013).

(Global Rating Group, JCR Group, and RAM). Moody's is the largest group because it includes at least twice the number of rating agencies included in any other group. Some reference groups include not only rating agencies but also other firms, in the industrial or service sectors, and in some cases these offer services related to the rating activity (see Table 6.4).

Among the other group members, the types of firms most frequently included are consultancy firms specializing in information technology, strategy, and organization. This finding is not surprising, because cross-selling opportunities exist where firms can maximize customer value by offering a bundled package of integrated services within the group (Bolton, Lemon, and Verhoef, 2004).

Rating agencies normally play a non-residual role in groups and can represent one of the main sources of group revenues (see Table 6.5).

Excluding the Nikkei Group and Morningstar, rating agencies contribute at least 25% of yearly revenues in the reference group, and for less sector-diversified groups (e.g. Fimalac, Global Rating, and Moody's) the revenue contribution is greater than 50%.

In the last five years the supply of ancillary services in the rating sector has increased significantly. Customers now frequently obtain consultancy services to better manage or organize the firm and thus obtain a better rating (Mishkin et al., 2004). Group affiliation normally restricts ancillary services from being offered due to regulatory constraints in the main financial markets (Champsaur, 2005).

With regard to the time trend of rating services with respect to overall group revenue, in some cases (like NICE, RAM and Xinhua Finance) the ratio is decreasing over time, even if the results are not always satisfied due to the high frequency of mergers and acquisitions for the group analyzed.

Table 6.4 Group Composition for the Main Rating Agencies

Group	Rating Agencies	Other Members
Fimalac	Apoyo y Asociados – Bankwatch Ratings S.A. – DCR Colombia – Fitch Ratings	Fitch Solutions – Fitch Trainings – Algoritmics
Global Rating	Rusrating – Kzrating – Amrating – AzeriRating	–
JCR Group	Japan Credit Rating Agency – Seoul Credit Rating & Information Inc. – JCR-VIS Credit Rating Co. Ltd. – JCR Eurasia Rating	Tokyo Shoko Research
McGraw-Hill Companies	CRISIL – Standard & Poor's – Taiwan Ratings	McGraw-Hill Education – McGraw-Hill School Education Group – McGraw-Hill Higher Education – McGraw-Hill – Professional – CTB/McGraw-Hill – Standard & Poor's – J.D. Power & Associates – Platts – McGraw-Hill Construction – Aviation Week – McGraw-Hill Broadcasting

(Continued…)

Table 6.4 Group Composition for the Main Rating Agencies (continued)

Group	Rating Agencies	Other Members
Moody's group	Moody's Investors Service – BRC Investor Services S.A. – Chengxin International Credit Rating Co. Ltd. – Ecuability, SA – Equilibrium Clasificadora de Riesgo – Interfax Rating Agency – Investment Information and Credit Rating Agency – P.T. PEFINDO Credit Rating Indonesia – Shanghai Far East Credit Rating Co. Ltd.	Moody's Analytics Inc. – Moody's Wall Street Analytics Inc. – The Moody's Foundation – Moody's Investors Service – Moody's Capital Markets Research Inc. – Moody's Risk Services Corp. – Moody's Advisors Inc.
Morningstar	Realpoint LLC	Corporate Fundamentals Inc. – Historis, LLC – Morningstar Global LLC – Ibbotson Associates Advisors, LLC – Morningstar Associates, LLC – Morningstar Investment Services Inc. – Morningstar Real-Time Data Inc. – MarketHistory.com Inc. – Logical Information Machines Inc. – Ibbotson Associates Inc. – Intech Pty Limited – Intech Research Pty Limited – Intech Fiduciaries Limited – Morningstar Australasia Pty Limited – Morningstar Direct Investments – Morningstar Research Inc. – Fundamental Data Limited – Hemscott Group Limited
NICE	National Information & Credit Evaluation	Seoul Electronics & Telecom – Seti – NICE e-Banking Services – NICE Information & Telecommunication – NICE R&C, ANR – NICE Data – NICE Investors Service – NICE – D&B – NICE Pricing Services – NICE F&I
Nikkei Group	Rating and Investment Information Inc.	Newspaper Division Sales – Newspaper Division Advertising – Newspaper Division Printing & Production – Newspaper Division Culture & Events – Newspaper Division Editorial – Publishing Division – Digital Media Division – Broadcasting division – Japan Center for Economic Research – Nikkei Adverting Research Institute – Nikkei Advanced Systems Inc. – Corporate Division General Affairs – Corporate Division International
RAM	RAM Rating Services Berhad – RAM Consultancy Services SdnBhd – RAM Ratings (Lanka) Limited (RAM Lanka)	–
SMERA	SIDBI	Dun & Bradstreet India – Indian leading banks
Xinhua Holding	Xinhua Finance	Market News International Inc. – Xinhua Financial Network Limited – Washington Analysis – XFM – China Finance Limited – Fortune China Public Relations Limited – FTSE/Xinhua Index Limited – Market News (Service) International Inc. – Mergent – Shanghai Tongxin Information Technology Consulting Co. Ltd.

If some regional divisions exists, the table presents only the reference division.
Source: Rating agency websites (accessed 03.01.2013).

Table 6.5 The Role of Rating Agencies in the Reference Groups (Millions of Reference Currency)

Group		2006	2007	2008	2009	2010	2011
Fimalac	Overall	744.80 €	559.10 €	586.90 €	559.20 €	608.90 €	545.00 €
	Rating	623.40 €	452.87 €	504.73 €	450.10 €	487.50 €	527.50 €
	%	83.70%	81.00%	86.00%	80.49%	80.06%	96.79%
Global Rating*	Overall	–	–	–	–	–	–
	Rating	–	–	–	–	–	–
	%	100%	100%	100%	100%	100%	100%
JCR Group*	Overall	–	–	–	–	–	–
	Rating	–	–	–	–	–	–
	%	–	–	–	–	–	–
McGraw-Hill Companies[†]	Overall	6255.10 $	6772.30 $	6355.10 $	5951.80 $	6168.30 $	6246.00 $
	Rating	2746.00 $	3046.00 $	1583.00 $	1537.30 $	1695.40 $	1767.00 $
	%	43.90%	44.98%	24.91%	25.83%	27.49%	28.29%
Moody's	Overall	2037.10 $	2259.00 $	1755.40 $	1797.20 $	2032.00 $	2280.07 $
	Rating	1894.30 $	1779.90 $	1204.70 $	1217.00 $	1405.00 $	1634.70 $
	%	92.99%	78.79%	68.63%	67.72%	69.14%	71.70%

Morningstar	Overall	315.18 $	435.11 $	502.46 $	479.00 $	555.35 $	641.40 $
	Rating	29.28$	43.14 $	45.68 $	39.45 $	49.67 $	64.14 $
	%	9.29%	9.91%	9.09%	8.24%	8.94%	10.0%
NICE	Overall	236,009.00 ₩	272,971.37 ₩	476,099.60 ₩	521,984.81 ₩	101,591.58 ₩	179,070.00 ₩
	Rating	149,518.00 ₩	155,493.98 ₩	172,716.41 ₩	175,749.58 ₩	44,047.23 ₩	83,665.09 ₩
	%	63.35%	56.96%	36.27%	33.67%	43.36%	46.72%
Nikkei Group[‡]	Overall	–	–	–	177,100 ¥	177,468 ¥	171,894 ¥
	Rating	–	–	–	4,490 ¥	4,252 ¥	4,454 ¥
	%	–	–	–	2.53%	2.40%	2.59%
RAM	Overall	31.19 RM	38.22 RM	48.28 RM	49.35 RM	40.78 RM	41.70 RM
	Rating	28.74 RM	24.02 RM	18.11 RM	18.36 RM	21.00 RM	32.63 RM
	%	92.14%	62.85%	37.51%	37.20%	51.50%	78.25%
SMERA*	Overall	–	–	–	–	–	–
	Rating	–	–	–	–	–	–
	%	–	–	–	–	–	–
Xinhua Finance[§]	Overall	20.84 $	29.41 $	25.43 $	17.02 $	14.21 $	19.56 $
	Rating	–	14.03 $	8.50 $	–	10.11 $	12.75 $
	%	–	47.71%	33.41%	–	71.15%	65.19%

*Balance sheets are not available.
[†]Data until 2007 do not consider only the rating service because the financial service macro-category does not give any breakdown on the single business areas.
[†]Data available in the English section of the website, allowing study only of the performance of the last years.
[‡]In 2009 the balance sheet did not provide revenues related to each business area.
Source: Rating agencies balance sheets.

BOX 6.5 Examples of Ethical Codes for Ancillary Services

Japan Credit Rating Agency

In carrying out ancillary business and other business operations, JCR shall ensure that it has procedures and mechanisms in place to identify, eliminate, manage or minimize matters that may unfairly affect the assignment or the provision of credit ratings.

The content of the ancillary business of JCR shall be made public on the website.

Rating and Investment Information

R&I shall keep its credit rating division independent from all other divisions in terms of information control and operational management. R&I shall ensure that its ancillary businesses do not necessarily present conflicts of interest with R&I's rating.

Activities have in place procedures and mechanisms designed to minimize the likelihood that conflicts of interest will arise. R&I shall define ancillary businesses and identify businesses it considers to be ancillary businesses.

Source: Rating agency websites (accessed 03.01.2013).

Even if ancillary services could be provided, supervisory authorities mandate that agency ethical codes clearly state that buying these extra services will not affect rating judgments (see Box 6.5).

6.6 PUBLIC INTERVENTION

The main international rating agencies are not usually interested in doing business in developing countries due to the high risk of reputation loss should they have to evaluate risky issuers or issues with insufficient data (Tourk, 2004). To develop a financial market and ease capital flows from foreign investors, public authorities in developing countries must increase the information transparency of the market through the development of a rating service (Nayar, 1993). A government can directly benefit from the development of a rating sector due to the lower returns they can then offer investors for Treasury bills or bond subscriptions due to the lower risk indicated by rating judgment. This is only one reason to support the rating sector, and empirical evidence shows that the coverage offered by the main rating agencies is generally high, even in developing countries (Kraussl, 2005).

The main reasons to support the rating sector can be ascribed to economic growth through easier access to credit, including that for firms not yet rated by the main international rating agencies. Empirical evidence shows that the presence of rating agencies in a country can significantly increase the amount of foreign capital invested in firms, especially listed ones (Sharma, 2001).

Another way countries can increase foreign capital investments is to create national credit agencies that offer rating services, thus reducing information

Table 6.6 Examples of Public Equity Ownership of Rating Agencies

CariCRIS		TRIS Corp.	
Brokerage firms	9.00%	Government Saving Bank	13.52%
Central banks	13.00%	Ministry of Finance	5.00%
Commercial banks	41.00%	Commercial Banks	45.33%
Insurance/conglomerates	9.00%	Stock Exchange of Thailand	13.34%
Multilateral	13.00%	Finance and securities companies	7.81%
Mutual funds	6.00%	Mutual fund management companies	5.00%
Stock exchange	1.00%	Insurance companies	5.00%
Technical consultant	8.00%	Asian Development Bank	5.00%

Source: Rating agency websites (accessed 03.01.2013).

asymmetry in the financial market (Gyntelberg, Ma, and Remolona, 2005). Since the costs related to starting a rating business and/or acquiring a reputation may be unsustainable for a small company, a government can support it through direct intervention in shareholder capital flows and/or indirect capital flows through publicly controlled companies (Ferri et al., 2009) (see Table 6.6).

Due to the financial crisis and the risks of collusion between rating agencies and evaluated entities, in the last years the main developed countries have begun to discuss opportunities to develop such publicly owned rating agencies. The main goal would be to provide the market with a judgment that is less affected by business relationships between issuers and rating agencies (Utzig, 2010).

Direct intervention in shareholder ownership is often criticized for the risk of a negative effect on firm independence and thus the objectivity of the service offered. In addition, public authorities may be interested in increasing ratings to achieve economic growth in certain sectors or geographical areas by giving these firms easier access to capital markets (Cheung and Chan, 2002). To avoid such risks, some countries have instead supported the development of a rating sector without direct intervention in agency capital ownership. A more effective solution is the development of a rating agency association that supports knowledge sharing; however, the success of such associations normally depends on the membership of some of the main players in the worldwide market (Park and Rhee, 2006). The main purpose of these associations is to develop high-quality standards for the rating procedure and to increase the information content of the services offered (Asian Bankers Association, 2000) (see Box 6.6).

BOX 6.6   Example of a Rating Agency Association: ACRAA

Brief History

ACRAA was organized on 14 September 2001 at the Asian Development Bank headquarters, Metro Manila, by 15 Asian credit rating agencies from 13 countries, a pioneering event to bring domestic credit rating agencies in a regional cooperative effort.

Objectives

The Association of Credit Rating Agencies in Asia is organized for the following purposes:

- To develop and maintain cooperative efforts that promote interaction and exchange of ideas, experiences, information, knowledge and skills among credit rating agencies in Asia, and that would enhance their capabilities and their role of providing reliable market information.
- To undertake activities aimed at promoting the adoption of best practices and common standards that ensure high quality and comparability of credit ratings throughout the region, following the highest norms of ethics and professional conduct.
- To undertake activities aimed at promoting the development of Asia's bond markets and cross-border investment throughout the region.

Members

As of October 2010, membership has increased to 28 members from 15 countries. ACRAA's members are the following:

Ahbor Rating (Ahbor)
Brickwork Ratings India Pvt. Ltd.
China Chengxin International
China Lianhe Credit Rating Co. Ltd.
Credit Analysis and Research Limited (CARE)
Credit Rating Agency of Bangladesh Limited (CRAB)
Credit Rating Co. Ltd. (CCXI)
Credit Rating Information & Services Limited (CRISL)
CRISIL Limited
Dagong Global Credit Rating Co. Ltd (Dagong)
ICRA Limited
Islamic International Rating Agency (IIRA)
Japan Credit Rating Agency Limited (JCR)
JCR-VIS Credit Rating Co. Limited (JCR-VIS)
JSC "Rating Agency of Regional Financial Center of Almaty City"
Korea Investors Service Inc. (KIS)
Korea Ratings Corporation (Korea Ratings)
Malaysian Rating Corporation Berhad (MARC)
NICE Investors Service Co. Ltd. (NICE)
Pakistan Credit Rating Agency Limited (PACRA)
PEFINDO Credit Rating Indonesia (PEFINDO)
Philippine Rating Services Corporation (PhilRatings)
RAM Ratings (Lanka) Ltd.
Rating Agency Malaysia Berhad (RAM)
Seoul Credit Rating & Information Inc. (SCRI)
Shanghai Brilliance Credit Rating & Investors Service Co. Ltd.
Shanghai Far East Credit Rating Co. Ltd. (SFECR)
Taiwan Ratings Corp (TRC)
TRIS Rating Co. Limited (TRIS)

(Continued)

> **BOX 6.6   Example of a Rating Agency Association: ACRAA (Continued)**
>
> Minimum requirements for membership of ACRAA are:
> - The Applicant must be organized and domiciled, and its operations based in Asia.
> - It must be duly accredited as a credit rating agency by the duly established regulatory authorities in the country of domicile. If there is no regulatory authority, the board will decide whether to waive this requirement or not.
> - It has been in operation for at least one year with a full-time staff of analysts or has assigned credit ratings to at least five accounts/entities, whichever comes first.
>
> *Source*: <*http://www.acraa.com/*> *(accessed 03.01.2013).*

6.7 CONCLUSIONS

Rating service objectivity can be ensured by creating external and internal monitoring procedures to avoid any risk of collusion between the evaluator and any stakeholders engaged in the evaluation process. Regarding the relationship between the agency and the entity evaluated, the main monitoring methods involve employee ethical codes, the identification of supervisors on the rating committee, and separating the rating and evaluation committee from all other business areas. Regarding other stakeholders, the most important features to control are ownership concentration and public intervention. The rating sector is normally characterized by a significant degree of ownership concentration and when an agency is affiliated with a group, the supervisory authorities must make sure this status is not used to avoid cross-selling constraints. Public intervention in the rating sector could be accomplished via direct shareholder owners or other types of indirect intervention that can better ensure the evaluator's independence.

Even if organizational methods can reduce the risk of collusion between issuers and rating agencies, the risk still exists and must be monitored by supervisory authorities by examining the business relationship between each customer and agency. The main issue normally evaluated is the construction of a monitoring index that allows one to properly measure the risk of collusion between customers and raters by looking at the concentration of customer portfolios.

The next chapter presents a detailed analysis of the relationship established between raters and customers, and evaluates, with a simulation approach, the fitness of the current solution adopted by regulators in evaluating the concentration of customer portfolios.

Chapter | seven

The Economic Independence of Rating Agencies

7.1 INTRODUCTION

Even though the rating agency market is not overly competitive, each player is interested in increasing its market share, acquiring clients from its competitors. To acquire new customers, a rating agency can increase the quality of service or define a judgment that, independently of the evaluation process, is positively biased (Flandreau, Gaillard, and Parker, 2010). In the first scenario, competition has a positive effect on the value of the service offered and the rating agencies will try to improve the quality of the evaluation process. In the second scenario, the rating can lose its objectivity and thus the service will not reduce information asymmetry in the market and can mislead unskilled financial investors. In this case, an effective supervisory approach can minimize the risk of rating shopping among rating agencies.

The regulator must measure the economic relevance of each customer for each rating agency to verify whether some customers are so relevant that the rating agency considers the risk of reputation loss preferable to losing them. On the basis of the current supervisory approach (e.g. SEC, 2007; European Commission, 2008; IOSCO, 2008), standard measures proposed in the marketing literature to evaluate the economic relevance of a customer can also be applied to the rating market.

Considering a representative sample of the worldwide rating market (Table 7.1), this chapter presents a detailed analysis of the customer–rater relationship from 2001 to 2012.

Section 7.2 analyzes the characteristics of the relationship between customers and firms in the rating industry, considering both the literature available and summary statistics constructed on the rating agency data. Section 7.3 presents the main approach proposed by the supervisory authorities to monitor rater independence and discusses the main issues related to its application in

The Independence of Credit Rating Agencies.
© 2014 Elsevier Inc. All rights reserved.

industry evaluation. Section 7.4 presents a simulation approach to evaluate the differences in the fitness of the model in a scenario of equal and differentiated fees. Section 7.5 summarizes the conclusions and main implications of the analysis.

7.2 CUSTOMER RELATIONSHIPS FOR RATING AGENCIES

Rating agencies can be considered external firm auditors that certify the quality of an issuer or issue. The auditing literature shows that there are many incentives for auditors to disregard their duties in pursuit of personal gain (Demski, 2003). The main aspects involved in measuring this risk of collusion pertain to the customer's relative size and the length of the relationship with the auditing firm (Reynolds and Francis, 2000).

The customer's relative size with respect to the rater can significantly affect judgment and, normally, the greater the economic role of the customer for the evaluator, the lower the rater's independence in the evaluation process (DeAngelo, 1981). The lower degree of independence can be explained by the negative impact that the loss of a main customer can have on the evaluator's yearly income.

The evaluation of independence must also consider a multi-period framework, because relationships in this type of service do not expire after a year and can last for many years. If the analysis considers a long-term relationship, the longer the relationship, the greater the probability of the evaluator losing independence (Berger and Nada, 1998).

In the rating sector, relationships between customers and agencies are always medium to long term and new or young firms normally survive and grow in the rating market only if they are able to increase customer loyalty (Sagner, 1995). The marketing literature measures customer loyalty on the basis of the number and amount of services bought yearly and the retention rate (Blattberg, Getz, and Thomas, 2001). Customer loyalty has to be analyzed considering the role of both new customers and lost ones.

Looking at the number of new customers acquired on a yearly time horizon, only small rating agencies suffer from a high turnover of their portfolio due to the high growth registered for the business in the time horizon considered (Table 7.1).

Excluding five raters (Capital Intelligence Ltd.; European Rating Agency; Global Credit Rating Co.; Shanghai Brilliance Credit Rating & Investors Service Co. Ltd.; and Xinhua Finance) that started in the time horizon analyzed, the average role of new customers is lower than 13%. Large raters (such as Fitch Rating, Moody's Investor Services, and Standard & Poor's) are less affected by the phenomenon. The role of new customers acquired is never higher than 20% and, on average, lower than 10% for all years.

Around 35% of the agencies show an increase in the number of customers served equal to zero in at least one year and some raters (10) are characterized

Table 7.1 Sample Description

A.M. Best Company	Japan Credit Rating Agency
Austin Rating	Korea Ratings Corporation
BRC Investor Services	Malaysian Rating Corporation Berhad
Canadian Bond Rating Service	Mikuni & Co.
Capital Intelligence	Moody's Investors Service
Chengxin International Credit Rating	National Information & Credit Evaluation
China Lianhe Credit Rating	P.T. PEFINDO Credit Rating Indonesia
Credit Analysis & Research	Philippine Rating Services
CRISIL	RAM Rating Services Berha
Dagong Global Credit Rating	Rating and Investment Information
Dominion Bond Rating Service	Rus Ratings
European Rating Agency	Shanghai Brilliance Credit Rating & Investors Service
Fitch Ratings	Standard & Poor's
Global Credit Rating	Thai Rating and Information Services
Investment Information and Credit Rating Agency	Xinhua Finance

Source: Bloomberg data processed by the author.

by more than one year of zero growth in their customer portfolios. Only one rater (Canadian Bond Rating Service) never acquired a new customer in the time horizon considered.

Given the numbers of customers lost by the raters (Table 7.2), the retention rate for the overall portfolios managed by rating agencies is always higher than 75% (except for Xinhua Finance, which, in the first years analyzed, was significantly affected by the turnover of their customer portfolio), demonstrating that the relationships between rating agencies and customers tend to be long term.

Many raters (seven) do not suffer at all from the loss of customers and for all 12 years considered none of the customers served decided to interrupt their relationship with the rating agency. The biggest players (Fitch Rating, Moody's Investor Services, and Standard & Poor's) never suffered a loss of customers in a year greater that 17% of the overall portfolio.

The value of the customer is affected not only by the current buying behavior but also by the number of new services requested during the lifetime of the customer relationship (Ryals, 2002) and normally all service industries comparable to the rating sector are characterized by long-term relationships with loyal customers. To complete the analysis of customer relationships in the rating industry, it is necessary to consider retained customer behavior and the number of services requested yearly from the rater (Table 7.4).

Table 7.2 Summary Statistics for New Customers Acquired Yearly

	Mean	Min		Max	
		Value	No. of Years	Value	No. of Years
A.M. Best Company	19.47%	0.38%	1	84.34%	1
Austin Rating	5.31%	0.00%	5	22.45%	1
BRC Investor Services	8.34%	0.00%	5	23.08%	1
Canadian Bond Rating Service	0.00%	0.00%	12	0.00%	12
Capital Intelligence	42.42%	2.42%	1	100.00%	1
Chengxin International Credit Rating	33.47%	0.00%	3	86.67%	1
Credit Analysis & Research	6.91%	0.00%	2	21.32%	1
CRISIL	15.30%	3.67%	1	50.81%	1
Dagong Global Credit Rating	34.61%	0.00%	4	76.71%	1
Dominion Bond Rating Service	11.23%	2.19%	1	25.23%	1
European Rating Agency	36.59%	0.00%	2	100.00%	1
Fitch Ratings	9.16%	3.21%	1	19.95%	1
Global Credit Rating	30.47%	0.00%	3	100.00%	1
Japan Credit Rating Agency	4.93%	1.95%	1	8.26%	1
Korea Ratings Corporation	13.09%	4.72%	1	20.07%	1
Malaysian Rating Corporation Berhad	16.57%	1.67%	1	54.17%	1
Mikuni & Co.	19.47%	0.38%	1	84.34%	1
Moody's Investors Service	5.57%	3.63%	1	7.80%	1
National Information & Credit Evaluation	5.47%	0.47%	1	11.80%	1
P.T. PEFINDO Credit Rating Indonesia	8.54%	1.35%	1	28.30%	1
Philippine Rating Services	4.84%	0.00%	2	14.71%	1
RAM Rating Services Berha	8.03%	1.81%	1	13.04%	1
Rating and Investment Information	3.92%	1.86%	1	6.02%	1
Rus Ratings	19.47%	0.38%	1	84.34%	1
Shanghai Brilliance Credit Rating & Investors Service	54.51%	30.25%	1	100.00%	1
Standard & Poor's	7.28%	4.26%	1	16.38%	1
Thai Rating and Information Services	19.44%	2.17%	1	89.29%	1
Xinhua Finance	26.06%	0.00%	4	100.00%	1

Source: Bloomberg data processed by the author.

Table 7.3 Summary Statistics for Lost Customers Yearly

	Mean	Min		Max	
		Value	No. of Years	Value	No. of Years
A.M. Best Company	0.96%	0.00%	4	2.54%	1
Austin Rating	0.00%	0.00%	12	0.00%	12
BRC Investor Services	0.00%	0.00%	12	0.00%	12
Canadian Bond Rating Service	0.00%	0.00%	12	0.00%	12
Capital Intelligence	0.19%	0.00%	8	1.21%	1
Chengxin International Credit Rating	0.00%	0.00%	12	0.00%	12
Credit Analysis & Research	0.77%	0.00%	6	3.73%	1
CRISIL	1.07%	0.00%	2	2.85%	1
Dagong Global Credit Rating	0.00%	0.00%	12	0.00%	12
Dominion Bond Rating Service	0.21%	0.00%	6	1.27%	1
European Rating Agency	0.00%	0.00%	6	0.00%	6
Fitch Ratings	2.75%	0.57%	1	5.12%	1
Global Credit Rating	0.00%	0.00%	8	0.00%	8
Investment Information and Credit Rating Agency	2.09%	0.00%	1	4.99%	1
Japan Credit Rating Agency	0.08%	0.00%	8	0.36%	1
Korea Ratings Corporation	10.59%	0.78%	1	24.77%	1
Malaysian Rating Corporation Berhad	0.32%	0.00%	9	1.64%	1
Mikuni & Co.	0.96%	0.00%	4	2.54%	1
Moody's Investors Service	0.02%	0.00%	2	0.05%	1
National Information & Credit Evaluation	0.20%	0.00%	9	1.31%	1
P.T. PEFINDO Credit Rating Indonesia	0.00%	0.00%	12	0.00%	12
Philippine Rating Services	0.00%	0.00%	12	0.00%	12
RAM Rating Services Berha	0.31%	0.00%	8	2.08%	1
Rating and Investment Information	4.29%	0.22%	1	9.06%	1
Rus Ratings	0.96%	0.00%	4	2.54%	1
Shanghai Brilliance Credit Rating & Investors Service	0.00%	0.00%	7	0.00%	7
Standard & Poor's	5.53%	2.87%	1	13.50%	1
Thai Rating and Information Services	0.16%	0.00%	10	1.12%	1
Xinhua Finance	16.39%	0.00%	7	91.61%	1

Source: Bloomberg data processed by the author.

Table 7.4 Percentage of Existing Customers Classified by Number of Services Requested

	Stable No. of Services			Increased No. of Services			Decreased No. of Services		
	Mean	Min	Max	Mean	Min	Max	Mean	Min	Max
A.M. Best Company	93.53%	53.41%	100.00%	5.44%	0.00%	44.63%	1.03%	0.00%	44.63%
Austin Rating	93.28%	68.75%	100.00%	6.72%	0.00%	31.25%	0.00%	0.00%	0.00%
BRC Investor Services	94.17%	50.00%	100.00%	5.83%	0.00%	50.00%	0.00%	0.00%	0.00%
Canadian Bond Rating Service	100.00%	100.00%	100.00%	0.00%	0.00%	0.00%	0.00%	0.00%	0.00%
Capital Intelligence	95.49%	80.68%	100.00%	4.29%	0.00%	18.09%	0.22%	0.00%	1.22%
Chengxin International Credit Rating	92.46%	76.92%	100.00%	7.54%	0.00%	23.08%	0.00%	0.00%	0.00%
Credit Analysis & Research	97.51%	90.97%	100.00%	1.55%	0.00%	5.16%	0.95%	0.00%	3.87%
CRISIL	94.38%	83.65%	100.00%	4.12%	0.00%	14.68%	1.51%	0.00%	3.48%
Dagong Global Credit Rating	92.97%	77.35%	100.00%	7.03%	0.00%	22.65%	0.00%	0.00%	0.00%
Dominion Bond Rating Service	93.10%	82.52%	99.17%	6.62%	0.83%	16.06%	0.29%	0.00%	1.42%
European Rating Agency	100.00%	100.00%	100.00%	0.00%	0.00%	0.00%	0.00%	0.00%	0.00%
Fitch Ratings	87.10%	78.82%	89.63%	9.10%	5.26%	19.64%	3.80%	0.81%	6.77%
Global Credit Rating	93.73%	66.67%	100.00%	6.27%	0.00%	33.33%	0.00%	0.00%	0.00%
Investment Information and Credit Rating Agency	91.03%	79.88%	99.74%	5.75%	0.26%	18.97%	3.22%	0.00%	8.16%

Japan Credit Rating Agency	93.60%	56.03%	99.02%	6.27%	0.98%	43.97%	0.13%	0.00%	0.59%
Korea Ratings Corporation	80.92%	56.79%	98.44%	3.19%	0.36%	14.11%	15.89%	1.17%	40.74%
Malaysian Rating Corporation Berhad	98.06%	94.87%	100.00%	1.61%	0.00%	5.13%	0.33%	0.00%	1.67%
Mikuni & Co.	93.53%	53.41%	100.00%	5.44%	0.00%	44.63%	1.03%	0.00%	2.72%
Moody's Investors Service	90.28%	77.77%	95.11%	9.69%	4.88%	22.21%	0.03%	0.00%	0.09%
National Information & Credit Evaluation	97.69%	95.31%	100.00%	1.91%	0.00%	3.89%	0.39%	0.00%	2.29%
P.T. PEFINDO Credit Rating Indonesia	96.85%	85.00%	100.00%	3.15%	0.00%	15.00%	0.00%	0.00%	0.00%
Philippine Rating Services	99.59%	97.44%	100.00%	0.41%	0.00%	2.56%	0.00%	0.00%	0.00%
RAM Rating Services Berha	98.46%	96.84%	100.00%	1.22%	0.00%	3.16%	0.32%	0.00%	2.13%
Rating and Investment Information	87.35%	29.21%	98.91%	7.34%	0.22%	66.74%	5.31%	0.54%	11.86%
Rus Ratings	93.53%	53.41%	100.00%	5.44%	0.00%	44.63%	1.03%	0.00%	2.72%
Shanghai Brilliance Credit Rating & Investors Service	83.71%	66.67%	100.00%	16.29%	0.00%	33.33%	0.00%	0.00%	0.00%
Standard & Poor's	86.20%	69.25%	93.23%	7.03%	1.12%	26.90%	6.76%	3.85%	16.35%
Thai Rating and Information Services	95.77%	87.18%	100.00%	3.75%	0.00%	12.82%	0.49%	0.00%	2.27%
Xinhua Finance	99.72%	97.22%	100.00%	0.00%	0.00%	0.00%	0.28%	0.00%	2.78%

Source: Bloomberg data processed by the author.

On average, the number of services requested by a customer does not vary significantly from year to year. In addition, independent of the rating agency considered, the average number of customers that do not change the amount of services requested is always greater than 79%. Regarding year-by-year results, the minimum percentage of stable ratings is provided by Shanghai Brilliance Credit Rating & Investors Service, for which in one year less than 30% of customers do not change their buying strategy with respect to the previous year. The majority of raters have at least one year in which there is perfect coherence between the customer's buying strategy in two consecutive years.

For more than 70% of the raters, in at least one year the percentage of customers that increased the number of services requested was equal to zero. For more than 85% of rating agencies, in at least one year customers did not increase the number of services requested.

Considering customers that change their buying strategy from year to year, excluding Korea Ratings Corporation and Xinhua Finance, the number of rated entities that, on average, increased the amount of services requested was always higher than the number of those that decided to reduce the amount of services requested.

7.3 MEASURING ECONOMIC INDEPENDENCE OF RATING AGENCIES

The marketing literature presents different approaches to measure the value of each customer, and the choice of the best approach depends on the characteristics of the firms and the purpose of the evaluation (Kumar, 2007).

The first measure proposed considers the yearly revenues relating to the customer on the basis of the amount and price of goods/services bought:

$$REV_{i,t} = Revenues_{it} = \sum_{j=1}^{n} p_{it}^j q_{it}^j, \qquad (7.1)$$

where overall revenues are the sum of the products of the price (p_{it}^j) and quantity (q_{it}^j) of n goods bought in year t. For rating agencies, revenues can be distinguished in those related to existing ratings and new issues. To consider the customer satisfaction discount policy adopted for top customers, revenues for new services requested could not always be correlated with the amount of services purchased. In other words,

$$REV_{i,t} = \min\left[nn_{it}fee_{it}, multiple\,fee_{it}\right] + ne_{it}Monitoring\,fee_{it}, \qquad (7.2)$$

where revenues related to the new rating requests are the minimum of the product of the fees and number of new ratings and the multiple-service fee ($\min[nn_{it}fee_{it}, multiple\,fee_{it}]$), while the revenues for existing ratings are usually proportional to the number of ratings available ($ne_{it}Monitoring\,fee_{it}$).

Data about commercial relationships between firms and their customers are sensitive data that are not normally public. In this context, the supervisory

---

BOX 7.1 Example of Customer Relationship Disclosure Rules

Basel Committee on Banking Supervision (2006)
[…] The ECAI must be financially viable so that it can operate free from economic and political pressures exerted by its owners/shareholders or rated entities. […]

European Commission (2008)
[…] A credit rating agency shall publicly disclose the names of the rated entities or related third parties from which it receives more than 5% of its annual revenue. […]
[…] On a yearly basis the following information:
(a) a list of the largest 20 clients of the credit rating agency by revenue;
(b) a list of those clients of the credit rating agency whose contribution to the growth rate in the revenue of the credit rating agency in the previous financial year exceeded the growth rate in the total revenues of the credit rating agency in that year by a factor of more than 1.5 times; each such client shall only be included on this list where in that year it accounted for more than 0.25% of the worldwide total revenues of the credit rating agency at global level […]

IOSCO (2008)
[…] A [credit rating agency] should disclose if it receives 10 percent or more of its annual revenue from a single issuer, originator, arranger, client or subscriber (including any affiliates of that issuer, originator, arranger, client or subscriber) […]

SEC (2007)
[…] Section 15E(a)(1)(B)(viii) of the Exchange Act requires that an application for registration as an NRSRO include, on a confidential basis, a list of the 20 largest issuers and subscribers that use the credit rating services provided by the credit rating agency by amount of net revenue received by the credit rating agency in the fiscal year immediately preceding the date of submission of the application […]

Source: Basel Committee on Banking Supervision (2006), European Commission (2008), IOSCO (2008), and SEC (2007).

---

authorities are the only institutions that can control customer portfolio concentrations and evaluate the rating agencies' independence from their customers. Rating agencies are obliged to transmit to the supervisory authorities confidential documentation about their commercial relationships, thus allowing an evaluation of the risk of collusion with their main customers (Autorité de Marchés Financiers, 2005).

Even if the approaches adopted by the supervisory authorities are quite heterogeneous, common guidelines exist in constructing the measure of customer portfolio concentration (see Box 7.1).

Rules do not normally define any threshold that would trigger direct intervention from the supervisory authorities, but only disclosure procedures for the more relevant counterparties. The supervisory authorities decide on the basis of the data whether direct intervention is necessary and whether any excessive concentration affects the objectivity of a judgment.

Analysis of the customers' portfolios is carried out within a yearly time horizon, focusing only on the top customers. The relevant counterparties are identified as the top 20 customers regardless of their economic value or as customers that represent an exposure higher than an established threshold (5% or 10%) of the overall yearly revenues.

The set of information requested of each customer may differ according to the history of the relationship established with the firm. If the customer's relevance has been increasing over time, more detailed information may be requested.

Aside from top customers, the supervisory authorities do not worry about the other customers, and no information is requested to study the characteristics of overall customer portfolios. If the role of main customers is comparable among a group of rating agencies, the supervisory authority will not distinguish among rating agencies characterized by higher customer portfolio segmentation.

7.4 MEASURING PORTFOLIO CONCENTRATION FOR RATING AGENCIES

7.4.1 Sample

The analysis considers 29 rating agencies listed in the Bloomberg database for the 10 years between 2001 and 2012, and looks at all ratings (issue and issuer ratings) available to identify the customers and the number of services requested (Figure 7.1).

The sample includes 20,389 firms that were evaluated by more than one rating agency and so the number of customers served varies from 26,742 in 2001 to 61,218 counterparties in 2012. The number of raters in the sample increased over time, from 24 to 29 raters, and the average number of firms evaluated by each rater increased over time, from 922 rated customers in 2001 to 2111 counterparties in 2012.

The difference between surveillance and new rating fees is not frequently disclosed by the rating agency and the information provided on websites sometimes allows only evaluation of the ratio between the maximum fees applied for new and existing ratings (Table 7.5).

Normally the ratio is significantly variable, with a maximum of 20:1, and normally the spread is higher for issuer rating than for issue rating. Excluding extreme values (20 and one), on average, multiple services requested cost half of single requests.

No information is provided on the discounting policy applied for the best customer and normally the cost of the service is always defined on the basis of a one-to-one negotiation.

7.4.2 Methodology

Due to the unavailability of details about the fees applied to each customer, a simulation of the effect of discounting policies for top customers was carried

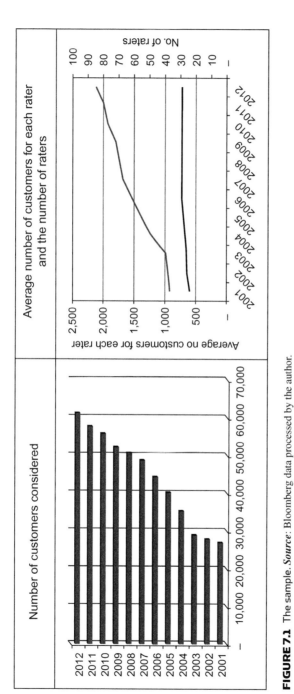

FIGURE 7.1 The sample. *Source*: Bloomberg data processed by the author.

Table 7.5 Fees and Discounting Policy Adopted by Rating Agencies for Multiple Ratings

	Issuer Rating (Maximum Fee, in Thousands)			Issue Rating (Maximum Fee, in Thousands or %)		
	New Ratings	Existing Rating	Ratio	New Ratings	Existing Rating	Ratio
A.M. Best Company	$500	$25	20	$120	$25	4.8
Austin Rating	n.a.	n.a.	n.a.	n.a.	n.a.	n.a.
BRC Investor Services	n.a.	n.a.	n.a.	n.a.	n.a.	n.a.
Canadian Bond Rating Service	n.a.	n.a.	n.a.	n.a.	n.a.	n.a.
Capital Intelligence	n.a.	n.a.	n.a.	n.a.	n.a.	n.a.
Chengxin International Credit Rating	n.a.	n.a.	n.a.	n.a.	n.a.	n.a.
Credit Analysis & Research	n.a.	n.a.	n.a.	n.a.	n.a.	n.a.
CRISIL	n.a.	n.a.	n.a.	n.a.	n.a.	n.a.
Dagong Global Credit Rating	n.a.	n.a.	n.a.	n.a.	n.a.	n.a.
Dominion Bond Rating Service	n.a.	n.a.	n.a.	n.a.	n.a.	n.a.
European Rating Agency	n.a.	n.a.	n.a.	n.a.	n.a.	n.a.
Fitch Ratings	$750	–	–	$750	n.a.	–
Global Credit Rating	n.a.	n.a.	n.a.	n.a.	n.a.	n.a.
Investment Information and Credit Rating Agency	n.a.	n.a.	n.a.	n.a.	n.a.	n.a.
Japan Credit Rating Agency	$1000	$950	1.16	0.10%	0.10%	1
Korea Ratings Corporation	n.a.	n.a.	n.a.	n.a.	n.a.	n.a.
Malaysian Rating Corporation Berhad	n.a.	n.a.	n.a.	0.6%	0.4%	1.5
Mikuni & Co.	n.a.	n.a.	n.a.	n.a.	n.a.	n.a.
Moody's Investors Service	$2500	n.a.	–	$2500	n.a.	–
National Information & Credit Evaluation	n.a.	n.a.	n.a.	n.a.	n.a.	n.a.
P.T. PEFINDO Credit Rating Indonesia	n.a.	n.a.	n.a.	n.a.	n.a.	n.a.
Philippine Rating Services	n.a.	n.a.	n.a.	n.a.	n.a.	n.a.
RAM Rating Services Berha	n.a.	n.a.	n.a.	n.a.	n.a.	n.a.
Rating and Investment Information	n.a.	n.a.	n.a.	n.a.	n.a.	n.a.
Rus Ratings	n.a.	n.a.	n.a.	n.a.	n.a.	n.a.
Shanghai Brilliance Credit Rating & Investors Service	n.a.	n.a.	n.a.	n.a.	n.a.	n.a.
Standard & Poor's	$200	n.a.	–	1.2%	–	
Thai Rating and Information Services	n.a.	n.a.	n.a.	n.a.	n.a.	n.a.
Xinhua Finance	n.a.	n.a.	n.a.	n.a.	n.a.	n.a.

Source: Rating agencies websites (accessed 03.01.2013).

out, using different discount rates and different thresholds for the identification of the more important counterparties:

$$New\ Rating\ Fee_t^{TOP} = New\ Rating\ Mean\ Fee_t \times (1 - Discount\%_{Hyp}^{TOP})\ (7.3)$$

$$Surveillance\ Fee_t^{TOP} = New\ Surveillance\ Fee_t^{TOP} \times (1 - Discount\%_{Hyp}^{TOP})$$
$$(7.4)$$

$$New\ Rating\ Fee_t^{OTHER} = New\ Rating\ Mean\ Fee_t \qquad (7.5)$$

$$Surveillance\ Fee_t^{OTHER} = Surveillance\ Mean\ Fee_t, \qquad (7.6)$$

where the discount applied to the top customers ($Discount\%_{Hyp}^{TOP}$) varies from 5% to 95% and the top customers are identified on the basis of outstanding ratings at time t. Top customer are identified considering both the top 1% and the top 5% of customers.[1]

Due to the high variability of the difference between *New Rating Mean Fee* and *Surveillance Mean Fee*, different hypotheses are tested, considering a ratio between the two types of fee that varies from 1:1 to 20:1.[2]

The analysis proposed considered all the measures proposed by the regulators in order to identify the most relevant customers that have to be monitored in order to avoid any risk of collusion.

The first three measures are constructed considering the ratio between revenues related to each customer with respect to the overall revenues and pointing out the following:

- The number of customers that represent more than 10% of revenues (IOSCO, 2008)
- The number of customers that represent more than 5% of revenues (European Commission, 2008)
- The role of the top 20 customers with respect to the overall portfolio (SEC, 2007).

For each of these, not only is the value for the current year considered, but also its persistence. The choice to evaluate persistence over time allows one to determine if the one-year time horizon underestimates the real risk of collusion and the higher the persistence of the results, the lower the usefulness of the current supervisory approach, based only on a one-year time horizon.

The last measure considered is the number of customers that increased their relevance by more than 150% in a one-year time horizon and so for that year they represent the customers with the highest growth potentiality (European Commission, 2008).

---

[1] The choice of a maximum threshold of 5% for the top customers is constrained by the data because, for a high number of raters, all the customers not included in the top 5% have the same buying behavior as that of all the other customers.

[2] In the main body of the book, the results are related to the assumption of double fees paid for single issue rating with respect to multiple ones. Results relating to other hypotheses on the difference of fees applied to retained customers and new ones are presented only in the Appendix (Table A.5).

7.4.3 Results

The customers' portfolio concentration under the hypothesis of equal fees reveals high portfolio fragmentation for the measures constructed on revenues (see Table 7.6).

The number of customers that represent a certain percentage of the portfolio is not normally relevant; only small raters can have customers that represent more than 10% of the overall portfolio, while for big raters this never happens. The results do not change due to the discounting policy used or the choice of threshold used to identify the best customers.

Regarding the persistence of the customers ranked as the most relevant (accounting for over 10% of the overall portfolio), on average 45% of the top customers maintain their status over time. Normally, persistence is negatively related to the size of the rater because the most persistent customers tend to be with the smaller agencies (BRC Investor Services, Chengxin International Credit Rating, Philippine Rating Services, and Xinhua Finance).

Using a less selective threshold to analyze customer portfolio concentration does not significantly change the results (Table 7.7).

For a threshold of 5% instead of 10%, only three other raters (Credit Analysis & Research, Global Credit Rating, and Malaysian Rating Corporation Berhad) are classified as concentrated for at least one year.

As expected, the maximum number of customers classified above the threshold increases with lower percentages of concentration analyzed and the increase is particularly significant: Using a threshold that is one-half with respect to the previous scenario increases the number of relevant customers, on average, more than 3.5 times.

The persistence of the rankings constructed using a threshold of 5% is higher with respect to the 10% threshold and the value even higher than 25%. Compared rater by rater, the ranking of the rating agencies based on the persistence of the top customers does not change significantly on the basis of the threshold used to identify the most important customers.

Considering together the 20 biggest customers served by each rater, the analysis of their average role on the overall portfolio and its turnover year by year allows one to evaluate in greater detail the differences between raters of different size (Table 7.8).

Smaller raters are characterized by a high concentration of the portfolio and top 20 customers that represent more than 90% of the overall portfolio (BRC Investor Services and European Rating Agency) and top 20 customers that represent more than 50% of the portfolio for five raters. On average, the role of the top customers is around 30% of the portfolio and the role of these counterparties is minimal for the three biggest players (1% for Fitch Ratings, Moody's Investor Services, and Standard & Poor's).

The persistence of the main 20 customers is negatively affected by a higher discount rate applied (on average, 4–5 percentage points lower) and positively affected by a higher percentage of top customers that obtain a special discount policy (on average, 2–3 percentage points higher).

Table 7.6 Statistics on the Maximum Number and Persistence of Customers that Represent More Than 10% of the Overall Customer Portfolio

Features	Best Customers, Top 1%				Best Customers, Top 5%			
	Value		Persistence		Value		Persistence	
Discount Rate Applied	5%	50%	5%	50%	5%	50%	5%	50%
A.M. Best Company	0	0	0%	0%	0	0	0%	0%
Austin Rating	2	2	17%	17%	2	2	17%	17%
BRC Investor Services	8	8	63%	63%	8	8	63%	63%
Canadian Bond Rating Service	0	0	0%	0%	0	0	0%	0%
Capital Intelligence	8	8	32%	32%	8	8	32%	32%
Chengxin International Credit Rating	2	2	50%	50%	2	2	50%	50%
Credit Analysis & Research	0	0	0%	0%	0	0	0%	0%
CRISIL	0	0	0%	0%	0	0	0%	0%
Dagong Global Credit Rating	4	4	33%	33%	4	4	33%	33%
Dominion Bond Rating Service	0	0	0%	0%	0	0	0%	0%
European Rating Agency	5	5	75%	75%	5	5	75%	75%
Fitch Ratings	0	0	0%	0%	0	0	0%	0%
Global Credit Rating	0	0	0%	0%	0	0	0%	0%
Investment Information and Credit Rating Agency	0	0	0%	0%	0	0	0%	0%
Japan Credit Rating Agency	0	0	0%	0%	0	0	0%	0%
Korea Ratings Corporation	0	0	0%	0%	0	0	0%	0%
Malaysian Rating Corporation Berhad	0	0	0%	0%	0	0	0%	0%
Mikuni & Co.	0	0	0%	0%	0	0	0%	0%
Moody's Investors Service	0	0	0%	0%	0	0	0%	0%
National Information & Credit Evaluation	0	0	0%	0%	0	0	0%	0%
P.T. PEFINDO Credit Rating Indonesia	1	1	0%	0%	1	1	0%	0%
Philippine Rating Services	5	5	63%	63%	5	5	63%	63%
RAM Rating Services Berha	0	0	0%	0%	0	0	0%	0%
Rating and Investment Information	0	0	0%	0%	0	0	0%	0%
Rus Ratings	2	2	33%	33%	2	2	33%	33%
Shanghai Brilliance Credit Rating & Investors Service	4	4	35%	35%	4	4	35%	35%
Standard & Poor's	0	0	0%	0%	0	0	0%	0%
Thai Rating and Information Services	1	1	33%	33%	1	1	33%	33%
Xinhua Finance	1	1	67%	67%	1	1	67%	67%

Source: Bloomberg data processed by the author.
This table presents for each rater the maximum number of customers that represent at least 10% of the portfolio from 2001 to 2012 and the percentage of persistence of the status of the most relevant customers. The analysis considers different discount hypotheses for the best customers (from 5% to 50%) and different definitions of the top customers (top 1% or top 5%, on the basis of the number of services requested). The ratio between new rating and surveillance fee is assumed equal to 2.

Table 7.7 Statistics on the Maximum Number and Persistence Over Time of the Customers that Represent More Than 5% of the Overall Customer Portfolio

| Features | Best Customers, Top 1% | | | | Best Customers, Top 5% | | | |
| | Value | | Persistence | | Value | | Persistence | |
Discount Rate Applied	5%	50%	5%	50%	5%	50%	5%	50%
A.M. Best Company	0	0	0%	0%	0	0	0%	0%
Austin Rating	9	9	64%	64%	9	9	64%	64%
BRC Investor Services	11	11	84%	84%	11	11	84%	84%
Canadian Bond Rating Service	0	0	0%	0%	0	0	0%	0%
Capital Intelligence	8	8	40%	40%	8	8	40%	40%
Chengxin International Credit Rating	2	2	40%	40%	2	2	40%	40%
Credit Analysis & Research	1	1	0%	0%	1	1	0%	0%
CRISIL	0	0	0%	0%	0	0	0%	0%
Dagong Global Credit Rating	6	6	33%	33%	6	6	33%	33%
Dominion Bond Rating Service	0	0	0%	0%	0	0	0%	0%
European Rating Agency	5	5	75%	75%	5	5	75%	75%
Fitch Ratings	0	0	0%	0%	0	0	0%	0%
Global Credit Rating	9	9	0%	0%	9	9	0%	0%
Investment Information and Credit Rating Agency	0	0	0%	0%	0	0	0%	0%
Japan Credit Rating Agency	0	0	0%	0%	0	0	0%	0%
Korea Ratings Corporation	0	0	0%	0%	0	0	0%	0%
Malaysian Rating Corporation Berhad	5	5	18%	18%	5	5	18%	18%
Mikuni & Co.	0	0	0%	0%	0	0	0%	0%
Moody's Investors Service	0	0	0%	0%	0	0	0%	0%
National Information & Credit Evaluation	0	0	0%	0%	0	0	0%	0%
P.T. PEFINDO Credit Rating Indonesia	4	4	0%	0%	4	4	0%	0%
Philippine Rating Services	15	15	82%	82%	15	15	82%	82%
RAM Rating Services Berha	0	0	0%	0%	0	0	0%	0%
Rating and Investment Information	0	0	0%	0%	0	0	0%	0%
Rus Ratings	14	14	17%	17%	14	14	17%	17%
Shanghai Brilliance Credit Rating & Investors Service	8	8	35%	35%	8	8	35%	35%
Standard & Poor's	0	0	0%	0%	0	0	0%	0%
Thai Rating and Information Services	7	7	34%	34%	7	7	34%	34%
Xinhua Finance	9	9	67%	67%	9	9	67%	67%

Source: Bloomberg data processed by the author.
This table presents for each rater the maximum number of customers that represent at least 5% of the portfolio from 2001 to 2012 and the percentage of persistence of the status of the most relevant customers. The analysis considers different discount hypotheses for the best customers (from 5% to 50%) and different definitions of the top customers (top 1% or top 5% on the basis of the number of services requested). The ratio between new rating and surveillance fee is assumed equal to 2.

Table 7.8 Statistics on the Maximum Number and Persistence of the Top 20 Customers

Features	Best Customers, Top 1%				Best Customers, Top 5%			
	Value		Persistence		Value		Persistence	
Discount Rate Applied	5%	50%	5%	50%	5%	50%	5%	50%
A.M. Best Company	4%	4%	52%	5%	4%	4%	52%	14%
Austin Rating	47%	47%	84%	84%	47%	47%	84%	84%
BRC Investor Services	98%	98%	92%	92%	98%	98%	92%	92%
Canadian Bond Rating Service	30%	30%	92%	92%	30%	30%	92%	92%
Capital Intelligence	45%	45%	37%	37%	45%	45%	37%	37%
Chengxin International Credit Rating	43%	43%	27%	27%	43%	43%	27%	27%
Credit Analysis & Research	21%	21%	81%	81%	21%	21%	81%	81%
CRISIL	9%	9%	34%	34%	9%	9%	35%	35%
Dagong Global Credit Rating	38%	39%	13%	13%	38%	38%	13%	13%
Dominion Bond Rating Service	4%	4%	26%	3%	4%	4%	27%	18%
European Rating Agency	100%	100%	75%	75%	100%	100%	75%	75%
Fitch Ratings	1%	1%	15%	1%	1%	1%	15%	1%
Global Credit Rating	33%	33%	68%	68%	33%	33%	68%	68%
Investment Information and Credit Rating Agency	12%	12%	37%	37%	12%	12%	37%	37%
Japan Credit Rating Agency	3%	3%	28%	11%	3%	3%	54%	54%
Korea Ratings Corporation	9%	9%	31%	24%	9%	9%	42%	42%
Malaysian Rating Corporation Berhad	23%	23%	70%	70%	23%	23%	70%	70%
Mikuni & Co.	10%	10%	91%	91%	10%	10%	91%	91%
Moody's Investors Service	1%	1%	15%	1%	1%	1%	15%	0%
National Information & Credit Evaluation	5%	5%	49%	44%	5%	5%	58%	58%
P.T. PEFINDO Credit Rating Indonesia	27%	27%	70%	70%	27%	27%	70%	70%
Philippine Rating Services	81%	81%	92%	92%	81%	81%	92%	92%
RAM Rating Services Berha	13%	13%	80%	80%	13%	13%	80%	80%
Rating and Investment Information	3%	3%	42%	52%	3%	3%	46%	46%
Rus Ratings	63%	63%	66%	66%	63%	63%	66%	66%
Shanghai Brilliance Credit Rating & Investors Service	53%	53%	38%	38%	53%	53%	38%	38%
Standard & Poor's	1%	1%	20%	0%	1%	1%	20%	0%
Thai Rating and Information Services	43%	43%	72%	72%	43%	43%	72%	72%
Xinhua Finance	39%	39%	64%	64%	39%	39%	64%	64%

Source: Bloomberg data processed by the author.
This table presents for each rater the average weight of the top 20 customers with respect to the overall portfolio from 2001 to 2012 and the percentage of persistence of the status of the most relevant customers. The analysis considers different discount hypotheses for the best customers (from 5% to 50%) and different definitions of the top customers (top 1% or top 5% on the basis of the number of services requested). The ratio between new rating and surveillance fee is assumed equal to 2.

Table 7.9 Statistics on Average and Maximum Percentages of Customers that Increase Their Business by More Than 150%

Features	Best Customers, Top 1%				Best Customers, Top 5%			
	Average		Maximum		Average		Maximum	
Discount Rate Applied	**5%**	**50%**	**5%**	**50%**	**5%**	**50%**	**5%**	**50%**
A.M. Best Company	4%	4%	36%	36%	4%	4%	36%	36%
Austin Rating	5%	5%	19%	19%	5%	5%	19%	19%
BRC Investor Services	1%	1%	9%	9%	1%	1%	9%	9%
Canadian Bond Rating Service	0%	0%	0%	0%	0%	0%	0%	0%
Capital Intelligence	1%	1%	7%	7%	1%	1%	7%	7%
Chengxin International Credit Rating	5%	5%	12%	12%	5%	5%	12%	12%
Credit Analysis & Research	1%	1%	3%	3%	1%	1%	3%	3%
CRISIL	3%	3%	8%	8%	3%	3%	8%	8%
Dagong Global Credit Rating	5%	8%	21%	34%	5%	5%	21%	21%
Dominion Bond Rating Service	4%	6%	10%	18%	4%	7%	10%	38%
European Rating Agency	0%	0%	0%	0%	0%	0%	0%	0%
Fitch Ratings	5%	5%	8%	9%	5%	7%	8%	16%
Global Credit Rating	5%	5%	26%	26%	5%	5%	26%	26%
Investment Information and Credit Rating Agency	3%	3%	18%	18%	2%	2%	6%	6%
Japan Credit Rating Agency	4%	6%	16%	28%	4%	4%	16%	16%
Korea Ratings Corporation	2%	2%	8%	8%	2%	2%	8%	8%
Malaysian Rating Corporation Berhad	1%	1%	3%	3%	1%	1%	3%	3%
Mikuni & Co.	0%	0%	0%	0%	0%	0%	0%	0%
Moody's Investors Service	5%	5%	12%	12%	5%	7%	12%	15%
National Information & Credit Evaluation	1%	1%	2%	2%	1%	1%	2%	2%
P.T. PEFINDO Credit Rating Indonesia	3%	3%	14%	14%	3%	3%	14%	14%
Philippine Rating Services	1%	1%	6%	6%	1%	1%	6%	6%
RAM Rating Services Berha	1%	1%	2%	2%	1%	1%	2%	2%
Rating and Investment Information	5%	5%	38%	38%	5%	5%	38%	38%
Rus Ratings	3%	3%	10%	10%	3%	3%	10%	10%
Shanghai Brilliance Credit Rating & Investors Service	2%	2%	10%	10%	2%	2%	10%	10%
Standard & Poor's	4%	4%	14%	14%	4%	6%	14%	23%
Thai Rating and Information Services	2%	2%	6%	6%	2%	2%	6%	6%
Xinhua Finance	1%	1%	6%	6%	1%	1%	6%	6%

Source: Bloomberg data processed by the author.
This table presents for each rater the average and maximum percentages of customers that increase their business by more than 150% in a one-year time horizon. The analysis considers different discount hypotheses for the best customers (from 5% to 50%) and different definitions of the top customers (top 1% or top 5% on the basis of the number of services requested). The ratio between new rating and surveillance fee is assumed equal to 2.

The last criterion proposed to identify the most relevant customers is based on the comparison between the relevance of each customer in two subsequent years and classifies it as a relevant counterparty if the customer increased its role by more than 150% (Table 7.9).

On average, the number of customers that significantly increase their role in a one-year time horizon is around 3% of the overall portfolio and the ratio is lowest for raters characterized by low customer turnover (e.g. Canadian Bond Rating Service, European Rating Agency, and Mikuni & Co).

Year by year, the number of customers that significantly increase the amount of services requested can vary significantly; in fact, the difference between the mean value and the maximum value registered from 2001 to 2012 is higher than 10% for eight raters.

There is no clear relation between the discounting policy adopted by the rating agency (both the discount rate and the criterion adopted to identify the most relevant counterparties) and the relevance of the change in the amount of services requested by each rated entity.

7.5 CONCLUSIONS

The commercial relationship between the rating agencies and their customers is normally a medium- to long-term relationship in which each issuer buys more than one service from the same provider (issuer and issue ratings). The retention rate is usually high due to the negative market impact of any ratings withdrawn, regardless of the reason.

The supervisory approach allows the use of simple measures (with a one-year time horizon) constructed on revenues obtained from the top customers and the increase in revenues registered in the last year.

Empirical evidence on customer portfolios managed by a set of rating agencies shows that the values of the measures constructed on the customers with an exposure higher than 5% or 10% of the overall portfolio are not normally useful in evaluating portfolio concentration because values of zero are frequently assumed. The threshold defined by regulators seems to be too high, especially for the larger raters, and does not allow one to properly measure increases or decreases in portfolio concentration.

The analysis of the role of the top 20 customers significantly increases their exposure during the one-year time horizon and allows better evaluation of the concentration dynamics of rating agencies' customer portfolios. The role of the top 20 customers is significantly affected by any characteristic of the discounting policy adopted, while the measure constructed on the highest growth of customer relevance is less sensitive to discount policy changes.

For all the measures constructed on the top customers, the persistence of the results achieved is significant; therefore, current one-year measures used to determine the economic independence of agencies may be biased due to the persistence of the ranking constructed. Multiple time-horizon measures allow one to better evaluate customers by considering the long-term horizon that characterizes the relationship (e.g. Gibilaro and Mattarocci, 2011b).

Conclusions

Rating is an information service that reduces the information asymmetry of financial markets due to the high degree of expertise and skills of agencies in collecting and using public and reserved information about the entity evaluated. The final output of the evaluation process is a synthetic judgment expressed using an alphanumeric scale that can be easily used by institutional investors, financial institutions, and individual investors.

Ratings significantly affect the dynamics of the financial market. An unexpected change in the judgment provided by a reference rater will significantly affect the performance achieved by bonds and stocks, and thus impact the cost of capital for the firm. The current financial crisis has revealed many limitations of the current rating market, and the capabilities of raters to properly evaluate signals offered by the market differ significantly.

The rating is a low competition market with a small number of players and three main agencies (Fitch, Moody's, and Standard & Poor's) that own more than 90% of the market share on the basis of volume of activity. Smaller agencies are normally specialized in one country or sector and can survive only if they develop distinctive skills in their market niche.

The business model of the rating agencies is not significantly different from that of other information providers, based on their economic and financial equilibria. The annual report analysis shows that the main differences concern the role of the core business and cash flow dynamics: Revenues are mostly related to the core business and all other business areas play a residual role in defining annual performance. In addition, the level of annual cash flow generated by a firm is related mostly to its operating activities.

Due to the characteristics of the market, revenues related to the core business of a rating agency are strictly related to the pricing policy adopted. The price of the service offered is normally determined on the basis of the value created for the customer, and different fees are applied to the different services offered due to the different degrees of complexity characterizing each type of issue or issuer rating. To maximize revenues and reduce the risk of free-riding, firms mainly adopt an issuer fee model, and only few firms adopt the user fee model. The issuer fee model increases the risk of collusion between the evaluator and the evaluated entity, which is increased by the strict relationship established during the evaluation process to collect a complete set of information necessary for the judgment.

To prevent the commercial relationship from affecting the quality and objectivity of the evaluation procedure, rating agencies must define an organizational structure that minimizes the risk of collusion. The supervisory authority must define an evaluation approach that, on the basis of accounting data, allows one to identify any excessive exposure of the rating agency to a customer.

To avoid conflicts of interest with different stakeholders, analysis of the organizational methods adopted by the rating agencies shows that the main features that must be taken into account involve internal organization, legal status and ownership, public intervention, and group affiliation.

Consistent with the best practices adopted in other sectors, rating agencies define an ethical code to regulate the relationships between employees directly engaged in the evaluation process and to prevent any risk of corruption. Moreover, to ensure the efficacy of the evaluation process, each rating agency must hire a sufficient number of analysts and supervisors to handle the volume of activities. To ensure that marketing policies do not affect an agency's rating judgment, the agency must establish firewalls to prevent any contact between the marketing areas and the evaluation and rating committee.

Rating agencies do not always adopt a legal status that ensures the limited liability of the owners, and generally ownership is significantly concentrated, especially for small agencies. Even when agencies have the appropriate legal status, they still do not satisfy the listing requirements relating to ownership dispersion, and thus few list on the stock market.

Public authorities can support the development of small, local rating agencies to increase foreign capital flows in their financial markets through the direct or indirect ownership of agency shares, but this method can lead to lower levels of objectivity of the judgment expressed. Therefore, an alternative method is being adopted by public authorities, which is to support the rating sector by creating alliances or associations between rating agencies, giving them the opportunity to grow faster through knowledge sharing.

Rating agencies are frequently a part of groups, and some of their customers can thus be served by other group members offering related services. The role of rating revenues in the overall group's revenues is normally prominent. Cross-selling opportunities and the relation between the rating judgment and the number of other goods/services bought from other group members must therefore be considered when evaluating customer relationships.

Analysis of the economic independence of rating agencies with respect to their customers can only be conducted with a complete dataset of the goods and services purchased by all customers. These data are not publicly available, and thus the monitoring of their economic exposure must be assigned to a supervisory authority that ensures that the data are used only for this purpose. The monitoring approach adopted uses simple measures of yearly revenue to identify more relevant customers and establish thresholds beyond which the risk of excessive concentration must be monitored and verified.

The simulation proposed of the portfolios of the main rating agencies demonstrates that concentration exposures are significantly different for different raters, and thresholds defined by regulators seem to be less effective, especially for the larger raters.

All the measures constructed on the top customers are characterized by a high persistence of the results achieved; therefore, current one-year measures used by regulators for monitoring the economic independence of agencies may be biased due to the persistence of the ranking constructed.

The information currently available, especially for smaller rating agencies, does not allow a more detailed analysis of the business and the market. During the financial crisis, attention on the rating sector has increased and the supervisory authorities (especially the SEC) have started publishing reports and information useful in evaluating the market and the characteristics of the main players. The legal status and choice to not be listed adopted by many rating agencies probably negatively affect the availability and comparability of the data.

The main information missing regarding organizational features pertains to groups and cross-selling and related opportunities. The availability of these data would allow one to replicate the analysis of customer relevance at the group level, instead of the agency level, to test whether group affiliation significantly affects the customer independence of rating agencies. Thus, organizational choices affect economic exposure.

As far as economic independence is concerned, the lack of detailed information about the pricing policies adopted for each customer does not allow one to conduct a more detailed analysis of the simulation proposed. The risks and profitability of different business sectors are not always the same (Partnoy, 2006), and the availability of detailed information, especially for riskier and more profitable businesses, would allow a better evaluation of the risk of collusion.

A complete dataset pertaining to the organizational and economic independence of rating agencies may also allow an examination of the role of these features in market reactions. The standard assumption is that the greater the agency independence, the higher the value of the service offered. However, there is no current empirical evidence that allows an examination of the advantages/disadvantages of rating agencies associated with the increase/decrease in independence recognized by the market and their impact on agency revenues and costs. Evidence of the relation between independence and rating agency reputation may support the choice made by many supervisory authorities to establish rules to monitor and disclose excessive customer portfolio concentrations.

Appendix

Table A.1 Payment Models Adopted by the Rating Agencies

Agency	Type
A.M. Best Company Inc.	Issuer fee model
Agusto & Co. Ltd.	Issuer fee model
Ahbor Rating	Issuer fee model
Apoyo & Asociados Internacionales S.A.C.	Issuer fee model
Bank Watch Ratings S.A.	Issuer fee model
BRC Investor Services S.A.	Issuer fee model
Calificadora de Riesgo, PCA	Issuer fee model
Capital Intelligence Ltd.	Issuer fee model
Capital Standards	Issuer fee model
Caribbean Information & Credit Rating Services Ltd.	Issuer fee model
Central European Rating Agency	Issuer fee model
Chengxin International Credit Rating Co. Ltd.	Issuer fee model
China Lianhe Credit Rating Co. Ltd.	Issuer fee model
Clasificadora de Riesgo Humphreys Ltda.	Issuer fee model
Class y Asociados S.A. Clasificadora de Riesgo	Issuer fee model
CMC International Ltd.	User fee model
Companhia Portuguesa de Rating, SA	Issuer fee model
Credit Analysis & Research Ltd.	Issuer fee model
Credit-Rating: A Ukrainian rating agency	Issuer fee model
Credit Rating Agency of Bangladesh Ltd.	Issuer fee model
Credit Rating Information and Services Ltd.	Issuer fee model
CRISIL Ltd.	Issuer fee model
Dagong Global Credit Rating Co. Ltd.	Issuer fee model
Demotech Inc.	Issuer fee model
Dominion Bond Rating Service	Issuer fee model
Duff & Phelps de Colombia, S.A., S.C.V	Issuer fee model

(Continued)

Table A.1 (Continued)

Agency	Type
Ecuability, SA	Issuer fee model
Egan-Jones Rating Company	User fee model
Emerging Credit ratings	Issuer fee model
Equilibrium Clasificadora de Riesgo	Issuer fee model
European Rating Agency	Issuer fee model
Feller Rate Clasificadora de Riesgo	Issuer fee model
Fitch Ratings Ltd.	Issuer fee model
Global Credit Rating Co.	User fee model
HR Ratings de Mexico, S.A. de C.V.	Issuer fee model
Interfax Rating Agency	User fee model
Investment Information and Credit Rating Agency	Issuer fee model
Islamic International Rating Agency, B.S.C.	Issuer fee model
Istanbul International Rating Services Inc.	Issuer fee model
Japan Credit Rating Agency Ltd.	Issuer fee model
JCR Avrasya Derecelendime A.S.	Issuer fee model
JCR-VIS Credit Rating Co. Ltd.	Issuer fee model
Kobirate	Issuer fee model
Korea Investors Service Inc.	Issuer fee model
Korea Ratings Corporation	Issuer fee model
LACE Financial Corp.	Issuer fee model
Lanka Rating Agency Ltd.	Issuer fee model
Malaysian Rating Corporation Berhad	Issuer fee model
Mikuni & Co. Ltd.	User fee model
Moody's Investors Service	Issuer fee model
National Information & Credit Evaluation Inc.	User fee model
ONICRA Credit Rating Agency of India Ltd.	Issuer fee model
P.T. Kasnic Credit Rating Indonesia	Issuer fee model
P.T. PEFINDO Credit Rating Indonesia	Issuer fee model
Pacific Credit Rating	Issuer fee model
Pakistan Credit Rating Agency Ltd.	Issuer fee model
Philippine Rating Services Corp.	Issuer fee model
RAM Rating Services Berha	Issuer fee model
Rapid Ratings International Inc.	User fee model

Table A.1 (Continued)

Agency	Type
Rating and Investment Information Inc.	Issuer fee model
Realpoint, LLC	Mixed model
Rus Ratings	Issuer fee model
Saha Kurumsal Yönetim ve Kredi Derecelendirme Hizmetleri	Issuer fee model
Seoul Credit Rating & Information Inc.	Issuer fee model
Shanghai Credit Information Services Co. Ltd	User fee model
Shanghai Far East Credit Rating Co. Ltd.	User fee model
SME Rating Agency of India Limited	Issuer fee model
Sociedad Calificadora de Riesgo Centroamericana, S.A.	Issuer fee model
Standard & Poor's	Issuer fee model
Taiwan Ratings Corp.	Issuer fee model
TCR Kurumsal Yonetim ve Kredi Derecelendirme Hizmetleri A.S.	Issuer fee model
Thai Rating and Information Services Co. Ltd.	Issuer fee model
Veribanc Inc.	Mixed model
Weiss Ratings Inc.	User fee model

Source: Rating agencies websites for all rating agencies listed on www.defaultrisk.com (accessed 03.01.2013).

Table A.2 Legal Status of the Rating Agencies

Rating Agency	Type of Firm	Code
A.M. Best Company Inc.	Incorporation	–
Agusto & Co. Ltd.	Limited	PC
Ahbor Rating	–	–
Apoyo & Asociados Internacionales S.A.C.	Sociedad Anónima	LTD
Bank Watch Ratings S.A.	Sociedad Anónima	LTD
BRC Investor Services S.A.	Sociedad Anónima	LTD
Calificadora de Riesgo, PCA	–	–
Capital Intelligence Ltd.	Limited	PC
Capital Standards Rating	–	–
Caribbean Information & Credit Rating Services Ltd.	Limited	PC
Central European Rating Agency	–	–
Chengxin International Credit Rating Co. Ltd.	Limited	PCU

(Continued)

Table A.2 (Continued)

Rating Agency	Type of Firm	Code
China Lianhe Credit Rating Co. Ltd.	Limited	PCU
Clasificadora de Riesgo Humphreys Ltda.	Limited	PCU
Class y Asociados S.A.	Sociedad Anónima	SRL
CMC International Ltd.	Limited	PCU
Companhia Portuguesa de Rating, SA	Sociedad Anónima	SRL
Credit Analysis & Research Ltd.	Public Limited Company	PCU
"Credit-Rating": A Ukrainian rating agency	–	–
Credit Rating Agency of Bangladesh Ltd.	Public Limited Company	PCU
Credit Rating Information and Services Ltd.	Public Limited Company	PCU
CRISIL Ltd.	Public Limited Company	PCU
Dagong Global Credit Rating Co. Ltd.	有限公司	PCU
Demotech Inc.	Incorporation	–
Dominion Bond Rating Service	Limited	PCU
Duff & Phelps de Colombia, S.A., S.C.V	Sociedad Anónima	PC
Ecuability, SA	Sociedad Anónima	PC
Egan-Jones Rating Company	Company	–
Emerging Credit Rating Ltd.	Limited	PCU
Equilibrium Clasificadora de Riesgo	Sociedad Anónima	PC
European Rating Agency	Akciová Spoločnosť	PC
Feller Rate Clasificadora de Riesgo	–	–
Fitch Ratings Ltd.	–	–
Global Credit Rating Co.	–	–
HR Ratings de Mexico, S.A. de C.V.	Sociedad Anónima	LTD
Interfax Rating Agency	–	–
Investment Information and Credit Rating Agency	–	–
Islamic International Rating Agency, B.S.C.	Baharain Shareholding Company	PC
Istanbul International Rating Services Inc.	Corporation	–
Japan Credit Rating Agency Ltd.	有限責任事業組合	PCU
JCR Avrasya Derecelendime A.S.	Anonim Şirket	PC
JCR-VIS Credit Rating Co. Ltd.	Anonim Şirket	PC
Kobirate	Anonim Şirket	PC

Table A.2 (Continued)

Rating Agency	Type of Firm	Code
Korea Investors Service Inc.	Incorporation	–
Korea Ratings Corporation	–	–
LACE Financial Corp.	Corporation	–
Lanka Rating Agency Ltd.	Limited	PCU
Malaysian Rating Corporation Berhad	Berhad	PCU
Mikuni & Co. Ltd.	有限責任事業組合	PCU
Moody's Investors Service	–	–
National Information & Credit Evaluation Inc.	Incorporation	–
ONICRA Credit Rating Agency of India Ltd.	Public Limited Company	PCU
P.T. PEFINDO Credit Rating Indonesia	Limited Liability Company	PCU
Pacific Credit Rating	Sociedade em Conta por Ações	PCU
Pakistan Credit Rating Agency Ltd.	Limited	PCU
Philippine Rating Services Corp.	Corporation	–
RAM Rating Services Berha	Limited	PCU
Rapid Ratings International Inc.	Incorporation	–
Rating and Investment Information Inc.	Incorporation	–
Realpoint, LLC	Limited Liability Company	LTD
Rus Ratings	–	–
Saha Kurumsal Yönetim ve Kredi Derecelendirme Hizmetleri A.Ş.	Anonim Şirket	PC
Seoul Credit Rating & Information Inc.	Incorporation	–
Shanghai Credit Information Services Co. Ltd	有限公司	PCU
Shanghai Far East Credit Rating Co. Ltd.	有限公司	PCU
SME Rating Agency of India Limited	Limited	PCU
Sociedad Calificadora de Riesgo Centroamericana, S.A.	Sociedad Anónima	LTD
Standard & Poor's	Incorporation	–
Taiwan Ratings Corp.	Incorporation	–
TCR Kurumsal Yonetim ve Kredi Derecelendirme Hizmetleri A.Ş.	Anonim Şirket	PC
Thai Rating and Information Services Co. Ltd.	Limited	PCU
Weiss Ratings Inc.	Incorporation	–
Veribanc Inc.	Incorporation	–

Source: Rating agencies websites for all rating agencies listed on www.defaultrisk.com (accessed 03.01.2013).
PC = public company listed; PCU = public company unlisted; LTD = limited partnership; – = information not available.

Table A.3 Firms Classified in the Sector Credit Reporting and Collection

Firm	Country of Origin
Accord Financial Corp.	Canada
AccuFacts Pre-Employment Screening Inc.	USA
Anxin Trust & Investment Co. Ltd.	China
Assured Guaranty Ltd.	Bermuda
Bank of Ikeda Ltd.	Japan
Baycorp Holdings Ltd.	New Zealand
Bentley International Inc.	USA
Casino & Credit Services Inc.	USA
ChoicePoint Inc.	USA
Computer Sciences Corp.	USA
Creditriskmonitor.com Inc.	USA
Creditrust Corp.	USA
CRS Corp.	USA
Culture Convenience Club Co. Ltd	Japan
Diverse Holdings Corp.	USA
Duff & Phelps Credit Rating Co.	USA
Dun & Bradstreet Corp (DE)	USA
Equifax Inc.	USA
Fair Isaac Corp.	USA
Financiera CMR S.A. (Peru)	Peru
Financiera Daewoo SA (Peru)	Peru
Financiere Marc de Lacharriere SA (FIMALAC SA)	France
First Advantage Corp.	USA
Gifu Bank Ltd. (The) (Japan)	Japan
Hydrogen Power Inc.	USA
Intersections Inc.	USA
Intrum Justitia N.V. (Netherlands Antilles)	Netherlands Antilles
Lawrie Group Plc	UK
Life Co. Ltd. (Japan)	Japan
Lifeguard ReInsurance Ltd. (New Zealand)	New Zealand
London Scottish Bank PLC	UK
Mie Bank Ltd. (The) (Japan)	Japan
Moody's Corp.	USA

(Continued)

Table A.3 (Continued)

Firm	Country of Origin
Namur-Assurances du Credit SA (Belgium)	Belgium
National Information & Credit Evaluation Inc.	South Korea
NCO Portfolio Management Inc.	USA
Retail Decisions Plc	UK
Shinki Co. Ltd. (Japan)	Japan
Trade Indemnity Group PLC	UK
TRW Inc.	USA
UCB Group PLC	UK
Veda Advantage Ltd.	Australia
Xinhua Finance Ltd.	Cayman Islands

Source: Compustat data processed by the author.

Table A.4 Rating Fee Disclosure for Rating Agencies

Agency	Fee Disclosure
A.M. Best Company Inc.	☐
Agusto & Co. Ltd.	☐
Ahbor Rating	☐
Apoyo & Asociados Internacionales S.A.C.	
Bank Watch Ratings S.A.	☐
BRC Investor Services S.A.	☐
Calificadora de Riesgo, PCA	☐
Capital Intelligence Ltd.	☐
Capital Standards	☑
Caribbean Information & Credit Rating Services Ltd.	☑
Central European Rating Agency	☐
Chengxin International Credit Rating Co. Ltd.	☐
China Lianhe Credit Rating Co. Ltd.	☐
Clasificadora de Riesgo Humphrey Ltda.	☐
Class y Asociados S.A. Clasificadora de Riesgo	☐
CMC International Ltd.	☐
Companhia Portuguesa de Rating, SA	☑

(Continued)

Table A.4 (Continued)

Agency	Fee Disclosure
Credit Analysis & Research Ltd.	☐
Credit-Rating: A Ukrainian rating agency	☐
Credit Rating Agency of Bangladesh Ltd.	☑
Credit Rating Information and Services Ltd.	☐
CRISIL Ltd.	☑
Dagong Global Credit Rating Co. Ltd.	☐
Demotech Inc.	☐
Dominion Bond Rating Service	☐
Duff & Phelps de Colombia, S.A., S.C.V	☐
Ecuability, SA	☑
Egan-Jones Rating Company	☐
Emerging Credit Ratings	☑
Equilibrium Clasificadora de Riesgo	☐
European Rating Agency	☐
Feller Rate Clasificadora de Riesgo	☐
Fitch Ratings Ltd.	☑
Global Credit Rating Co.	☑
HR Ratings de Mexico, S.A. de C.V.	☐
Interfax Rating Agency	☐
Investment Information and Credit Rating Agency	☐
Islamic International Rating Agency, B.S.C.	☐
Istanbul International Rating Services Inc.	☐
Japan Credit Rating Agency Ltd.	☐
JCR Avrasya Derecelendime A.S.	☐
JCR-VIS Credit Rating Co. Ltd.	☑
Kobirate	☐
Korea Investors Service Inc.	☐
Korea Ratings Corporation	☐
LACE Financial Corp.	☐
Lanka Rating Agency Ltd.	☐
Malaysian Rating Corporation Berhad	☑
Mikuni & Co. Ltd.	☐

(Continued)

Table A.4 (Continued)

Agency	Fee Disclosure
Moody's Investors Service	☑
National Information & Credit Evaluation Inc.	☑
ONICRA Credit Rating Agency of India Ltd.	☐
P.T. Kasnic Credit Rating Indonesia	☐
P.T. PEFINDO Credit Rating Indonesia	☐
Pacific Credit Rating	☐
Pakistan Credit Rating Agency Ltd.	☑
Philippine Rating Services Corp.	☐
RAM Rating Services Berha	☐
Rapid Ratings International Inc.	☐
Rating and Investment Information Inc.	☐
Realpoint, LLC	☐
Rus Ratings	☐
Saha Kurumsal Yönetim ve Kredi Derecelendirme Hizmetleri	☐
Seoul Credit Rating & Information Inc.	☐
Shanghai Credit Information Services Co. Ltd.	☑
Shanghai Far East Credit Rating Co. Ltd.	☐
SME Rating Agency of India Limited	☑
Sociedad Calificadora de Riesgo Centroamericana, S.A.	☐
Standard & Poor's☑	☑
Taiwan Ratings Corp.	☐
TCR Kurumsal Yonetim ve Kredi Derecelendirme Hizmetleri A.S.	☐
Thai Rating and Information Services Co. Ltd.	☐
Veribanc Inc.	☑
Weiss Ratings Inc.	☑

Source: Rating agencies websites for all rating agencies listed on www.defaultrisk.com (accessed 03.01.2013).

DETAILS ABOUT RATING FEES POLICY ADOPTED BY AGENCIES

A.M. Best Company Inc.

Annual fees may range up to $500,000 per entity/group and are determined by various factors including, but not limited to, size, types of business written, and complexity of the entity/group.

Debt rating fees:

- Corporate Debt/Shelf Registrations/Note and Commercial Paper Programs: Fees may range up to maximum of $120,000 per issue. Surveillance fees may range up to $25,000.
- Insurance-Linked Structured Transactions: Fees typically range from 6 to 10 basis points of par amount and are based on the size and complexity of the transaction.

Surveillance fees generally range from $5000 to $50,000 and are based on the size and complexity of the transaction.

Note: A.M. Best does not charge rated entities any fees for publishing the rated entity's Best Ratings on A.M. Best's publicly available website.

Agusto & Co. Ltd.

Our fee structure is arrived at using basis point, which depends on the size and complexity of the transaction involved. However, we have a minimum base fee when the amount being raised is small and the transaction is simple.

We also charge a relatively smaller fee for annual rating reviews.

Our fees plus the VAT at the prevailing rate of 5% are payable in advance.

Capital Standards

The rating fees charged by Capital Intelligence typically vary in accordance with the size and complexity of the entity and the type of rating being assigned.

Caribbean Information & Credit Rating Services Ltd.

Rating fees are of two types: initial rating fees (IRF) and surveillance fees (SF). CariCRIS charges IRF for all new ratings assigned. For all "accepted" ratings, CariCRIS charges SF throughout the life of the instrument. The current fee structure is indicated below, but may be subject to change from time to time:

- Initial rating fees: 0.10% (10 basis points) of the issue size of the rated instrument.
- Surveillance fees: 0.05% (5 basis points) of the issue size of the rated instrument. In case the instrument is partly redeemed, SF is payable only on the outstanding amount.

VAT or any other tax as applicable is added as per prevailing rates.

Out-of-pocket expenses, as per actual expenditure incurred, are for the client's account.

Floor: Both IRF and SF are subject to floors of US$20,000 and US$10,000 per instrument/issuer.

This fee structure is not applicable to private credit assessments and the fees for these are as negotiated between the CEO and the client, taking size and complexity of the firm into consideration.

CariCRIS bills an issuer IRF when the issuer approaches CariCRIS with a mandate for rating its issue. IRF is to be collected before the case is presented to the Rating Committee. Surveillance fees are payable in arrears and are chargeable after 12 months from the date of assignment of the initial rating.

Companhia Portuguesa de Rating, SA

Fee is defined case by case on the basis of the complexity of the rating evaluation, and before starting the rating process CPR will provide to the issuer a price proposal for the service requested. Normally the degree of complexity and the price estimate can be released on the basis of the last balance sheet and income statement of the issuer.

Credit Rating Agency of Bangladesh Ltd.

Fees for corporate entity rating:
- **Category-I.** Corporate with asset size Tk = 75 crore and above: initial rating fee (year 1) Tk = 5.50 Lac and annual review (from year 2 onwards) Tk = 4.00 Lac.
- **Category-II.** Corporate with asset size less than 75 crore and more than 40 crore: initial rating fee (year 1) Tk = 4.50 Lac and annual review (from year 2 onwards) Tk = 3.00 Lac.
- **Category-III.** Corporate with asset size less than 40 crore but more than 20 crore: initial rating fee (year 1) Tk = 2.50 Lac and annual review (from year 2 onwards) Tk = 2.00 Lac.
- **Category-IV.** Corporate with asset size less than 10 crore: initial rating fee (year 1) Tk = 2.00 Lac and annual review (from year 2 onwards) Tk = 1.50 Lac.
  Fees for project rating:
- Project loan above 25 crore: initial rating fee (year 1) 0.08% of the proposed external financing and annual review (from year 2 onwards) 0.06% of the proposed external financing.
- Project loan below 25 crore: initial rating fee (year 1) Tk = 2.00 Lac and annual review (from year 2 onwards) Tk = 1.50 Lac.

CRISIL Ltd.

Fee structures are summarized in fee schedules that are communicated and finalized before the rating assignment.

CRISIL Ratings charges an initial rating fee at the time of the initial rating exercise and an annual surveillance fee subsequently for such time as the rating remains outstanding. Precise fee amounts are determined by various factors including, but not limited to, the principal amount of the debt issuance that is rated. The rating fees in all cases are negotiated by the business development team and this team is not involved in analytical or rating committee processes. The business development team also considers alternative fee arrangements for volume issuers and other entities.

Within the general nature of compensation arrangements with rated entities CRISIL Ratings reserves the right to charge specific fees to issuers. Fee schedules are available to issuers upon request.

Ecuability, SA

Fee for issue credit ratings. Issue rating one basis point (bps) of the issue value.

Clasificación del Emisor. From the minimum US $5000 to the maximum US $25,000 on the basis of the value of the total assets.

Fee for issuer credit ratings. Lowest charge $5000, highest charge $25,000.

Global risk assessments. Free quote will be given upon request.

Emerging Credit Ratings

Banks. Asset size lower than BDT 4 billion: initial rating 450,000; annual surveillance 375,000. Asset size 4–7 billion: initial rating 600,000; annual surveillance 500,000. Asset size 7–10 billion: initial rating 675,000; annual surveillance 550,000. Asset size 10–15 billion: initial rating 725,000; annual surveillance 600,000. Asset size above 10 billion: initial rating 800,000; annual surveillance 700,000.

Financial institutions. Asset size below 4 billion: initial rating 500,000; annual surveillance 450,000. Asset size equal to or greater than 4 billion: initial rating 655,000; annual surveillance 550,000.

Corporations. Asset size below 400 million: initial rating 450,000; annual surveillance 325,000. Asset size 400–750 million: initial rating 500,000; annual surveillance 420,000. Asset size equal to or greater than 750 million: initial rating 675,000; annual surveillance 550,000.

Insurance, general. Turnover less that 400 million: initial rating 450,000; annual surveillance 325,000. Turnover 400–750 million: initial rating 500,000; annual surveillance 420,000. Turnover equal to or greater than 750 million: initial rating 675,000; annual surveillance 550,000.

Life insurance banks. Turnover less that 400 million: initial rating 450,000; annual surveillance 325,000. Turnover 400–750 million: initial rating 500,000; annual surveillance 425,000. Turnover equal to or greater than 750 million: initial rating 600,000; annual surveillance 500,000.

Working capital/facility ratings. Asset size below 200 million: initial rating 250,000; annual surveillance 200,000. Asset size 200–500 million: 250,000 plus 0.2% of the incremental amount; annual surveillance 200,000 plus 0.2% of the incremental amount. Asset size 500–750 million: 450,000 plus 0.2% of the incremental amount; annual surveillance 350,000 plus 0.2% of the incremental amount. Asset size 750–1000 million: 500,000 plus 0.2% of the incremental amount; annual surveillance 400,000 plus 0.2% of the incremental amount. Asset size equal to or greater than 1 billion: 550,000 plus 0.2% of the incremental amount; annual surveillance 450,000 plus 0.2% of the incremental amount.

Corporate bond/structured finance products. Value lower than 500 million initial rating 450,000; annual surveillance 350,000. Value of 500–1000 million initial rating 500,000 plus 0.2% of the incremental amount; annual surveillance 350,000 plus 0.2% of the incremental amount. Value not lower than 1 billion initial rating 700,000 plus 0.2% of the incremental amount; annual surveillance 500,000 plus 0.2% of the incremental amount.

Other ratings/private ratings. Free quotes will be given upon request.

Fitch Ratings Ltd.

Fitch receives fees from issuers, insurers, guarantors, other obligors, and underwriters for rating securities. Such fees generally vary from US$1000 to US$750,000 (or the applicable currency equivalent) per issue. In certain cases, Fitch will rate all or a number of issues issued by a particular issuer, or insured or guaranteed by a particular insurer or guarantor, for a single annual fee. Such fees are expected to vary from US$10,000 to US$1,500,000 (or the applicable currency equivalent).

Global Credit Rating Co.

The Subscription Service is based on regions across Africa, comprising COMESA, ECOWAS, SADC and South Africa, as well as the sectors covered by GCR within those regions. The sectors currently comprise Corporates and Public Sector Debt, Insurance, Structured and Securitisations, and Financial Institutions. The annual cost to subscribe to one sector in one region is currently between US$3500 and US$5000, depending on the level of GCR's coverage. A discount of between 10% and 30% can be applied for subscriptions to more than one sector in a particular region. GCR can also tailor a subscription to a client's specific needs. Please refer to "Services and Support" for contact information in this regard.

JCR-VIS Credit Rating Co. Ltd.

Commercial banks/DFIs. Total assets ≥5% of the overall banking assets: initial rating 1,000,000; surveillance 950,000. Total assets 2–5% of the overall banking assets: initial rating 800,000; surveillance 750,000. Total assets ≤2% of the the overall banking assets: initial rating 600,000; surveillance 550,000.

Microfinance banks. Initial rating 550,000; surveillance fee 500,000.

Leasing companies, investment banks, security firms, housing finance companies. Initial rating 500,000; surveillance fee 450,000.

Modarabas. Initial rating 350,000; surveillance fee 300,000.

Industrial corporations. Initial rating 350,000–750,000; surveillance fee 300,000–700,000.

Mutual fund rankings/fund stability ratings. One basis point (bps) of the Net Assets at the end of the latest financial year, subject to a minimum of 100,000 and a maximum of 200,000 for rankings and minimum of Rs 250,000 and maximum of Rs 400,000 for fund stability ratings.

Asset management companies. Assets under management ≥10 billion: initial rating 550,000; surveillance fee 500,000. Assets under management <10 billion: initial rating 350,000; surveillance fee 300,000.

Insurer financial strength ratings of insurance companies. Gross premium written ≥1 billion: initial rating 500,000; surveillance fee 450,000. Gross premium written <1 billion: initial rating 350,000; surveillance fee 300,000.

Long-term corporate debt instruments. Same fees are charged for both the initial and the surveillance rating. Issue size lower that 1 billion 10 bps of the issue amount with a minimum threshold of 300,000. Issue size 1–3 billion 1 million 5 bps of the issue amount exceeding 1 billion. Issue size 3–7 billion 2 million 2 bps of the issue amount exceeding 3 billion. Issue size 7–15 billion 2.8 million 2 bps of the issue amount exceeding 7 billion. Over 15 billion 3.6 million plus 0.75 of the issue amount exceeding 15 billion.

Short-term corporate debt instruments. Fees will be charged based on the instrument amount.

Real estate developers. Initial rating 450,000; surveillance rating 400,000.

Corporate governance/NPO governance ratings. Initial rating 500,000; surveillance rating 450,000.

Financial risk assessment. JCR-VIS conducts Financial Risk Assessments (FRAs) for entities who wish to know where they stand prior to going for a proper rating. For FRAs, JCR-VIS charges 80% of the normal rating fee. In case the entity decides to go for a normal rating, this fee is adjusted against the normal rating fee.

Malaysian Rating Corporation Berhad

Private debt securities (PDS). Initial rating: 0.06% on the debt size (minimum RM 150,000); surveillance fee: 0.06% on the debt size (minimum RM 100,000).

Asset-backed securities. Initial fee: RM 120,000 plus 0.06% on debt size (minimum RM 150,000); surveillance fee: 0.04% on debt size (minimum RM 100,000).

Project finance rating. Initial rating: 0.06% on debt size (minimum RM 150,000); surveillance fee: 0.04% on debt size (minimum RM 100,000).

Corporate credit rating. Free quote will be given upon request.

Financial institutions/insurance/financial strength. Free quote will be given upon request.

Islamic financial institution governance rating. Free quote will be given upon request.

Sovereign issuer credit rating. Free quote will be given upon request.

Moody's Investors Service

From $1500 to $2,500,000 depending on the type of issue or issuer.

Pakistan Credit Rating Agency Ltd.

Commercial banks. Small banks (having total assets <2% of overall banking assets) PKR 600,000; medium banks (having total assets <5% and ≥2% of overall banking assets) PKR 800,000; large banks (having total assets ≥5% of overall banking assets) PKR 1,000,000.

Microfinance banks. Small banks PKR 350,000; large banks (usually banks having nationwide license) PKR 500,000.

Non-banking financial institutions/DFI. Small entities (having equity of up to PKR 1.0 bln) PKR 350,000; large entities (having equity >PKR 1.0 bln) PKR 500,000.

Modarabas. Small modarabas PKR 350,000; large modarabas PKR 500,000.

Insurer financial strength (IFS) rating of insurance companies. Small (having GPW <PKR 1.0 bln) PKR 350,000; large (having GPW ≥PKR 1.0 bln) PKR 500,000.

Corporations. Small companies PKR 350,000; medium companies PKR 500,000; large companies PKR 600,000–750,000.

Real estate project grading. Small (project up to PKR 1.0 bln) PKR 350,000; medium (project ≥PKR 1.0 bln and <PKR 5.0 bln) PKR 500,000; large (project ≥PKR 5.0 bln) PKR 750,000.

Instrument rating. Long-term corporate debt instruments (TFCs, Sukuks, etc.): The rating fee depends upon the issue size subject to a minimum fee of PKR 300,000. Short-term corporate debt instruments (short-term TFCs, commercial papers, etc.): Instrument amount up to PKR 1.0 bln 10 bps of the issue amount, subject to a minimum of PKR 300,000; over PKR 1.0 bln and up to PRK 3.0 bln PKR 1,000,000 plus 5.0 bps of the amount exceeding PKR 1.0 bln; over PKR 3.0 bln and up to PRK 7.0 bln PKR 2,000,000 plus 2.0 bps of the amount exceeding PKR 3.0 bln; over 7.0 bln and up to 15.0 bln PKR 2,800,000 plus 1.0 bps of the amount exceeding 7.0 bln; over 15.0 bln PKR 3,600,000 plus 0.75 bps of the amount exceeding 15.0 bln.

Asset management. Small AM (having AUM of <PKR 10.0 bln) PKR 350,000; large AM (having AUM ≥PKR 10.0 bln) PKR 500,000.

Mutual funds. One basis point (bps) of the Net Asset Value at the end of the latest financial year, subject to following minimum and maximum. Capital Protection Rating: minimum PKR 100,000 and maximum PKR 200,000. Fund stability rating: minimum PKR 150,000 and maximum PKR 250,000. Fund performance ranking: minimum PKR 100,000 and maximum PKR 200,000.

Indicative ratings. Indicative ratings merely indicate the rating band or category in which the entity's long-term rating is likely to fall, if a formal rating review were to be conducted. These are not meant for public dissemination and are for the consumption of the management of the entity. PACRA charges 50% of the formal rating fee for indicative rating. This fee is adjustable against the formal rating fee, if the entity so desires, within 3 months of indicative rating.

Shanghai Credit Information Services Co. Ltd.

Query cost: 30 US$.

SME Rating Agency of India Limited

SME rating. Turnover <50 Lacs: 45,000 Rs; turnover 50–200 Lacs: 50,600 Rs; turnover >200 Lacs: 67,400 Rs.

NSIC-D&B-SMERA rating fees. Turnover <50 Lacs: 9100 Rs; turnover 50–200 Lacs: 11,800 Rs; turnover >200 Lacs: 15,500 Rs.

Greenfield and brownfield grading rating fees. Turnover <50 Lacs: 45,000 Rs; turnover 50–200 Lacs: 50,600 Rs; turnover >200 Lacs: 67,400 Rs.

Microfinance institution rating fees. Free quote will be given upon request.

Green rating fees. Free quote will be given upon request.

Maritime training institution rating fees. Free quote will be given upon request.

Bond rating fees. Free quote will be given upon request.

IPO grading rating fees. Free quote will be given upon request.

Bank loan rating fees. Free quote will be given upon request.

Standard & Poor's

Corporations (includes industrial and financial service companies). Up to 5.50 basis points for most transactions with a minimum fee $85,000.

Public finance. Varies based upon the sector, par amount, structure, and complexity of the transaction. Fees generally range from $7500 to $495,000 and fees on large transactions (>$500 million) are determined on a case-by-case basis.

Sovereigns. Fees typically range from $45k to $200k.

Structured finance. Fees range up to 12 basis points.

Complex transactions. Higher fees apply to more complex transactions.

Frequent issuer and multi-year fee arrangements. S&P will consider alternative fee arrangements for volume issuers and other entities that want multi-year ratings services agreements. Entities may request information about qualifying for such fee arrangements.

Veribanc Inc.

Individual institutions. Instant rating $5; short form report $30; briefing report $65; research report $50; Veritrend report $55 (only for banks); holding company short form $40; holding company research report $95.

Group of institutions. Blue ribbon report $40; banker dozen $40; state ratings report $120; competitors report $120.

Weiss Rating

Banks and thrifts. Annual $449, single issue $249.

Health insurers. Annual $449, single issue $249.

Life and annuity insurers. Annual $449, single issue $249.

Property and casualty insurers. Annual $449, single issue $249.

Consumer guides. Annual $499, half a year $359.

Bank fees and service charges. Single issue $359.

Credit unions. Annual $499, single issue $249.

Investing guides. Annual $499, single issue $249.

Bond and money market mutual funds. Annual $499, single issue $249.

Exchange traded funds. Annual $499, single issue $249.

Stock mutual funds. Annual $499, single issue $249.

Ultimate guided tour of investing. Annual $499, single issue $249.

One by one ratings are also offered and the price is defined through restricted negotiations

Bank and thrift ratings and reports. One-year subscription €449 and two-year subscription €898.

All bank, thrift, and insurance company ratings. One-year subscription €998 and two-year subscription €1976.

Table A.5a Statistics on the Maximum Number and Persistence Over Time of the Customers that Represent More Than 10% of the Overall Customer Portfolio

| Features | Best Customers, Top 1% | | | | Best Customers, Top 5% | | | |
| | Value | | Persistence | | Value | | Persistence | |
Discount rate applied	5%	50%	5%	50%	5%	50%	5%	50%
A.M. Best Company	0	0	0%	0%	0	0	0%	0%
Austin Rating	2	2	17%	17%	2	2	17%	17%
BRC Investor Services	8	8	81%	81%	8	8	81%	81%
Canadian Bond Rating Service	0	0	0%	0%	0	0	0%	0%
Capital Intelligence	5	5	40%	40%	5	5	40%	40%
Chengxin International Credit Rating	2	2	50%	50%	2	2	50%	50%
Credit Analysis & Research	0	0	0%	0%	0	0	0%	0%
CRISIL	0	0	0%	0%	0	0	0%	0%
Dagong Global Credit Rating	6	6	33%	33%	6	6	33%	33%

(Continued)

Table A.5a (Continued)

| Features | Best Customers, Top 1% | | | | Best Customers, Top 5% | | | |
| | Value | | Persistence | | Value | | Persistence | |
Discount rate applied	5%	50%	5%	50%	5%	50%	5%	50%
Dominion Bond Rating Service	0	0	0%	0%	0	0	0%	0%
European Rating Agency	5	0	75%	0%	0	0	0%	0%
Fitch Ratings	0	0	0%	0%	0	0	0%	0%
Global Credit Rating	0	0	0%	0%	0	0	0%	0%
Investment Information and Credit Rating Agency	0	0	0%	0%	0	0	0%	0%
Japan Credit Rating Agency	0	0	0%	0%	0	0	0%	0%
Korea Ratings Corporation	0	0	0%	0%	0	0	0%	0%
Malaysian Rating Corporation Berhad	0	0	0%	0%	0	0	0%	0%
Mikuni & Co.	0	0	0%	0%	0	0	0%	0%
Moody's Investors Service	0	0	0%	0%	0	0	0%	0%
National Information & Credit Evaluation	0	0	0%	0%	0	0	0%	0%
P.T. PEFINDO Credit Rating Indonesia	0	0	0%	0%	0	0	0%	0%
Philippine Rating Services	5	5	63%	63%	5	5	63%	63%
RAM Rating Services Berha	0	0	0%	0%	0	0	0%	0%
Rating and Investment Information	0	0	0%	0%	0	0	0%	0%
Rus Ratings	2	2	33%	33%	2	2	33%	33%
Shanghai Brilliance Credit Rating & Investors Service	5	5	40%	40%	5	5	40%	40%
Standard & Poor's	0	0	0%	0%	0	0	0%	0%
Thai Rating and Information Services	2	2	33%	33%	2	2	33%	33%
Xinhua Finance	1	1	67%	67%	1	1	67%	67%

Source: Bloomberg data processed by the author.
The table presents for each rater the maximum number of customers that represent at least 5% of the portfolio in the time period 2001–2012 and the percentage of persistence over time of the status of the most relevant customers. The analysis is conducted considering different discount hypotheses for the best customers (from 5% to 50%) and different definitions of top customers (top 1% or top 5% on the basis of the number of services requested). The ratio between new rating and surveillance fee is assumed equal to 1.

Table A.5b Statistics on the Maximum Number and Persistence Over Time of the Customers that Represent More Than 10% of the Overall Customer Portfolio

	Best Customers, Top 1%				Best Customers, Top 5%			
Features	Value		Persistence		Value		Persistence	
Discount rate applied	5%	50%	5%	50%	5%	50%	5%	50%
A.M. Best Company	0	0	0%	0%	1	1	0%	0%
Austin Rating	4	4	8%	8%	4	4	8%	8%
BRC Investor Services	8	8	63%	63%	8	8	63%	63%
Canadian Bond Rating Service	0	0	0%	0%	0	0	0%	0%
Capital Intelligence	8	8	20%	20%	8	8	20%	20%
Chengxin International Credit Rating	2	2	50%	50%	2	2	50%	50%
Credit Analysis & Research	0	0	0%	0%	0	0	0%	0%
CRISIL	0	0	0%	0%	0	0	0%	0%
Dagong Global Credit Rating	4	4	0%	0%	4	4	0%	0%
Dominion Bond Rating Service	0	0	0%	0%	0	0	0%	0%
European Rating Agency	3	3	50%	50%	3	3	50%	50%
Fitch Ratings	0	0	0%	0%	0	0	0%	0%
Global Credit Rating	0	0	0%	0%	0	0	0%	0%
Investment Information and Credit Rating Agency	0	0	0%	0%	0	0	0%	0%
Japan Credit Rating Agency	0	0	0%	0%	0	0	0%	0%
Korea Ratings Corporation	0	0	0%	0%	0	0	0%	0%
Malaysian Rating Corporation Berhad	1	1	0%	0%	1	1	0%	0%
Mikuni & Co.	0	0	0%	0%	0	0	0%	0%
Moody's Investors Service	0	0	0%	0%	0	0	0%	0%
National Information & Credit Evaluation	0	0	0%	0%	0	0	0%	0%
P.T. PEFINDO Credit Rating Indonesia	2	2	0%	0%	2	2	0%	0%
Philippine Rating Services	3	3	33%	33%	3	3	33%	33%
RAM Rating Services Berha	0	0	0%	0%	0	0	0%	0%
Rating and Investment Information	0	0	0%	0%	0	0	0%	0%

(Continued)

Table A.5b (Continued)

| Features | Best Customers, Top 1% | | | | Best Customers, Top 5% | | | |
| | Value | | Persistence | | Value | | Persistence | |
Discount rate applied	5%	50%	5%	50%	5%	50%	5%	50%
Rus Ratings	2	2	20%	20%	2	2	20%	20%
Shanghai Brilliance Credit Rating & Investors Service	4	4	7%	7%	4	4	7%	7%
Standard & Poor's	0	0	0%	0%	0	0	0%	0%
Thai Rating and Information Services	7	7	0%	0%	7	7	0%	0%
Xinhua Finance	1	1	67%	67%	1	1	67%	67%

Source: Bloomberg data processed by the author.
The table presents for each rater the maximum number of customers that represent at least 5% of the portfolio in the time period 2001–2012 and the percentage of persistence over time of the status of the most relevant customers. The analysis is conducted considering different discount hypotheses for the best customers (from 5% to 50%) and different definitions of top customers (top 1% or top 5% on the basis of the number of services requested). The ratio between new rating and surveillance fee is assumed equal to 5.

Table A.5c Statistics on the Maximum Number and Persistence Over Time of the Customers that Represent More Than 10% of the Overall Customer Portfolio

| Features | Best Customers, Top 1% | | | | Best Customers, Top 5% | | | |
| | Value | | Persistence | | Value | | Persistence | |
Discount rate applied	5%	50%	5%	50%	5%	50%	5%	50%
Discount rate applied	5%	50%	5%	50%	5%	50%	5%	50%
A.M. Best Company	0	0	0%	0%	0	0	0%	0%
Austin Rating	4	4	8%	8%	4	4	8%	8%
BRC Investor Services	8	8	42%	42%	8	8	42%	42%
Canadian Bond Rating Service	0	0	0%	0%	0	0	0%	0%
Capital Intelligence	8	8	0%	0%	8	8	0%	0%
Chengxin International Credit Rating	1	1	25%	25%	1	1	25%	25%
Credit Analysis & Research	2	2	0%	0%	2	2	0%	0%
CRISIL	0	0	0%	0%	0	0	0%	0%
Dagong Global Credit Rating	4	4	0%	0%	4	4	0%	0%
Dominion Bond Rating Service	0	0	0%	0%	0	0	0%	0%

(Continued)

Table A.5c (Continued)

| Features | Best Customers, Top 1% | | | | Best Customers, Top 5% | | | |
| | Value | | Persistence | | Value | | Persistence | |
Discount rate applied	5%	50%	5%	50%	5%	50%	5%	50%
European Rating Agency	2	2	0%	0%	2	2	0%	0%
Fitch Ratings	0	0	0%	0%	0	0	0%	0%
Global Credit Rating	0	0	0%	0%	0	0	0%	0%
Investment Information and Credit Rating Agency	0	0	0%	0%	0	0	0%	0%
Japan Credit Rating Agency	0	0	0%	0%	0	0	0%	0%
Korea Ratings Corporation	0	0	0%	0%	0	0	0%	0%
Malaysian Rating Corporation Berhad	2	2	0%	0%	2	2	0%	0%
Mikuni & Co.	0	0	0%	0%	0	0	0%	0%
Moody's Investors Service	0	0	0%	0%	0	0	0%	0%
National Information & Credit Evaluation	0	0	0%	0%	0	0	0%	0%
P.T. PEFINDO Credit Rating Indonesia	3	3	0%	0%	3	3	0%	0%
Philippine Rating Services	3	3	27%	27%	3	3	27%	27%
RAM Rating Services Berha	0	0	0%	0%	0	0	0%	0%
Rating and Investment Information	0	0	0%	0%	0	0	0%	0%
Rus Ratings	4	4	20%	20%	4	4	20%	20%
Shanghai Brilliance Credit Rating & Investors Service	7	7	7%	7%	7	7	7%	7%
Standard & Poor's	0	0	0%	0%	0	0	0%	0%
Thai Rating and Information Services	7	7	0%	0%	7	7	0%	0%
Xinhua Finance	1	1	50%	50%	1	1	50%	50%

Source: Bloomberg data processed by the author.
This table presents for each rater the maximum number of customers that represent at least 5% of the portfolio in the time period 2001–2012 and the percentage of persistence over time of the status of the most relevant customers. The analysis is conducted considering different discount hypotheses for the best customers (from 5% to 50%) and different definitions of top customers (top 1% or top 5% on the basis of the number of services requested). The ratio between new rating and surveillance fee is assumed equal to 10.

Table A.5d Statistics on the Maximum Number and Persistence Over Time of the Customers that Represent More Than 5% of the Overall Customer Portfolio

	Best Customers, Top 1%				Best Customers, Top 5%			
Features	Value		Persistence		Value		Persistence	
Discount rate applied	5%	50%	5%	50%	5%	50%	5%	50%
A.M. Best Company	0	0	0%	0%	0	0	0%	0%
Austin Rating	6	6	76%	76%	6	6	76%	76%
BRC Investor Services	11	11	89%	89%	11	11	89%	89%
Canadian Bond Rating Service	0	0	0%	0%	0	0	0%	0%
Capital Intelligence	9	9	43%	43%	9	9	43%	43%
Chengxin International Credit Rating	2	2	40%	40%	2	2	40%	40%
Credit Analysis & Research	1	1	0%	0%	1	1	0%	0%
CRISIL	0	0	0%	0%	0	0	0%	0%
Dagong Global Credit Rating	6	6	29%	29%	6	6	29%	29%
Dominion Bond Rating Service	0	0	0%	0%	0	0	0%	0%
European Rating Agency	5	0	75%	0%	0	0	0%	0%
Fitch Ratings	0	0	0%	0%	0	0	0%	0%
Global Credit Rating	9	9	0%	0%	9	9	0%	0%
Investment Information and Credit Rating Agency	0	0	0%	0%	0	0	0%	0%
Japan Credit Rating Agency	0	0	0%	0%	0	0	0%	0%
Korea Ratings Corporation	0	0	0%	0%	0	0	0%	0%
Malaysian Rating Corporation Berhad	2	2	38%	38%	2	2	38%	38%
Mikuni & Co.	0	0	0%	0%	0	0	0%	0%
Moody's Investors Service	0	0	0%	0%	0	0	0%	0%
National Information & Credit Evaluation	0	0	0%	0%	0	0	0%	0%
P.T. PEFINDO Credit Rating Indonesia	2	2	0%	0%	2	2	0%	0%
Philippine Rating Services	15	15	82%	82%	15	15	82%	82%

(*Continued*)

Table A.5d (Continued)

| Features | Best Customers, Top 1% | | | | Best Customers, Top 5% | | | |
| | Value | | Persistence | | Value | | Persistence | |
Discount rate applied	5%	50%	5%	50%	5%	50%	5%	50%
RAM Rating Services Berha	0	0	0%	0%	0	0	0%	0%
Rating and Investment Information	0	0	0%	0%	0	0	0%	0%
Rus Ratings	15	15	50%	50%	15	15	50%	50%
Shanghai Brilliance Credit Rating & Investors Service	10	10	52%	52%	10	10	52%	52%
Standard & Poor's	0	0	0%	0%	0	0	0%	0%
Thai Rating and Information Services	10	10	62%	62%	10	10	62%	62%
Xinhua Finance	9	9	67%	67%	9	9	67%	67%

Source: Bloomberg data processed by the author.
This table presents for each rater the maximum number of customers that represents at least 5% of the portfolio in the time period 2001–2012 and the percentage of persistence over time of the status of the most relevant customers. The analysis is conducted considering different discount hypotheses for the best customers (from 5% to 50%) and different definitions of top customers (top 1% or top 5% on the basis of the number of services requested). The ratio between new rating and surveillance fee is assumed equal to 1.

Table A.5e Statistics on the Maximum Number and Persistence Over Time of the Customers that Represent More Than 5% of the Overall Customer Portfolio

| Features | Best Customers, Top 1% | | | | Best Customers, Top 5% | | | |
| | Value | | Persistence | | Value | | Persistence | |
Discount rate applied	5%	50%	5%	50%	5%	50%	5%	50%
A.M. Best Company	0	0	0%	0%	0.05	0.05	0%	0%
Austin Rating	7	7	34%	34%	7	7	34%	34%
BRC Investor Services	11	11	84%	84%	11	11	84%	84%
Canadian Bond Rating Service	0	0	0%	0%	0	0	0%	0%
Capital Intelligence	8	8	32%	32%	8	8	32%	32%
Chengxin International Credit Rating	2	2	40%	40%	2	2	40%	40%
Credit Analysis & Research	6	6	0%	0%	6	6	0%	0%
CRISIL	1	1	0%	0%	1	1	0%	0%

(Continued)

Table A.5e (Continued)

Features	Best Customers, Top 1%				Best Customers, Top 5%			
	Value		Persistence		Value		Persistence	
Discount rate applied	5%	50%	5%	50%	5%	50%	5%	50%
Dagong Global Credit Rating	9	9	0%	0%	9	9	0%	0%
Dominion Bond Rating Service	0	0	0%	0%	0	0	0%	0%
European Rating Agency	5	5	75%	75%	5	5	75%	75%
Fitch Ratings	0	0	0%	0%	0	0	0%	0%
Global Credit Rating	9	9	0%	0%	9	9	0%	0%
Investment Information and Credit Rating Agency	1	1	0%	0%	1	0	0%	0%
Japan Credit Rating Agency	0	0	0%	0%	0	0	0%	0%
Korea Ratings Corporation	0	0	0%	0%	0	0	0%	0%
Malaysian Rating Corporation Berhad	7	7	4%	4%	7	7	4%	4%
Mikuni & Co.	0	0	0%	0%	0	0	0%	0%
Moody's Investors Service	0	0	0%	0%	0	0	0%	0%
National Information & Credit Evaluation	0	0	0%	0%	0	0	0%	0%
P.T. PEFINDO Credit Rating Indonesia	9	9	0%	0%	9	9	0%	0%
Philippine Rating Services	12	12	70%	70%	12	12	70%	70%
RAM Rating Services Berha	0	0	0%	0%	0	0	0%	0%
Rating and Investment Information	0	0	0%	0%	0	0	0%	0%
Rus Ratings	14	14	14%	14%	14	14	14%	14%
Shanghai Brilliance Credit Rating & Investors Service	11	11	10%	10%	11	11	10%	10%
Standard & Poor's	0	0	0%	0%	0	0	0%	0%
Thai Rating and Information Services	10	10	4%	4%	10	10	4%	4%
Xinhua Finance	9	9	50%	50%	9	9	50%	50%

Source: Bloomberg data processed by the author.
This table presents for each rater the maximum number of customers that represents at least 5% of the portfolio in the time period 2001–2012 and the percentage of persistence over time of the status of the most relevant customers. The analysis is conducted considering different discount hypotheses for the best customers (from 5% to 50%) and different definitions of top customers (top 1% or top 5% on the basis of the number of services requested). The ratio between new rating and surveillance fee is assumed equal to 2.

Table A.5f Statistics on the Maximum Number and Persistence Over Time of the Customers that Represent More Than 5% of the Overall Customer Portfolio

Features	Best Customers, Top 1%				Best Customers, Top 5%			
	Value		Persistence		Value		Persistence	
Discount rate applied	5%	50%	5%	50%	5%	50%	5%	50%
A.M. Best Company	0	0	0%	0%	0	0	0%	0%
Austin Rating	7	7	34%	34%	7	7	34%	34%
BRC Investor Services	11	11	73%	73%	11	11	73%	73%
Canadian Bond Rating Service	0	0	0%	0%	0	0	0%	0%
Capital Intelligence	8	8	20%	20%	8	8	20%	20%
Chengxin International Credit Rating	2	2	40%	40%	2	2	40%	40%
Credit Analysis & Research	6	6	0%	0%	6	6	0%	0%
CRISIL	1	1	0%	0%	1	1	0%	0%
Dagong Global Credit Rating	9	9	0%	0%	9	9	0%	0%
Dominion Bond Rating Service	0	0	0%	0%	0	0	0%	0%
European Rating Agency	3	3	50%	50%	3	3	50%	50%
Fitch Ratings	0	0	0%	0%	0	0	0%	0%
Global Credit Rating	9	9	0%	0%	9	9	0%	0%
Investment Information and Credit Rating Agency	5	5	0%	0%	5	5	0%	0%
Japan Credit Rating Agency	0	0	0%	0%	0	0	0%	0%
Korea Ratings Corporation	0	0	0%	0%	0	0	0%	0%
Malaysian Rating Corporation Berhad	9	9	0%	0%	9	9	0%	0%
Mikuni & Co.	0	0	0%	0%	0	0	0%	0%
Moody's Investors Service	0	0	0%	0%	0	0	0%	0%
National Information & Credit Evaluation	0	0	0%	0%	0	0	0%	0%
P.T. PEFINDO Credit Rating Indonesia	9	9	1%	1%	9	9	1%	1%

(Continued)

Table A.5f (Continued)

Features	Best Customers, Top 1%				Best Customers, Top 5%			
	Value		Persistence		Value		Persistence	
Discount rate applied	5%	50%	5%	50%	5%	50%	5%	50%
Philippine Rating Services	12	12	70%	70%	12	12	70%	70%
RAM Rating Services Berha	7	7	0%	0%	7	7	0%	0%
Rating and Investment Information	0	0	0%	0%	0	0	0%	0%
Rus Ratings	14	14	14%	14%	14	14	14%	14%
Shanghai Brilliance Credit Rating & Investors Service	11	11	10%	10%	11	11	10%	10%
Standard & Poor's	0	0	0%	0%	0	0	0%	0%
Thai Rating and Information Services	10	10	5%	5%	10	10	5%	5%
Xinhua Finance	9	9	40%	40%	9	9	40%	40%

Source: Bloomberg data processed by the author.
This table presents for each rater the maximum number of customers that represents at least 5% of the portfolio in the time period 2001–2012 and the percentage of persistence over time of the status of the most relevant customers. The analysis is conducted considering different discount hypotheses for the best customers (from 5% to 50%) and different definitions of top customers (top 1% or top 5% on the basis of the number of services requested). The ratio between new rating and surveillance fee is assumed equal to 10.

Table A.5g Statistics on the Maximum Number and Persistence Over Time of Top 20 Customers

Features	Best Customers, Top 1%				Best Customers, Top 5%			
	Value		Persistence		Value		Persistence	
Discount rate applied	5%	50%	5%	50%	5%	50%	5%	50%
A.M. Best Company	4%	4%	71%	71%	4%	4%	71%	71%
Austin Rating	46%	46%	88%	88%	46%	46%	88%	88%
BRC Investor Services	97%	97%	92%	92%	97%	97%	92%	92%
Canadian Bond Rating Service	30%	30%	92%	92%	30%	30%	92%	92%
Capital Intelligence	42%	42%	82%	82%	42%	42%	82%	82%
Chengxin International Credit Rating	41%	41%	73%	73%	41%	41%	73%	73%
Credit Analysis & Research	18%	18%	86%	86%	18%	18%	86%	86%
CRISIL	8%	8%	85%	85%	8%	8%	85%	85%

(Continued)

Table A.5g (Continued)

Features	Best Customers, Top 1%				Best Customers, Top 5%			
	Value		Persistence		Value		Persistence	
Discount rate applied	5%	50%	5%	50%	5%	50%	5%	50%
Dagong Global Credit Rating	36%	36%	30%	30%	36%	36%	55%	55%
Dominion Bond Rating Service	3%	3%	80%	80%	3%	3%	80%	80%
European Rating Agency	100%	0%	75%	0%	0%	0%	0%	0%
Fitch Ratings	1%	1%	77%	75%	1%	1%	78%	77%
Global Credit Rating	31%	31%	79%	79%	31%	31%	79%	79%
Investment Information and Credit Rating Agency	11%	11%	65%	65%	11%	0%	78%	78%
Japan Credit Rating Agency	3%	3%	90%	90%	0%	0%	0%	0%
Korea Ratings Corporation	7%	7%	66%	66%	7%	7%	77%	77%
Malaysian Rating Corporation Berhad	22%	22%	85%	85%	22%	22%	85%	85%
Mikuni & Co.	10%	10%	91%	91%	10%	10%	91%	91%
Moody's Investors Service	0%	0%	74%	65%	0%	0%	74%	73%
National Information & Credit Evaluation	4%	4%	92%	92%	4%	4%	92%	92%
P.T. PEFINDO Credit Rating Indonesia	23%	23%	86%	86%	23%	23%	86%	86%
Philippine Rating Services	81%	81%	92%	92%	81%	81%	92%	92%
RAM Rating Services Berha	9%	9%	92%	92%	9%	9%	92%	92%
Rating and Investment Information	3%	3%	69%	69%	3%	3%	76%	76%
Rus Ratings	63%	63%	68%	68%	63%	63%	68%	68%
Shanghai Brilliance Credit Rating & Investors Service	51%	51%	75%	75%	51%	51%	75%	75%
Standard & Poor's	1%	1%	77%	77%	1%	1%	77%	77%
Thai Rating and Information Services	42%	42%	79%	79%	42%	42%	79%	79%
Xinhua Finance	36%	36%	84%	84%	36%	36%	84%	84%

Source: Bloomberg data processed by the author.
This table presents for each rater the average weight of the top 20 customers with respect to the overall portfolio in the time period 2001–2012 and the percentage of persistence over time of the status of the most relevant customers. The analysis is conducted considering different discount hypotheses for the best customers (from 5% to 50%) and different definitions of top customers (top 1% or top 5% on the basis of the number of services requested). The ratio between new rating and surveillance fee is assumed equal to 1.

Table A.5h Statistics on the Maximum Number and Persistence Over Time of Top 20 Customers

	Best Customers, Top 1%				Best Customers, Top 5%			
Features	Value		Persistence		Value		Persistence	
Discount rate applied	5%	50%	5%	50%	5%	50%	5%	50%
Discount rate applied	5%	50%	5%	50%	5%	50%	5%	50%
A.M. Best Company	0%	0%	0%	0%	5%	5%	3%	1%
Austin Rating	52%	52%	84%	84%	52%	52%	84%	84%
BRC Investor Services	98%	98%	92%	92%	98%	98%	92%	92%
Canadian Bond Rating Service	30%	30%	92%	92%	30%	30%	92%	92%
Capital Intelligence	49%	49%	28%	28%	49%	49%	28%	28%
Chengxin International Credit Rating	45%	45%	25%	25%	45%	45%	25%	25%
Credit Analysis & Research	29%	29%	71%	71%	29%	29%	71%	71%
CRISIL	13%	13%	4%	4%	13%	13%	4%	4%
Dagong Global Credit Rating	41%	41%	13%	13%	41%	41%	13%	13%
Dominion Bond Rating Service	7%	7%	1%	1%	6%	7%	1%	1%
European Rating Agency	100%	100%	75%	75%	100%	100%	75%	75%
Fitch Ratings	2%	2%	1%	1%	2%	2%	1%	1%
Global Credit Rating	37%	37%	60%	60%	37%	37%	60%	60%
Investment Information and Credit Rating Agency	17%	17%	12%	12%	17%	0%	12%	0%
Japan Credit Rating Agency	5%	5%	3%	3%	5%	5%	4%	4%
Korea Ratings Corporation	14%	14%	5%	5%	14%	14%	5%	5%
Malaysian Rating Corporation Berhad	33%	33%	53%	53%	33%	33%	53%	53%
Mikuni & Co.	10%	10%	91%	91%	10%	10%	91%	91%
Moody's Investors Service	1%	1%	0%	0%	1%	1%	0%	0%
National Information & Credit Evaluation	8%	9%	9%	9%	8%	8%	9%	9%
P.T. PEFINDO Credit Rating Indonesia	38%	38%	69%	69%	38%	38%	69%	69%

(Continued)

Table A.5h (Continued)

| Features | Best Customers, Top 1% | | | | Best Customers, Top 5% | | | |
| | Value | | Persistence | | Value | | Persistence | |
Discount rate applied	5%	50%	5%	50%	5%	50%	5%	50%
Philippine Rating Services	83%	83%	92%	92%	83%	83%	92%	92%
RAM Rating Services Berha	24%	24%	28%	28%	24%	24%	28%	28%
Rating and Investment Information	6%	6%	2%	2%	6%	6%	2%	2%
Rus Ratings	71%	71%	66%	66%	71%	71%	66%	66%
Shanghai Brilliance Credit Rating & Investors Service	57%	57%	38%	38%	57%	57%	38%	38%
Standard & Poor's	1%	1%	1%	1%	1%	1%	1%	1%
Thai Rating and Information Services	54%	54%	72%	72%	54%	54%	72%	72%
Xinhua Finance	44%	44%	64%	64%	44%	44%	64%	64%

Source: Bloomberg data processed by the author.
This table presents for each rater the average weight of the top 20 customers with respect to the overall portfolio in the time period 2001–2012 and the percentage of persistence over time of the status of the most relevant customers. The analysis is conducted considering different discount hypotheses for the best customers (from 5% to 50%) and different definitions of top customers (top 1% or top 5% on the basis of the number of services requested). The ratio between new rating and surveillance fee is assumed equal to 5.

TABLE A.5i Statistics on the Maximum Number and Persistence Over Time of Top 20 Customers

| Features | Best Customers, Top 1% | | | | Best Customers, Top 5% | | | |
| | Value | | Persistence | | Value | | Persistence | |
Discount rate applied	5%	50%	5%	50%	5%	50%	5%	50%
A.M. Best Company	5%	5%	0%	0%	5%	5%	0%	0%
Austin Rating	52%	52%	84%	84%	52%	52%	84%	84%
BRC Investor Services	98%	98%	92%	92%	98%	98%	92%	92%
Canadian Bond Rating Service	30%	30%	92%	92%	30%	30%	92%	92%
Capital Intelligence	52%	52%	28%	28%	52%	52%	28%	28%
Chengxin International Credit Rating	47%	47%	25%	25%	47%	47%	25%	25%
Credit Analysis & Research	37%	37%	71%	71%	37%	37%	71%	71%

(Continued)

Table A.5i (Continued)

Features	Best Customers, Top 1%				Best Customers, Top 5%			
	Value		Persistence		Value		Persistence	
Discount rate applied	5%	50%	5%	50%	5%	50%	5%	50%
CRISIL	18%	18%	4%	4%	18%	18%	4%	4%
Dagong Global Credit Rating	42%	42%	13%	13%	42%	42%	13%	13%
Dominion Bond Rating Service	9%	9%	1%	1%	9%	9%	1%	1%
European Rating Agency	100%	100%	75%	75%	100%	100%	75%	75%
Fitch Ratings	3%	3%	1%	1%	3%	3%	1%	1%
Global Credit Rating	40%	40%	60%	60%	40%	40%	60%	60%
Investment Information and Credit Rating Agency	24%	24%	12%	12%	24%	24%	12%	12%
Japan Credit Rating Agency	8%	8%	2%	2%	8%	8%	2%	2%
Korea Ratings Corporation	19%	19%	5%	5%	19%	19%	5%	5%
Malaysian Rating Corporation Berhad	42%	42%	53%	53%	42%	42%	53%	53%
Mikuni & Co.	10%	10%	91%	91%	10%	10%	91%	91%
Moody's Investors Service	2%	2%	0%	0%	2%	2%	0%	0%
National Information & Credit Evaluation	13%	14%	9%	9%	13%	13%	9%	9%
P.T. PEFINDO Credit Rating Indonesia	49%	49%	69%	69%	49%	49%	69%	69%
Philippine Rating Services	85%	85%	92%	92%	85%	85%	92%	92%
RAM Rating Services Berha	33%	33%	28%	28%	33%	33%	28%	28%
Rating and Investment Information	6%	6%	2%	2%	6%	6%	2%	2%
Rus Ratings	78%	78%	66%	66%	78%	78%	66%	66%
Shanghai Brilliance Credit Rating & Investors Service	59%	59%	38%	38%	59%	59%	38%	38%
Standard & Poor's	2%	2%	1%	1%	2%	2%	1%	1%
Thai Rating and Information Services	64%	64%	72%	72%	64%	64%	72%	72%
Xinhua Finance	48%	48%	64%	64%	48%	48%	64%	64%

Source: Bloomberg data processed by the author.
This table presents for each rater the average weight of the top 20 customers with respect to the overall portfolio in the time period 2001–2012 and the percentage of persistence over time of the status of the most relevant customers. The analysis is conducted considering different discount hypotheses for the best customers (from 5% to 50%) and different definitions of top customers (top 1% or top 5% on the basis of the number of services requested). The ratio between new rating and surveillance fee is assumed equal to 10.

Table A.5j Statistics on Average and Maximum Percentage of Customers that Increase Their Business by More Than 150%

Features	Best Customers, Top 1%				Best Customers, Top 5%			
	Average		Maximum		Average		Maximum	
Discount rate applied	5%	50%	5%	50%	5%	50%	5%	50%
A.M. Best Company	4%	4%	36%	36%	4%	4%	36%	36%
Austin Rating	2%	2%	15%	15%	2%	2%	15%	15%
BRC Investor Services	0%	0%	0%	0%	0%	0%	0%	0%
Canadian Bond Rating Service	0%	0%	0%	0%	0%	0%	0%	0%
Capital Intelligence	0%	0%	0%	0%	0%	0%	0%	0%
Chengxin International Credit Rating	2%	2%	15%	15%	2%	2%	15%	15%
Credit Analysis & Research	1%	1%	3%	3%	1%	1%	3%	3%
CRISIL	2%	2%	9%	9%	2%	2%	9%	9%
Dagong Global Credit Rating	5%	5%	21%	21%	5%	5%	21%	21%
Dominion Bond Rating Service	3%	3%	8%	8%	3%	3%	8%	8%
European Rating Agency	0%	0%	0%	0%	0%	0%	0%	0%
Fitch Ratings	3%	3%	4%	4%	3%	3%	4%	4%
Global Credit Rating	4%	4%	19%	19%	4%	4%	19%	19%
Investment Information and Credit Rating Agency	1%	1%	6%	6%	1%	1%	3%	3%
Japan Credit Rating Agency	3%	3%	17%	17%	0%	0%	0%	0%
Korea Ratings Corporation	2%	2%	11%	11%	2%	2%	11%	11%
Malaysian Rating Corporation Berhad	1%	1%	3%	3%	1%	1%	3%	3%
Mikuni & Co.	0%	0%	0%	0%	0%	0%	0%	0%
Moody's Investors Service	4%	4%	8%	8%	4%	4%	8%	8%
National Information & Credit Evaluation	1%	1%	3%	3%	1%	1%	3%	3%
P.T. PEFINDO Credit Rating Indonesia	4%	4%	14%	14%	4%	4%	14%	14%
Philippine Rating Services	1%	1%	6%	6%	1%	1%	6%	6%
RAM Rating Services Berha	1%	1%	2%	2%	1%	1%	2%	2%

(Continued)

Table A.5j (Continued)

Features	Best Customers, Top 1%				Best Customers, Top 5%			
	Average		Maximum		Average		Maximum	
Discount rate applied	5%	50%	5%	50%	5%	50%	5%	50%
Rating and Investment Information	1%	1%	4%	4%	1%	1%	4%	4%
Rus Ratings	3%	3%	10%	10%	3%	3%	10%	10%
Shanghai Brilliance Credit Rating & Investors Service	0%	0%	0%	0%	0%	0%	0%	0%
Standard & Poor's	1%	1%	3%	3%	1%	1%	3%	3%
Thai Rating and Information Services	3%	3%	12%	12%	3%	3%	12%	12%
Xinhua Finance	1%	1%	6%	6%	1%	1%	6%	6%

Source: Bloomberg data processed by the author.
This table presents for each rater the average and the maximum percentage of customers that increase their business by more than 150% in a one-year time horizon. The analysis is conducted considering different discount hypotheses for the best customers (from 5% to 50%) and different definitions of top customers (top 1% or top 5% on the basis of the number of services requested). The ratio between new rating and surveillance fee is assumed equal to 1.

Table A.5k Statistics on Average and Maximum Percentage of Customers that Increase Their Business by More Than 150%

Features	Best Customers, Top 1%				Best Customers, Top 5%			
	Average		Maximum		Average		Maximum	
Discount rate applied	5%	50%	5%	50%	5%	50%	5%	50%
A.M. Best Company	0%	0%	0%	0%	3%	3%	17%	17%
Austin Rating	12%	12%	69%	69%	12%	12%	69%	69%
BRC Investor Services	1%	1%	9%	9%	1%	1%	9%	9%
Canadian Bond Rating Service	0%	0%	0%	0%	0%	0%	0%	0%
Capital Intelligence	2%	2%	12%	12%	2%	2%	12%	12%
Chengxin International Credit Rating	5%	5%	12%	12%	5%	5%	12%	12%
Credit Analysis & Research	1%	1%	3%	3%	1%	1%	3%	3%
CRISIL	8%	8%	45%	45%	8%	8%	45%	45%

(Continued)

Table A.5k (Continued)

| Features | Best Customers, Top 1% | | | | Best Customers, Top 5% | | | |
| | Average | | Maximum | | Average | | Maximum | |
Discount rate applied	5%	50%	5%	50%	5%	50%	5%	50%
Dagong Global Credit Rating	8%	8%	36%	36%	8%	8%	36%	36%
Dominion Bond Rating Service	11%	11%	64%	64%	11%	11%	64%	64%
European Rating Agency	0%	0%	0%	0%	0%	0%	0%	0%
Fitch Ratings	7%	7%	15%	15%	7%	7%	15%	15%
Global Credit Rating	24%	24%	82%	82%	24%	24%	82%	82%
Investment Information and Credit Rating Agency	4%	4%	19%	19%	4%	4%	19%	19%
Japan Credit Rating Agency	5%	5%	34%	34%	5%	5%	34%	34%
Korea Ratings Corporation	2%	2%	8%	8%	2%	2%	8%	8%
Malaysian Rating Corporation Berhad	5%	5%	39%	39%	5%	5%	39%	39%
Mikuni & Co.	0%	0%	0%	0%	0%	0%	0%	0%
Moody's Investors Service	7%	7%	17%	17%	8%	7%	17%	18%
National Information & Credit Evaluation	1%	1%	2%	2%	1%	1%	2%	2%
P.T. PEFINDO Credit Rating Indonesia	9%	9%	66%	66%	9%	9%	66%	66%
Philippine Rating Services	9%	9%	92%	92%	9%	9%	92%	92%
RAM Rating Services Berha	1%	1%	2%	2%	1%	1%	2%	2%
Rating and Investment Information	5%	5%	39%	39%	5%	5%	39%	39%
Rus Ratings	5%	5%	12%	12%	5%	5%	12%	12%
Shanghai Brilliance Credit Rating & Investors Service	5%	5%	20%	20%	5%	5%	20%	20%
Standard & Poor's	13%	13%	75%	75%	13%	13%	75%	75%
Thai Rating and Information Services	2%	2%	6%	6%	2%	2%	6%	6%
Xinhua Finance	8%	8%	38%	38%	8%	8%	38%	38%

Source: Bloomberg data processed by the author.
This table presents for each rater the average and the maximum percentage of customers that increase their business by more than 150% in a one-year time horizon. The analysis is conducted considering different discount hypotheses for the best customers (from 5% to 50%) and different definitions of top customers (top 1% or top 5% on the basis of the number of services requested). The ratio between new rating and surveillance fee is assumed equal to 5.

Table A.5l Statistics on Average and Maximum Percentage of Customers that Increase Their Business by More Than 150%

	Best Customers, Top 1%				Best Customers, Top 5%			
Features	**Average**		**Maximum**		**Average**		**Maximum**	
Discount rate applied	**5%**	**50%**	**5%**	**50%**	**5%**	**50%**	**5%**	**50%**
A.M. Best Company	18%	18%	70%	70%	18%	18%	70%	70%
Austin Rating	12%	12%	69%	69%	12%	12%	69%	69%
BRC Investor Services	8%	8%	82%	82%	8%	8%	82%	82%
Canadian Bond Rating Service	0%	0%	0%	0%	0%	0%	0%	0%
Capital Intelligence	14%	14%	79%	79%	14%	14%	79%	79%
Chengxin International Credit Rating	5%	5%	12%	12%	5%	5%	12%	12%
Credit Analysis & Research	13%	13%	76%	76%	13%	13%	76%	76%
CRISIL	14%	14%	67%	67%	14%	14%	67%	67%
Dagong Global Credit Rating	8%	8%	36%	36%	8%	8%	36%	36%
Dominion Bond Rating Service	11%	11%	64%	64%	11%	11%	64%	64%
European Rating Agency	0%	0%	0%	0%	0%	0%	0%	0%
Fitch Ratings	13%	13%	70%	70%	13%	13%	70%	70%
Global Credit Rating	24%	24%	82%	82%	24%	24%	82%	82%
Investment Information and Credit Rating Agency	4%	4%	19%	19%	4%	4%	19%	19%
Japan Credit Rating Agency	5%	5%	34%	34%	5%	5%	34%	34%
Korea Ratings Corporation	8%	7%	66%	62%	8%	8%	66%	66%
Malaysian Rating Corporation Berhad	5%	5%	39%	39%	5%	5%	39%	39%
Mikuni & Co.	0%	0%	0%	0%	0%	0%	0%	0%
Moody's Investors Service	8%	8%	18%	18%	8%	8%	18%	18%
National Information & Credit Evaluation	1%	1%	2%	2%	1%	1%	2%	2%
P.T. PEFINDO Credit Rating Indonesia	18%	18%	91%	91%	18%	18%	91%	91%

(Continued)

Table A.5I (Continued)

Features	Best Customers, Top 1%				Best Customers, Top 5%			
	Average		Maximum		Average		Maximum	
Discount rate applied	5%	50%	5%	50%	5%	50%	5%	50%
Philippine Rating Services	17%	17%	92%	92%	17%	17%	92%	92%
RAM Rating Services Berha	1%	1%	2%	2%	1%	1%	2%	2%
Rating and Investment Information	5%	5%	39%	39%	5%	5%	39%	39%
Rus Ratings	16%	16%	68%	68%	16%	16%	68%	68%
Shanghai Brilliance Credit Rating & Investors Service	6%	6%	20%	20%	6%	6%	20%	20%
Standard & Poor's	13%	13%	75%	75%	13%	13%	75%	75%
Thai Rating and Information Services	16%	16%	82%	82%	16%	16%	82%	82%
Xinhua Finance	17%	17%	91%	91%	17%	17%	91%	91%

Source: Bloomberg data processed by the author.
This table presents for each rater the average and the maximum percentage of customers that increase their business by more than 150% in a one-year time horizon. The analysis is conducted considering different discount hypotheses for the best customers (from 5% to 50%) and different definitions of top customers (top 1% or top 5% on the basis of the number of services requested). The ratio between new rating and surveillance fee is assumed equal to 10.

References

Admati, A. R. & Pfleiderer, P. (1986). A monopolistic market for information. *Journal of Economic Theory, 39*(2), 400–438.

Alcubilla, R. G. & Del Pozo, J. R. (2012). *Credit rating agencies on the watch list: Analysis of European regulation.* Oxford: Oxford University Press.

Altman, E. (2005). An emerging market credit scoring system for corporate bonds. *Emerging Markets Review, 6*(4), 311–323.

Altman, E. & Karlin, B. (2009). Defaults and returns in the high-yield bond market: The year 2008 in review and outlook, New York University Salomon Center Special Report. Available from <http://www.law.utoronto.ca/documents/conferences2/CreditMeltdown10_altman-lecture.pdf> Accessed 03.01.13.

Ang, J. A. & Patel, K. A. (1975). Bond rating methods: Comparison and validation. *Journal of Finance, 30*(2), 631–640.

Arbuthnott, J. (1710). An argument for divine providence, taken from the constant regularity observed in the births of both sexes. *Philosophical Transaction of the Royal Society of London, 27,* 186–190.

Arnold, G. (2002). *Corporate financial management.* Harlow: Prentice Hall.

Ashbaugh-Skaife, H., Collins, D. W., & LaFond, R. (2006). The effects of corporate governance on firms credit rating. *Journal of Accounting and Economics, 42*(1), 203–243.

Asian Bankers Association (2000). Development of regional standards for Asian credit rating agencies: issues, challenges and strategic options. Available from <http://www.linkpdf.com/ebook-viewer.php?url=http://www.ctasc.org.tw/conference/Other%20Papers_files%5CCredit%20Ratings_files%5CCRAstudy.pdf> Accessed 03.01.13.

Autorité de Marchés Financiers (2005). 2004 AMF report on rating agencies. Available from <http://www.amf-france.org/documents/general/5891_1.pdf> Accessed 03.01.13.

Bai, L. (2010). On regulating conflict of interests in the credit rating industry. *NYU Journal of Legislation and Public Policy, 13*(2), 254–313.

Baker, K. H. & Mansi, S. A. (2002). Assessing credit rating agencies by bond issuers and institutional investors. *Journal of Business Finance and Accounting, 29*(9), 1367–1398.

Bannier, C. E., Behr, P., & Guttler, A. (2010). Rating opaque borrowers: Why are unsolicited ratings lower? *Review of Finance, 14*(2), 263–294.

Bannier, C. & Tyrell, M. (2005). Modelling the role of credit rating agencies: Do they spark off a virtuous circle? Available from <http://www.finance.uni-frankfurt.de/wp/1020.pdf> Accessed 03.01.13.

Barron, M. J., Clare, A. D., & Thomas, S. H. (1997). The effect of bond rating changes and new ratings on UK stock returns. *Journal of Business Finance and Accounting, 24*(3/4), 497–509.

Basel Committee on Banking Supervision (2006). International convergence of capital measurements and capital standards, June.

Bates, B. J. (1990). Information as an economic good: A re-evaluation of theoretical approaches. In B. D. Ruben & L. A. Lievrouw (Eds.), *Information and behaviour.* New Brunswick: Transaction Publishers.

Beaver, W. H., Shakespeare, C., & Soliman, M. T. (2006). Differential properties in the ratings of certified versus non-certified bond-rating agencies. *Journal of Accounting and Economics, 42*(3), 303–334.

Behr, P. & Guttler, A. (2008). The informational content of unsolicited ratings. *Journal of Banking and Finance, 32*(4), 587–599.

Benmelech, E. & Dlugosz, J. (2009). The credit rating crisis. NBER working paper no. 15045. Available from <http://www.nber.org/papers/w15045> Accessed 03.01.13.

Berger, P. D. & Nada, I. N. (1998). Customer lifetime value: Marketing models and applications. *Journal of Interactive Marketing*, *12*(1), 17–30.

Bhattacharyya, D. (2010). *Financial statement analysis*. New Delhi: Pearson Education.

Billett, M. (1996). Targeting capital structure: The relationship between risky debt and the firm's likelihood of being acquired. *Journal of Business*, *69*(2), 173–192.

Bird, M. M. (1989). Gift-giving and gift-taking in industrial companies. *Industrial Marketing Management*, *19*(2), 91–94.

BIS (2000). Credit rating and complimentary sources of credit quality information. BCBS working paper 3-2000. Available from <http://www.bis.org/publ/bcbs_wp3.pdf> Accessed 03.01.13.

Blattberg, R. C., Getz, G., & Thomas, J. S. (2001). *Customer equity: Building and managing relationships as valuable assets*. Boston, MA: Harvard Business School Press.

Blume, M. E., Lim, F., & Mackinlay, C. (1998). The declining credit quality of U.S. corporate debt: Myth or reality? *Journal of Finance*, *53*(4), 1389–1413.

Bolton, R. N., Lemon, K. N., & Verhoef, P. C. (2004). The theoretical underpinnings of customer asset management: A framework and propositions for future research. *Journal of the Academy of Marketing Science*, *32*(3), 271–292.

Bond Market Association (2006). *Rate the raters – issuers poll*, February. Paris: Bond Market Association.

Boot, A. W. A., Milbourn, T. T., & Schmeits, A. (2006). Credit ratings as coordination mechanisms. *Review of Financial Studies*, *19*(1), 81–118.

Brearley, R. A., Myers, S. C., Allen, F., & Sandri, S. (2010). *Principi di finanza aziendale*. Milan: McGraw Hill.

Bussani, M. (2010). Credit rating agencies' accountability: Short notes on a global issue. *Global Jurist*, *10*(1), 2–16.

Butler, A. W. & Rodgers, K. J. (2003). Relationship rating: How do bond rating agencies process information? EFA 2003 annual conference paper no. 491. Available from <http://papers.ssrn.com/sol3/papers.cfm?abstract_id=345860> Accessed 03.01.13.

Byoun, S. & Yoon, S. S. (2002). Unsolicited credit ratings: Theory and empirical analysis. Proceedings of the Midwest Business Economics Association 2002. Available from <http://69.175.2.130/~finman/Reno/Papers/Unsolicited_Ratings_FMA.pdf> Accessed 03.01.13.

Cannata, F. (2001). Rating esterni e dati di bilancio: un'analisi statistica. *Studi e Note di Economia*, *3*, 37–65.

Cantor, R. & Parker, F. (1995). The credit rating industry. *Journal of Fixed Income*, *5*(3), 10–34.

Cantor, R. & Parker, F. (1996). Multiple rating and credit standards: Differences of opinion in the credit rating industry. Federal Bank of New York Staff Report no. 12-1996. Available from <http://www.newyorkfed.org/research/staff_reports/sr12.pdf> Accessed 03.01.13.

Cantor, R., Parker, F., & Cole, K. (1997). Split ratings and the pricing of credit risk. *Journal of Fixed Income*, *7*(3), 72–82.

Caramiello, C., Di Lazzaro, F., & Fiori, G. (2003). *Indici di bilancio: Strumenti per l'analisi della gestione aziendale*. Varese: Giuffrè Editore.

Carretta, A. (1982). *Il finanziamento delle aziende commerciali*. Varese: Giuffrè Editore.

Caton, G. & Goh, J. (2003). Are all rivals affected equally by bond rating downgrades? *Review of Quantitative Finance and Accounting*, *20*(1), 49–62.

Cavalieri, E. & Ferraris, F. R. (2005). *Economia aziendale*. Turin: Giappichelli Editore.

Cavalieri, E. & Ranalli, F. (1995). *Appunti di economia aziendale*. Rome: Kappa.

CEBS (2006). Guidelines on the recognition of external credit assessment institutions. Available from <http://www.c-ebs.org/formupload/41/413b2513-5084-4293-a386-16385b80411d.pdf> Accessed 03.01.13.

Champsaur, A. (2005). The regulation of credit rating agencies in the U.S. and the E.U.: Recent initiatives and proposals. Harvard Law School working paper. Available from <www.law.harvard.edu/programs/about/pifs/llm/sp19.pdf> Accessed 03.01.13.

Chandy, P. R., Hsueh, L. P., & Liu, Y. A. (1993). Effects of preferred stock re-rating on common stock prices: Further evidence. *Financial Review*, *28*(4), 449–467.

Cheick, W. (2011). Credit and credibility: Triple-A failure and the subprime mortgage crisis. *Review of Business Research, 11*(4), 1–12.

Cheng, M. & Neamtiu, M. (2009). An empirical analysis of changes in credit rating properties: Timeliness, accuracy and volatility. *Journal of Accounting and Economics, 47*(1–2), 108–130.

Cheng, N. S. & Pike, R. (2003). Trade credit decision: Evidence of U.K. firms. *Managerial and Decision Economics, 24*(6–7), 419–438.

Cheung, S. Y. L. & Chan, B. Y. (2002). Bond markets in the pacific RIM development, market structure and relevant issuer in fixed income securities markets. *Asia-Pacific Development Journal, 9*(1), 1–21.

Coffee, J. C. (2004). What caused Enron? A capsule social and economic history of the 1990s. *Cornell Law Review, 89*(2), 272–308.

Committee of European Securities Regulators (2004). CESR's technical advice to the European Commission on possible measures concerning credit rating agencies. Consultation paper. Available from <http://www.treasurers.org/system/files/cesr_consultation.pdf> Accessed 03.01.13.

Coskun, D. (2008). Credit rating agencies in a post-Enron world: Congress revisits the NRSRO concept. *Journal of Banking Regulation, 9*(4), 164–183.

Coval, J. D., Jurek, J. W., & Stafford, E. (2009). The economics of structured finance. *Journal of Economic Perspectives, 23*(1), 3–25.

Covitz, D. M. & Harrison, P. (2003). Testing conflicts of interest at bond rating agencies with market anticipation: Evidence that reputation incentives dominate. Board of Governors of the Federal Reserve System (U.S.) – Finance and Economics Discussion Series with number 2003-68. Available from <http://www.federalreserve.gov/pubs/feds/2003/200368/200368abs.html> Accessed 03.01.13.

Cowan, A. R. (1991). Inside information and debt rating changes. *Journal of the Midwest Finance Association, 20*(1), 47–58.

Creighton, A., Gower, L., & Richards, A. J. (2007). The impact of rating changes in Australian financial markets. *Pacific-Basin Finance Journal, 15*(1), 11–17.

Crouhy, M., Galai, D., & Mark, R. (2001). Prototype risk rating system. *Journal of Banking and Finance, 25*(1), 47–95.

Csikos, P. (2005). Emergence d'une nouvelle gouvernance internationale privee/publique: les cas des agences de notation financiere et des norme comptables. Universityof Lausanne – Travaux de science politique no. 19. Available from <http://www.csikos.com/download/csikos_publication_%20memoire.pdf> Accessed 03.01.13.

Daft, R. L. (2008). *Organization theory and design.* Mason: South-Western Cengage Learning.

Dale, R. S. & Thomas, S. H. (1991). The regulatory use of credit ratings in international financial markets. *Journal of International Securities Markets, 5*(3), 9–18.

Dallocchio, M. & Salvi, A. (2005). *Finanza d'azienda: analisi per le decisioni di impresa.* EGEA, Milan.

Darbellay, A. & Partnoy, F. (2012). Credit rating agencies and regulatory reform. In C. A. Hill, J. L. Krusemark, B. H. McDonnell & S. Robbins (Eds.), *Research handbook on the economics of corporate law.* Cheltenham: Edward Elgar Publishing.

DeAngelo, L. E. (1981). Auditor size and audit quality. *Journal of Accounting Economics, 3*(3), 183–199.

De Laurentis, G. (1999). I processi di rating e i modelli di scoring. In A. Sironi & M. Marsella (Eds.), *La misurazione e la gestione del rischio di credito.* Rome: Bancaria editrice.

De Laurentis, G. (2001). *Rating interni e credit risk management.* Rome: Bancaria editrice.

De Meijer, C. R. W. & Saaf, M. H. W. (2008). The credit crunch and the credit rating agencies: Are they really striving towards more transparency? *Journal of Securities Law, Regulation and Compliance, 1*(4), 322–336.

Demski, J. (2003). Corporate conflicts of interest. *Journal of Economic Perspectives, 17*(2), 51–72.

Demski, J. S., Lewis, T. R., Yao, D., & Yildirim, H. (1999). Practice for managing information flows within organizations. *Journal of Law, Economics and Organization, 15*(1), 107–131.

Dermine, J. & Neto de Carvalho, C. (2006). Bank loan losses-given-default: A case study. *Journal of Banking and Finance, 30*(4), 1219–1243.

Diamond, D. W. (1989). Reputation acquisition in debt market. *Journal of Political Economy, 97*(4), 828–862.

Diamond, D. W. & Rajan, R. G. (2009). The credit crisis: Conjectures about causes and remedies. *American Economic Review, 99*(2), 606–610.

Eamount, P. H. (2003). *Financial Engineering Principles.* Indianapolis: John Wiley.

Ebenroth, C. T. & Dillon, T. J. (1993). The international rating game: An analysis of the liability of rating agencies in Europe, England, and the United States. *Law and Policy in International Business, 24,* 783–834.

Ederington, L. H. (1974). The yield spread on new issues of corporate bonds. *Journal of Finance, 29*(5), 1531–1543.

Ederington, L. H. (1986). Why split ratings occur. *Financial Management, 15*(1), 37–47.

Ederington, L. H. & Goh, J. C. (1998). Bond rating agencies and stock analysts: Who knows what when? *Journal of Financial and Quantitative Analysis, 33*(4), 569–585.

Ederington, L. H. & Yawitz, J. (1987). The fund rating process. In E. Altman (Ed.), *Handbook of financial markets.* New York: Wiley.

El-Shagi, M. (2010). The role of rating agencies in financial crises: Event studies from the Asian flu. *Cambridge Journal of Economics, 34*(4), 671–685.

Ellis, N. S., Fairchild, L. M., & D'Souza, F. (2012). Is imposing liability on credit rating agencies a good idea? Credit rating agency reform in the aftermath of the Global Financial Crisis. *Stanford Journal of Law, Business and Finance, 17,* 175–310.

Ellis, R. (1998). Different sides of the same story: Investors' and issuers' views of credit ratings. *Journal of Fixed Income, 7*(4), 35–45.

European Commission (2008). Proposal for a regulation of the European parliament and of the council on credit rating agencies. Available from <http://register.consilium.europa.eu/pdf/en/09/st06/st06930.en09.pdf> Accessed 03.01.13.

Fabozzi, F. (2007). *Bond markets, analysis, and strategies.* Upper Saddle River: Pearson Prentice Hall.

Fayez, A. E., Wei, H. H., & Meyer, T. O. (2003). The informational content of credit rating announcements for share prices in a small market. *Journal of Economics and Finance, 27*(3), 337–356.

Feinberg, M., Shelor, R., & Jiang, J. (2004). The effect of solicitation and independence on corporate bond ratings. *Journal of Business, Finance and Accounting, 31*(9–10), 1327–1353.

Fender, I. & Mitchell, J. (2005). Structured finance: Complexity, risk and the use of ratings. *BIS Quarterly Review, 3*(1), 67–79.

Ferrero, G., Dezzani, F., Pisoni, P., & Puddu, L. (2006). *Analisi di bilancio e rendiconti finanziari.* Varese: Giuffrè Editore.

Ferri, G. (2004). More analysts, better ratings: Do rating agencies invest enough in less developed countries? *Journal of Applied Economics, 7*(1), 77–98.

Ferri, G., Kang, T. S., Lacitignola, P., & Lee, J. Y. (2009). Foreign ownership and the credibility of national rating agencies: evidence from Korea. ADBI working paper. Available from <http://istituti.unicatt.it/teoria_economica_metodi_quantitativi_100209.pdf> Accessed 03.01.13.

Ferri, G. & Lacitignola, P. (2009). *Le Agenzie di Rating.* Bologna: Il Mulino.

Ferri, G. & Liu, L. G. (2003). How do global credit-rating agencies rate firms from developing countries? *Asian Economic, Papers 2*(3), 30–56.

Fight, A. (2001). *The rating game.* London: John Wiley.

Flandreau, M., Gaillard, N., & Packer, F. (2010). To err is human: Rating agencies and the interwar foreign government debt crisis. BIS working paper no. 335. Available from <http://www.bis.org/publ/work335.htm> Accessed 03.01.13.

Fridson, M. (2010). Bond rating agencies: Conflict and competences. *Journal of Applied Corporate Finance, 22*(3), 56–64.

Frost, C. A. (2007). Credit rating agencies in capital markets: A review of research evidence on selected criticisms of the agencies. *Journal of Accounting, Auditing and Finance, 22*(3), 469–492.

Gaillard, N. (2012). *A century of sovereign ratings*. New York: Springer.

Galil, K. (2002). The quality of corporate credit rating: An empirical investigation. Tel Aviv University working paper. Available from <http://www.tau.ac.il/~koresh/Galil_Job_Market_Paper.pdf> Accessed 03.01.13.

Gallaugher, J. M., Augerb, P., & BarNirc, A. (2001). Revenue streams and digital content providers: An empirical investigation. *Information and Management, 38*(7), 473–485.

Geng, X., Stinchcombe, M. B., & Whinston, A. B. (2005). Bundling information goods of decreasing value. *Management Science, 51*(4), 662–667.

Gibilaro, L. & Mattarocci, G. (2011a). Pricing policies and customers' portfolio concentration for rating agencies: Evidence from Fitch, Moody's and S&P. *Academy of Banking Studies Journal, 10*(1), 23–52.

Gibilaro, L. & Mattarocci, G. (2011b). Measuring customers' portfolio concentration for rating agencies: Evidence from Fitch, Moody's and S&P. *International Journal of Bank Marketing, 29*(4), 333–356.

Goh, J. C. & Ederington, L. H. (1993). Is bond rating downgrade bad news, good news or no news for stockholders. *Journal of Finance, 48*(5), 2001–2008.

Goh, J. C. & Ederington, L. H. (1999). Cross-sectional variation in the stock market reaction to bond rating changes. *Quarterly Review of Economics and Finance, 39*(1), 109–112.

Golin, J. (2001). *The bank credit analysis handbook: A guide for analysts, bankers and investors*. London: John Wiley.

Goodhart, C. A. E. (2008). The regulatory response to the financial crisis. *Journal of Financial Stability, 4*(4), 351–358.

Grandori, A. (1991). Negotiating efficient organization forms. *Journal of Economic Behaviour and Organization, 16*(3), 319–340.

Greenwood, R., Li, S. X., Prakash, R., & Deephouse, D. L. (2005). Reputation, diversification, and organizational explanations of performance in professional service firms. *Organization Science, 16*(6), 661–672.

Gropp, R. E. & Richards, A. (2001). Rating agency actions and the pricing of debt and equity of European banks: What can we infer about private sector monitoring of bank soundness? European Central Bank working paper no. 76. Available from <http://www.ecb.europa.eu/pub/pdf/scpwps/ecbwp076.pdf> Accessed 03.01.20.

Grundfest, J. A. & Hochenberg, E. E. (2009). Investor owned and controlled rating agencies: A summary introduction. Stanford University Law School, law and economics online working paper Series No. 391. Available from <http://ssrn.com/abstract=1494527> Accessed 01.03.13.

Gudzowski, M. (2010). Mortgage credit ratings and the financial crisis: The need for a State-run mortgage security credit rating agency. *Columbia Business Law Review, 25*(1), 101–132.

Guttler, A. (2005). Using a bootstrap approach to rate the raters. *Financial Markets and Portfolio Management, 19*(3), 277–295.

Guttler, A. & Wahrenburg, M. (2007). The adjustment of credit ratings in advance of defaults. *Journal of Banking and Finance, 31*(3), 751–767.

Gwinner, K. P., Gremler, D. D. & Bitner, M. J. (1998). Relational benefits in services industries: The customer's perspective. *Journal of the Academy of Marketing Science, 26*(2), 101–114.

Gyntelberg, J., Ma, G. & Remolona, E. M. (2005). Corporate bond market in Asia. *BIS Quarterly Review, 6*(4), 83–95.

Hand, J. R., Holthausen, R. W. & Leftwich, R. W. (1992). The effect of bond rating agency announcements on bond and stock prices. *Journal of Finance, 47*(2), 733–752.

He, J., Qian, J. & Strahan, P. E. (2012). Are all ratings created equal? The impact of issuer size on the pricing of mortgage-backed securities. *Journal of Finance, 67*(6), 2097–2137.

Herfindahl, O. C. (1950). Concentration in the U.S. steel industry. Columbia University mimeo.

Hicks, J. (1982). Limited liability: The pros and cons. In T. Orhnial (Ed.), *Limited liability and the corporation*. Norfolk: Biddles.

Hill, C. A. (2002). Rating agencies behaving badly: The case of Enron. *Cornell Law Review*, *35*, 1145–1155.

Hill, C. A. (2004). Regulating rating agencies. *Washington University Law Quarterly*, *82*, 43–85.

Hill, C. A. (2010). Why did rating agencies do such a bad job rating subprime securities? *University of Pittsburgh Law Review*, *71*(1), 585–608.

Hirschman, A. O. (1945). *National power and the structure of foreign trade*. Berkeley: University of California Press.

Holthausen, R. W. & Leftwich, R. W. (1986). The effect of bond rating changes on common stock prices. *Journal of Financial Economics*, *17*(1), 57–89.

Hsueh, L. P. & Kidwell, D. S. (1972). Bond ratings: Are two better than one? *Financial Management*, *17*(1), 46–53.

Hunt, J. P. (2009). Credit rating agencies and the 'worldwide credit crisis': The limits of reputation, the insufficiency of reform, and a proposal for improvement. *Columbia Business Law Review*, *1*(1), 109–209.

Impson, C. M., Karafiath, I. & Glascock, J. (1992). Testing beta stationarity across bond rating change. *Financial Review*, *27*(4), 607–618.

IOSCO (2004). Code of conduct fundamentals for credit rating agencies. Available from <http://www.iosco.org/library/pubdocs/pdf/IOSCOPD180.pdf> Accessed 03.01.13.

IOSCO (2008). Code of conduct fundamentals for credit rating agencies. Available from <http://www.iosco.org/library/pubdocs/pdf/IOSCOPD271.pdf> Accessed 03.01.13.

Jameson, R. & McNee, A. (2002). The rating game. Available from <http://www.riskmania.com/pdsdata/The%20Rating%20Game-erisk.pdf> Accessed 03.01.13.

Jewell, J. & Livingston, M. (1999). A comparison of bond ratings from Moody's S&P and Fitch IBCA. *Financial Markets, Institutions and Instruments*, *8*(4), 1–45.

John, K., Lynch, A. W., & Puri, M. (2003). Credit ratings, collateral, and loan characteristics: Implications for yield. *Journal of Business*, *76*(3), 371–410.

John, K., Ravid, S. A., & Reisel, N. (2010). The notching rule for subordinated debt and the information content of debt rating. *Financial Management*, *39*(2), 489–513.

Johnson, R. (2003). An examination of rating agencies around the investment-grade boundary. Federal Reserve of Kansas City working paper no. 03-01. Available from <http://papers.ssrn.com/sol3/papers.cfm?abstract_id=394800> Accessed 03.01.13.

Jorion, P., Liu, Z., & Shi, S. (2005). Informational effects of regulation FD: Evidence from rating agencies. *Journal of Financial Economics*, *76*(2), 309–330.

Kaplan, R. S. & Urwitz, G. (1979). Statistical models of bond ratings: A methodological inquiry. *Journal of Business*, *52*(2), 231–261.

Kerwer, D. (2002). Standardising as governance: The case of credit rating agencies. In A. Heritier (Ed.), *Common goods: Reinventing european and international governance*. Boston: Rowan & Littlefield.

Kerwer, D. (2005). Holding global regulators accountable: The case of credit rating agencies. *Governance*, *18*(3), 453–475.

Klinger, D. & Sarig, O. (2000). The information value of bond ratings. *Journal of Finance*, *55*(6), 2879–2902.

Kotecha, M., Freifeld, J., Wang, F., et al. (2013). Assessing the importance and value of an NRSRO rating: Investor and NRSRO views. *Journal of Structured Finance*, *18*(4), 103–111.

Krahnen, J. P. & Weber, M. (2001). Generally accepted rating principles. *Journal of Banking and Finance*, *25*(1), 3–23.

Kraussl, R. (2005). Do rating agencies add to the dynamics of emerging market crises? *Journal of Financial Stability*, *1*(3), 355–385.

Kreps, D. M. & Wilson, R. (1982). Reputation and imperfect information. *Journal of Economic Theory*, *27*(2), 253–279.

Kuhner, C. (2001). Financial rating agencies: Are they credible? Insight into the reporting incentives of rating agencies in times of enhanced systemic risk. *Schmalenbach Business Review*, *53*(1), 2–26.

Kumar, A., Chuppe, T. M., & Perttunen, P. (1997). The regulation of non-bank financial institution. World Bank discussion paper no. 362.

Kumar, V. (2007). Customer lifetime value. The path to profitability. *Foundations and Trend in Marketing*, 2(1), 1–96.

Langhor, H. & Langhor, P. (2008). *The rating agencies and their credit rating: What they are, how they work and why they are relevant*. Chichester: John Wiley.

Lanzoni, P. & Patarnello, A. (2010). The rating industry and the role of national credit rating agencies: New markets and new rules after the EC regulation. In G. Bracchi & D. Masciandaro (Eds.), *Le banche italiane sono speciali? nuovi equilibri tra finanza, imprese e stato*. Rome: Bancaria Editrice.

Leonard, B. (2009). *Summary report of issues identified in the security and exchange commission staffs examinations of select credit rating agencies*. Darby: DIANE publishing.

Levine, R. (2012). The governance of financial regulation: Reform lessons from the recent crisis. *International Review of Finance*, 12(1), 39–56.

Leyens, P. C. (2011). Intermediary independence. Auditors, financial analysts and rating agencies. *Journal of Corporate Law Studies*, 11(1), 33–66.

Listokin, Y. & Taibleson, B. (2010). If you misrate, then you lose: Improving credit rating accuracy through incentive compensation. *Yale Journal of Regulation*, 27(1), 91–113.

Liu, P., Seyyed, F. J., & Smith, S. D. (1999). The independent impact of credit rating changes – The case of Moody's refinement on yield premiums. *Journal of Business, Finance and Accounting*, 26(3–4), 337–363.

Livingston, M., Naranjo, A., & Zhou, L. (2010). Split bond ratings and information opacity premiums. *Financial Management*, 39(2), 515–532.

Loffler, G. (2004). Rating versus market-based measures of default risk in portfolio governance. *Journal of Banking and Finance*, 24(11), 2715–2744.

Loffler, G. (2005). Avoiding the rating bounce: Why rating agencies are slow to react to new information. *Journal of Economic Behaviour and Organization*, 56(3), 365–381.

Lowe, M. (1999). *Business information at work*. London: Taylor & Francis.

Lucas, D. J., Goodman, L. S., & Fabozzi, F. J. (2008). How to save rating agencies. *Journal of Structured Finance*, 14(2), 21–26.

Mahlmann, T. (2008). Rating agencies and the role of rating publication rights. *Journal of Banking and Finance*, 32(11), 2412–2422.

Mann, R. J. (1999). Verification institutions in financing transactions. *Georgetown Law Journal*, 87, 2–45.

Manns, J. (2009). Rating risk after the subprime mortgage crisis: A user fee approach for rating agency accountability. *North Carolina Law Review*, 87, 1011–1089.

Massari, M. (1990). Gli strumenti per le analisi finanziarie. In G. Pivato (Ed.), *Trattato di finanza aziendale*. Milan: Franco Angeli.

Mathis, J., McAndrews, J., & Rochet, J. C. (2009). Rating the raters: Are reputation concerns powerful enough to discipline rating agencies? *Journal of Monetary Economics*, 56(5), 657–674.

Matolcsy, Z. P. & Lianto, T. (1995). The incremental information content of bond rating revisions: The Australian evidence. *Journal of Banking and Finance*, 19(5), 891–902.

Mattarocci, G. (2005). Il rapporto tra impresa e agenzia di rating: La soluzione del multirating. NEWFIN working paper no. 02–05.

McVea, H. (2010). Credit rating agencies, the subprime mortgage debacle and global governance: The EU strikes back. *International and Comparative Law Quarterly*, 59(3), 701–730.

Mella, P. (1998). *Indici di bilancio*. Milan: Il Sole 24Ore.

Mikkelson, W. H., Partch, M. M., & Shah, K. (1997). Ownership and operating performance of companies that go to public. *Journal of Financial Economics*, 44(3), 281–307.

Mishkin, F. S., Crockett, A., White, E., & Harris, T. A. L. (2004). Conflicts of Interest in the Financial Service Industry. Centre for Economic Policy Research – Geneva Report on the World Economy.

Morgan, D. P. (2002). Rating banks: Risk and uncertainty in an opaque industry. *American Economic Review*, 92(4), 874–888.

Mukhopadhyay, B. (2006). Existence of unsolicited rating. *Asia Pacific Financial Markets*, 13(3), 207–233.

Mukhopadhyay, B. (2009). Are competitive rating agencies efficient? *Journal of Emerging Financial Markets*, 8(1), 67–85.

Mulligan, C. M. (2009). From AAA to F: How the credit rating agencies failed America and what can be done to protect investors. *Boston College Law Review*, 50(4), 1275–1305.

Nayar, N. (1993). Asymmetric information, voluntary ratings and the rating agency of Malaysia. *Pacific Basin Finance Journal*, 1(4), 369–380.

Nayar, N. & Rozeff, M. S. (1994). Ratings, commercial paper, and equity returns. *Journal of Finance*, 49(4), 1431–1449.

Nickell, P., Perraudin, W., & Varotto, S. (2000). Stability of credit ratings transitions. *Journal of Banking and Finance*, 40(1–2), 203–227.

OICV-IOSCO (2003). Report on the activities of credit rating agencies. Available from <http://www.iosco.org/library/pubdocs/pdf/IOSCOPD153.pdf> Accessed 03.01.13.

Pagano, M. & Volpin, P. (2003). Credit ratings failures and policy options. *Economic Policy*, 25(4), 401–431.

Park, D. & Rhee, C. (2006). Building infrastructure for Asian bond markets: Settlement and credit rating. In Asian Bond Markets: Issues and Prospects, BIS paper no. 30. Available from <http://papers.ssrn.com/sol3/papers.cfm?abstract_id=1519822> Accessed 03.01.13.

Partnoy, F. (1999). The Siskel and Ebert of financial markets? Two thumbs down for the credit rating agencies. *Washington University Law Quarterly*, 77(3), 619–711.

Partnoy, F. (2001). The paradox of credit ratings. University of San Diego law and economic research paper no. 20. Available from <http://www.usdrinc.com/downloads/Credit-Rating-Agencies.pdf> Accessed 03.01.13.

Partnoy, F. (2006). How and why credit rating agencies are not like other gatekeepers. San Diego legal studies paper no. 07-46. Available from <http://www.usdrinc.com/down-loads/Credit-Rating-Agencies.pdf> Accessed 03.01.13.

Pavarani, E. (2002). *Analisi finanziaria*. Milan: McGraw Hill.

Pinches, G. E. & Mingo, K. A. (1973). A multivariate analysis of industrial bond ratings. *Journal of Finance*, 28(1), 1–28.

Pinches, G. E. & Singleton, C. J. (1978). The adjustment of stock prices to bond rating changes. *Journal of Finance*, 33(1), 29–44.

Pinto, A. R. (2006). Control and responsibility of credit rating agencies in the United States. *American Journal of Comparative Law*, 54(3), 341–356.

Poddighe, F. (2004). *Analisi di bilancio per indici: aspetti operativi*. Padova: CEDAM.

Pogue, T. F. & Soldofsky, R. M. (1969). What's in a bond rating? *Journal of Financial and Quantitative Analysis*, 4(2), 201–228.

Poon, W. P. H. (2003). Are unsolicited credit ratings biased downward? *Journal of Banking and Finance*, 27(4), 593–614.

Poon, W. P. H. & Firth, M. (2005). Are unsolicited credit ratings lower? International evidence from bank rating. *Journal of Business Finance and Accounting*, 32(9), 1741–1771.

Posch, P. N. (2011). Time to change. Rating changes and policy implications. *Journal of Economic Behavior and Organization*, 80(3), 641–656.

Purda, L. D. (2005). Mergers in the bond rating industry: Does rating provider matter? *Journal of Multinational Financial Management*, 15(2), 155–169.

Raiborn, C. A. (2010). *Core concepts of accounting*. Charlottesville: John Wiley.

Ramakrishnan, S. T. R. & Thakor, V. A. (1984). Information reliability and a theory of financial intermediation. *Review of Economic Studies*, 5(3), 415–432.

Ranalli, F. (2005). *Il bilancio di esercizio*. Rome: ARACNE.

Resti, A. & Omacini, C. (2001). Che cosa determina i rating creditizi delle aziende europee? *Banche e Banchieri*, 28(3), 197–216.

Reynolds, J. K. & Francis, J. R. (2000). Does size matter? The influence of large clients on office-level auditor reporting decisions. *Journal of Accounting and Economics*, 30(3), 375–400.

Richardson, M. & White, L. J. (2009). The rating agencies. Is regulation the answer? In V. V. Acharya & M. Richardson (Eds.), *Restoring financial stability: How to repair a failed system*. Hoboken: John Wiley.

Ritter, D. J. & Miranda, R. (2000). *An elected official guide to rating agency presentations*. Chicago: GFOA.

Rodgers, P. (2007). *International accounting standards: From UK standards to IAS*. Oxford: CIMA.

Rom, M. C. (2009). The credit rating agencies and the subprime mess: Greedy, ignorant, and stressed? *Public Administration Review*, 69(4), 640–650.

Rona-Tas, A. & Hiss, S. (2010). The role of ratings in the subprime mortgage crisis: The art of corporate and the science of consumer credit rating. In M. Lounsbury (Ed.), *Research in the Sociology of Organizations*. Bingley: Emerald.

Rosner, J. (2009). Towards an understanding: NRSRO failings in structured ratings and discreet recommendations to address agency conflicts. *Journal of Structured Finance*, 14(3), 7–22.

Rossignoli, B. (1991). Flusso dei fondi e fabbisogno finanziario. Elementi per la programmazione e il controllo. In C. Bisoni & B. Rossignoli (Eds.), *Letture di finanza aziendale*. Milan: Giuffrè Editore.

Rousseau, S. (2006). Enhancing the accountability of credit rating agencies: The case for a disclosure-based approach. *McGill Law Journal*, 51(1), 616–664.

Ryals, L. (2002). Are your customers worth more than money? *Journal of Retailing and Consumer Services*, 9(5), 241–251.

Sagner, J. S. (1995). Who rates the rating agencies? *Healthcare Financial Management*, 49(7), 86.

Sangiorgi, F., Sobokin, J., & Spatt, C. (2009). Credit-rating shopping, selection and the equilibrium structure of ratings. Unpublished. Available from <http://refic.mccombs.utexas.edu/research/Spatt_selection--22.pdf> Accessed 03.01.13.

Saunders, A. & Allen, L. (2010). *Credit risk: Measurement in and out of the financial crisis*. Hoboken: John Wiley.

Schwarz, S. L. (2001). The role of rating agencies in the global market regulation. In E. Ferrari & C. A. E. Goodhart (Eds.), *Regulating financial services and markets in the twenty first century*. Portland: Hart.

Schwarz, S. L. (2002). Private ordering of public markets: The rating agency paradox. *University of Illinois College of Law Review*, 53(1), 1–28.

Schwarz, S. L. (2008). Disclosure's failure in the subprime mortgage crisis. *University of Utah Law Review*, 60(3), 1109–1122.

SEC (2007). Final rule: Oversight of credit rating agencies registered as nationally recognized statistical rating organizations. 17 CFR Parts 240 and 249b, Release No. 34-55857. Available from <http://www.sec.gov/rules/final/2007/34-55857.pdf> Accessed 03.01.13.

SEC (2008). Summary report of issues identified in the commission staff's examinations of select credit rating agencies. Available from <www.sec.gov/news/studies/2008/craexamination070808.pdf> Accessed 03.01.13.

SEC (2009). Annual report on nationally recognized statistical rating organizations. Available from <http://www.sec.gov/divisions/marketreg/ratingagency/nrsroannrep0909.pdf> Accessed 03.01.13.

SEC (2010). Annual report on nationally recognized statistical rating organizations. Available from <http:/www.sec.gov/divisions/marketreg/ratingagency/nrsroannrep0111.pdf> Accessed 03.01.13.

SEC (2011). Annual report on nationally recognized statistical rating organizations. Available from <https://www.sec.gov/divisions/marketreg/ratingagency/nrsroannrep1212.pdf> Accessed 03.01.13.

SEC (2012). Report to Congress credit rating standardization study. Available from <www.sec.gov> Accessed 03.01.13.

Shapiro, C. & Varian, H. (1998). *Information rules*. Boston, MA: Harvard Business School Press.

Sharma, N. (2001). The underlying constraints on corporate bond market development in Southeast Asia. *World Development*, 29(8), 1405–1419.

Shimoda, N. & Kawai, Y. (2007). Credit rating gaps in Japan: Differences between solicited and unsolicited ratings, and 'rating splits'. Bank of Japan working paper no. 07-E-11.

Available from <http://www.boj.or.jp/en/type/ronbun/ron/wps/data/wp07e11.pdf> Accessed 03.01.13.

Shiren, N. & Crosignani, M. (2009). The new rating regime for structured finance investment in Europe. *Journal of Structured Finance*, *15*(3), 52–55.

Sinclair, T. J. (2001). The infrastructure of global governance: Quasi regulatory governance and the new global finance. *Global Governance*, *7*(4), 441–451.

Sinclair, T. J. (2003). Global monitor. Bond rating agencies. *New Political Economy*, *8*(1), 147–161.

Sinclair, T. J. (2005). *The new masters of capital: American bond rating agencies and the politics of creditworthiness*. Ithaca: Cornell University Press.

Sironi, A. & Resti, A. (2007). *Rischio e valore nelle banche: risk management e capital allocation*. Milan: Egea.

Skreta, V. & Veldkamp, L. (2009). Ratings shopping and asset complexity: A theory of ratings inflation. *Journal of Monetary Economics*, *56*(5), 678–695.

Smith, R. C. & Walter, I. (2001). Rating agencies: Is there an agency issue? NYU working paper no. FIN-01-003. Available from <http://archive.nyu.edu/handle/2451/26781> Accessed 03.01.13.

Stevens, B. (1994). An analysis of corporate ethical code studies: Where do we go from here? *Journal of Business Ethics*, *13*(1), 63–69.

Stiglitz, J. E. & Weiss, A. (1981). Credit rationing in markets with imperfect information. *American Economic Review*, *71*(3), 393–410.

Stolowy, H. & Lebas, M. J. (2006). *Financial accounting and reporting: A global perspective*. Andover: Cengage Learning.

Strier, F. (2008). Rating the raters: Conflicts of interest in the credit rating firms. *Business and Society Review*, *113*(4), 533–553.

Sufi, A. (2009). The real effects of debt certification: Evidence from the introduction of bank loan ratings. *Review of Financial Studies*, *22*(4), 1659–1691.

Sylla, R. (2002). An historical primer on the business of credit rating. In R. M. Levich, R. Majnoni & C. Reinhart (Eds.), *Ratings, rating agencies and the global financial system*. Boston: Kluwer Academic.

Thompson, G. R. & Vaz, P. (1990). Dual bond ratings: A test of the certification function of rating agencies. *Financial Review*, *25*(3), 457–471.

Todhanakasem, W. (2001). A domestic credit rating agency in an emerging Asian country: The TRIS experience: *Bond market development in Asia*. Paris: OECD.

Tourk, K. (2004). The political economy of east Asian economic integration. *Journal of Asian Economics*, *15*(5), 843–888.

Utzig, S. (2010). The financial crisis and the regulation of the credit rating agencies: A European banking perspective. ADBI working paper no. 188. Available from <http://www.adbi.org/files/2010.01.26.wp188.credit.rating.agencies.european.banking.pdf> Accessed 03.01.13.

Van Roy, P. (2006). Is there a difference between solicited and unsolicited bank ratings and if so, why? National Bank of Belgium working paper no. 79, Brussels. Available from <http://www.nbb.be/doc/oc/repec/reswpp/WP79.pdf> Accessed 03.01.13.

Vander Vennet, R. (2002). Cost and profit efficiency of financial conglomerates and universal banks. *European Journal of Money, Credit and Banking*, *34*(1), 254–282.

Varian, H. R. (2000). Buying, sharing and renting information goods. *Journal of Industrial Economics*, *48*(4), 473–488.

Vink, D. & Thibeault, A. E. (2008). ABS, MBS, and CDO pricing comparisons: An empirical analysis. *Journal of Structured Finance*, *14*(2), 27–45.

Voorhees, R. (2012). Rating the raters: Restoring confidence and accountability in credit rating agencies. *Case Western Reserve Journal of International Law*, *44*, 875–955.

Wakeman, L. M. (1984). The real function of bond rating agencies. In M. C. Jensen & C. W. Smith Jr (Eds.), *The modern theory of corporate finance*. New York: McGraw-Hill.

Weber, R. H. & Darbellay, A. (2008). The regulatory use of credit ratings in bank capital requirement regulations. *Journal of Banking Regulation*, *10*(1), 1–16.

Wessendorf, E. M. (2008). Regulating the credit rating agencies. *Entrepreneurial Business Law Journal, 3*(1), 155–175.

West, R. R. (1973). Bond ratings, bond yields and financial regulation: Some findings. *Journal of Law and Economics, 16*(1), 159–168.

Westbrook, R. A. (1987). Product/consumption-based affective responses and post purchase processes. *Journal of Marketing Research, 24*(3), 258–270.

White, G. I., Sondhi, A. C., & Fried, D. (2003). *The analysis and use of financial statement.* Charlottesville: John Wiley.

White, H. (1981). Where do markets come from? *American Journal of Sociology, 87*(3), 517–547.

White, L. J. (2002). The credit rating industry: An industrial organization analysis. In R. M. Levich, G. Majnoni & C. Reinhart (Eds.), *Ratings, rating agencies and the global financial system.* Boston: Kluwer Academic.

White, L. J. (2007). A new law for the bond rating industry. *Regulation, 30*(1), 48–52.

White, L. J. (2010). The credit rating agencies. *Journal of Economic Perspectives, 24*(2), 211–226.

Williamson, O. E. (1969). Allocative efficiency and the limits of the antitrust. *American Economic Review, 59*(2), 105–118.

Williamson, O. E. (2002). The theory of the firm as governance structure: From choice to contract. *Journal of Economic Perspectives, 16*(3), 171–195.

Woelfel, C. J. (1994). *Financial statement analysis.* New York: McGraw Hill.

Ziebart, D. A. & Reiter, S. A. (1992). Bond ratings, bond yields and financial information. *Contemporary Accounting Research, 9*(1), 252–282.

Index

Note: Page numbers followed by *"b," "f," and "t"* refer to boxes, figures, and tables, respectively.

Printed and bound by CPI Group (UK) Ltd, Croydon, CR0 4YY

08/05/2025

01864770-0002